KEN HOM'S
CHINESE
KITCHEN

With A Consumer's Guide
to Essential Ingredients

KEN HOM'S
CHINESE
KITCHEN

With A Consumer's Guide to Essential Ingredients

Photographs by Graham Kirk

PAVILION

To Gordon Wing
a great chef and colleague.
With grateful thanks for
more than ten years.

An author can only be as enthusiastic as the people he works with. I am fortunate to work with people who love food as much as I do and thank them for all their support.

I begin with thanks to Gerry Cavanaugh and Megan Jenks who helped in the editorial process, as well as offering constructive comments.

I am grateful to my literary agents, Carole Blake and Julian Friedmann who believed in the idea of this book and worked hard to make it a reality.

It was my luck to have Colin Webb as my publisher again, his words of encouragement and support were invaluable. The enthusiasm at Pavilion Books was infectious and I owe thanks to Gillian Young and Emma Lawson for their skillful editorial guidance, as well as Norma MacMillan for her work.

Graham Kirk's photographs breathe life into this book and for that I am very appreciative. And a big thank you to Helen Payne, Jane Stevenson and Allyson Birch.

Finally a tremendous salute to Gordon Wing to whom this book is dedicated. With his usual wit and keenly astute sense of food, he helped guide and shape this book, as well as many others we have worked on. I owe him a debt which can never be repaid.

Also by Ken Hom
Ken Hom's Encyclopaedia of Chinese Cookery Techniques (Ebury Press)
Ken Hom's Chinese Cookery (BBC Books)
Ken Hom's Vegetable & Pasta Book (BBC Books)
Ken Hom's East Meets West Cuisine (Macmillan)
Fragrant Harbour Taste (Bantam Press)
Ken Hom's Quick & Easy Chinese Cookery (BBC Books)
The Taste of China (Pavilion)
Sainsbury's the Cooking of China (Martin Books)
Ken Hom's Illustrated Chinese Cookery (BBC Books)

First published in
Great Britain in 1994 by
Pavilion Books Limited
26 Upper Ground
London
SE1 9PD

Text copyright © Taurom Incorporated 1994
Photographs copyright © Graham Kirk 1994

The moral right of the author has been asserted.

Produced by Write Image Limited, London
Stylist: Helen Payne
Home Economists: Allyson Birch and Jane Stevenson

A CIP catalogue record for this book is available from the British Library.

ISBN 1 85145 9510 (hbk)
ISBN 1 85793 8453 (pbk)

Printed and bound in Spain by Bookprint, Barcelona
6 8 10 9 7 5

This book may be ordered by post direct from the publisher. Please contact the Marketing Department. But try your bookshop first.

CONTENTS

INTRODUCTION 6

PART ONE

A CONSUMER'S GUIDE
TO ESSENTIAL INGREDIENTS 9

PART TWO

THE RECIPES

SOUPS 97

FISH AND SHELLFISH 107

POULTRY 127

MEAT 145

EGGS 161

VEGETABLES 169

RICE AND NOODLES 188

INDEX 197

INTRODUCTION

After more than two decades of teaching and demonstrating Chinese cookery throughout the world, and after publishing eight cookbooks, one would think I would have exhausted the subject. However, there is an essential aspect of Chinese cuisine that still needs to be discussed. As more and more people cook with Chinese ingredients, and as Chinese flavors have become more popular, much confusion has arisen about what ingredients to buy, where one should look for them, how to choose the best, and what particular brands are preferred. This book is, therefore, a guide to these niceties and details. My aim is to provide basic information in regard to ingredients, sauces and unusual preparations. Here I offer my informed and, I hope, unbiased view to guide you through the thicket of ingredients that are readily available in supermarkets and Chinese groceries today. This is *the guide* to take with you when shopping for the essential ingredients of your Chinese kitchen, as they are used in my own kitchen. I trust this little guide will be a companion to your other Chinese cookery books, to be used as a quick reference.

Over the centuries the Chinese have developed a unique style, an approach, a philosophy, concerning food. Most apparent is an accent on the freshness of ingredients and the balance of tastes. The Chinese use spices and flavorings but never overwhelmingly so: ginger, spring onions or scallions, garlic, soy sauce, chilli sauce, and other seasonings are clearly but never obtrusively present. Whenever I travel to Chinatowns throughout the world or to Hong Kong, Taiwan or China themselves, whether in markets, restaurants, or private homes, I always encounter Chinese cuisine in all its variety and pungency and in an atmosphere redolent with taste and flavors. In stores and Chinese supermarkets in almost every country, for example, there may be dozens of varieties of chilli bean pastes and sauces. Sometimes, in the best Chinese markets, the number of different condiments is impossible to count.

In China, Hong Kong, Taiwan, Australia and parts of Europe, as well as in North America, I have observed the wide variety of readily available Chinese foods and ingredients. Despite regional variations, one senses a unity of style that comes from shared techniques, flavors, ingredients, and philosophy, all of which are unique to Chinese cuisine. This style derives from more than the emphatic use of ginger, spring onions and garlic, the basic trinity of Chinese seasonings; nor is its uniqueness reducible to applications of soy sauce. The matter is at once more complex and more straightforward than that.

In China, the freshest ingredients are always the best, and the Chinese join these with the most appropriate seasonings, spices, and sauces. One would think there would be a limit to the number of dishes resulting from this masterful combination, yet I have witnessed again and again on many visits that there are always surprises. If you pursue your interest in Chinese cuisine, you too will be amazed and delighted by the limitless possibilities open to you.

Almost all the ingredients called for in this book can now be obtained in ordinary supermarkets and almost certainly in Chinese groceries or supermarkets. I have listed acceptable substitutes if the original cannot be had; however, in most cases, the search for the authentic is most desirable. You will find advice on what to look for when shopping for these exotic ingredients, how to use them, and how to store them, as well as which particular brand of sauce or condiment you should buy and why. With the illustrative photos in hand, along with the information I offer, you will be guided to the right ingredients that will enable you to achieve the same results as good Chinese cooks everywhere.

The food markets of China are full of exotic vegetables – wild rice shoots, fresh straw mushrooms, fresh bamboo shoots, smoked garlic, pea shoots, yellow cucumbers – whose range is impossible to find in the West. The good news, however, is that *most* ingredients, seasonings and vegetables used in Chinese cookery *are* available and are becoming increasingly so with expanding trade and the spread of an international style of cuisine. Today, with little effort, you can duplicate many of the culinary wonders of China quite easily. All the recipes included in this book were tested with easily obtained ingredients.

This guide is not meant to be an encyclopedia; nor is it meant to encompass all ingredients. However, I have endeavored to include the most commonly used ones as well as those that have aroused the most curiosity, such as bird's nest and shark's fin, which appear on Chinese restaurant menus.

It is my hope that with this book you will be tempted to try some of the more complex Chinese recipes. And, with the knowledge of good ingredients, you will understand the flavors of this fascinating cuisine and enjoy it as much as the Chinese do. I want to share this wonderful world of tasty and healthy food with you.

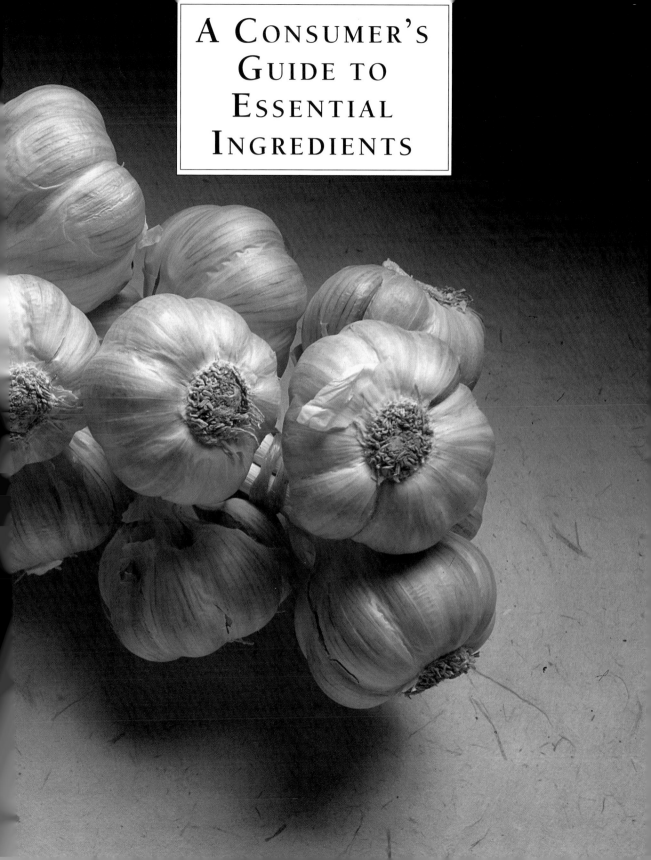

A CONSUMER'S
GUIDE TO
ESSENTIAL
INGREDIENTS

AUBERGINE/EGGPLANT

SOLANUM MELONGENA

A popular and inexpensive food found throughout China, the white-skinned variety was the first that English-speaking people encountered, hence the name eggplant. Nonetheless, this versatile food may be ivory, purple, or even light green in color. It is native to India and Southeast Asia and has been cultivated in China since 600 B.C. The original Chinese name translates as 'Malayan purple melon', indicating that Chinese traders brought it from the Malay peninsula. Although it is botanically a fruit, it is consumed as a vegetable. The size and shape varies from large and plump to small and thin. The most common type, the large purple variety, is easily available; the Chinese prefer the more delicate flavor of the smaller, thin aubergine. These are becoming more readily available in the West.

Shopping Tips

Try to find the long, thin, light purple variety known as Chinese or Japanese aubergines. They look like young courgettes [US zucchini] and tend to be sweet and tender with very few seeds. They are also easier to prepare, as they don't need to be salted before cooking. Look for aubergines with unwrinkled, firm, smooth, unblemished skin. They should sound hollow when tapped.

Storage Notes

The large variety found in supermarkets can be kept, unwrapped, in the bottom part of your refrigerator for at least 2 weeks. However, the thinner, Chinese variety should be eaten within a few days of purchase.

Useful Hints

Chinese normally do not peel aubergines since the skin preserves texture, taste, and shape. Large aubergines most often found in supermarkets should be cut according to the recipe, sprinkled with a little salt, and left to sit for 20-30 minutes. They should then be rinsed and any liquid blotted dry with paper towels, or rinsed carefully and dried. This process extracts bitter juices and excess moisture from the vegetable before it is cooked, giving a truer taste to a dish. The aubergine will also absorb less moisture. This procedure is unnecessary if you are using Chinese aubergines.

BAMBOO SHOOTS

DENDROCALAMUS; PHYLLOSTACHYS

Bamboo shoots are the young edible shoots of certain kinds of bamboo (part of the grass family). There are as many different types of bamboo shoots as there are kinds of bamboo – that is, over 100 – and at least 10 of the 100 or so are marketed. They generally fall into two broad categories: spring shoots and winter shoots, the winter being smaller and more tender than the spring ones, which can be quite large. Fresh bamboo shoots are sweet and crunchy with an unforgettable, distinctive taste. Because they can tolerate long cooking, their texture remains intact while their flavors blend well with other foods. Fresh bamboo shoots are expensive and are only found seasonally in markets in Hong Kong, Taiwan, and China, as well as other parts of Southeast Asia. They are too fragile to export, and I have only rarely seen them in Chinese markets in the West. We have to be satisfied with the canned varieties, which are at least more reasonably priced. Canned bamboo shoots tend to be pale yellow with a crunchy texture and, in some cases, a slightly sweet flavor. They come peeled and either whole or thickly sliced. In some Chinese markets, bamboo shoots preserved in brine are available and these tend to have much more flavor than the canned variety.

Shopping Tips

Many of the brands from China are tasty, especially the winter shoots; the May Ling brand is recommended. I have generally found brands from Taiwan to be relatively bland. Purchase the preserved-in-brine variety if they are available (in open bins in the refrigerated section of Chinese grocers). Buy whole bamboo shoots rather than sliced ones as they tend to hold their flavor better.

Storage Notes

Transfer any left-over shoots to a jar, cover them with fresh water, and refrigerate. If the water is changed daily they will keep 2 or 3 days.

Useful Hints

● Fresh bamboo shoots are prepared by first stripping off all their leaves and then trimming the hard base. Only the center core is edible, which is cut and then blanched in boiling water for at least 5 minutes to remove its bitterness. Prepare the core according to the recipe. The bamboo shoots are now ready to be stir-fried or cooked.

● Rinse canned bamboo shoots thoroughly and blanch them for 2 minutes in boiling water before use.

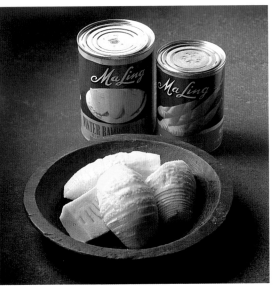

BEAN CURD

LEGUMINOSAE GLYCINE MAX

Bean curd, which is also known by its Chinese name, doufu, or by its Japanese name, tofu, has played an important part in Chinese cookery since it was discovered during the Han Dynasty (206 B.C. - A.D. 220). It became known as 'meat without bones' because it is highly nutritious and rich in protein, and it works well with other foods. It is also low in saturated fats and cholesterol, easy to digest, and inexpensive. Bean curd has a distinctively smooth, light, almost creamy texture but a bland taste. However, it is extremely versatile and lends itself to all types of cooking. It is made from yellow soybeans that are soaked, ground, mixed with water, and then cooked briefly before being solidified. Fresh bean curd is usually sold in two forms – as firm, small blocks or in a soft, custard-like variety – but it is also available in several dried forms and in a fermented version. The soft bean curd (sometimes called silken tofu) is used for soups and other dishes, while the solid type is used for stir-frying, braising, and deep-frying. Solid bean curd blocks are white in color and are packed in water in plastic containers.

Shopping Tips

If possible, purchase bean curd fresh from a Chinese market or grocer. Many commercial forms of bean curd available in supermarkets and health food stores, while nutritious, are ordinarily without the subtle, distinctive flavor prized by bean curd lovers in China.

Storage Notes

Fresh bean curd, once opened, may be kept in the refrigerator for up to 5 days, provided the covering water is changed daily. It is best to use the bean curd within 2 or 3 days of purchase.

Useful Hints

To cut solid bean curd, use a sharp knife and cut gently as the bean curd is fragile. It also needs to be cooked gently as too much stirring can cause it to disintegrate. This does not, however, affect its nutritional value. Deep-frying bean curd transforms its texture to a sponge-like web, allowing it to absorb sauces when it is cooked again the second time.

FERMENTED BEAN CURD, RED, CHILLI, AND REGULAR

This is a cheese-like form of bean curd that has been preserved in rice wine, in brine with rice wine, or with chillies and condiments. It is sold in glass jars at Chinese markets or grocers. It is very popular in China where it is eaten by itself, with rice or rice porridge, used as an ingredient in cooking, or featured as a seasoning. It is often used as a flavoring agent, especially with braised meat dishes or vegetables. A little adds zest to any vegetable dish. Once it begins to cook, it produces a fragrant aroma that enriches the vegetables. Used in braised meat dishes, it blends with the sauce to give it an extraordinary aromatic taste and flavor. It comes in several forms: red fermented bean curd, which has been cured in a brine with Shaoxing rice wine and fermented red rice (a reddish flavoring that is made by adding annatto seeds to rice wine lees left after brewing rice wine); chilli-fermented bean curd, which is flavored with crushed, dried chilli peppers; and regular fermented bean curd which is made with just Shaoxing rice wine. You can find all these only at Chinese markets or grocers.

Shopping Tips

Many Hong Kong brands are good and recommended, as are the brands from China and Taiwan. It is best to try several to find the one that suits your particular taste – they are extremely inexpensive. Some have a stronger winy taste, while others are salty and more briny in flavor.

Storage Notes

Once the jar has been opened, fermented bean curd will keep indefinitely if re-sealed and refrigerated.

PRESSED SEASONED BEAN CURD

When water is extracted from fresh bean curd cakes by pressing them with a weight, the bean curd becomes firm and compact. Simmered in water with soy sauce, star anise, and sugar, the pressed bean curd acquires a smooth, resilient texture that is quite unusual. Cut into small pieces, it can be stir-fried with meat or vegetables; when cut into larger pieces it can be simmered. Pressed seasoned bean curd is wonderful used in pure vegetarian dishes. In China, it is a popular offering at many food stalls.

Shopping Tips

It can be found at Chinese grocers and supermarkets, usually in the refrigerated sections. Locally made Chinese brands tend to be quite good.

Storage Notes

Pressed seasoned bean curd is often vacuum-packed, and as such it should keep in the refrigerator for at least 1 week. Once opened it should be used within 2 or 3 days.

Useful Hints

For vegetarian dishes, simply brush the bean curd cakes with oil and grill [US broil] them. Or add them instead of meat to vegetables for a tasty main course.

BEAN SAUCE

YELLOW BEAN SAUCE, BROWN BEAN SAUCE, BEAN PASTE, SOYBEAN CONDIMENT

S easonings made from germinated soybeans are one of the oldest forms of food flavoring in China. Before 200 B.C., the ancient Chinese used a form of salted and fermented soybeans, as well as another type of thin, salty sauce. These were precursors of the bean sauce of today, which is made from dried yellow or black soybeans that are partially decomposed by adding a mold culture and then they are salted, dried, or mixed with brine. Bean sauce is thick, spicy, and aromatic. Correctly blended, it is quite salty but provides a distinctive flavor to Chinese sauces and is a frequent addition in Chinese cookery. The traditional bean sauce follows the ancient recipe for pickled yellow soybeans in a salty liquid. There are two forms: whole beans in a thick sauce and mashed, ground or puréed beans (sold as crushed or yellow bean sauce).

Shopping Tips

If labeled plain 'bean sauce', it is likely to be whole beans. This is the preferred sauce, as it is rounder in flavor and has more of a textural bite. Often the pureed version is very salty. In China, bean sauce is often purchased from local food shops, which make sauce to a favorite local recipe. People buy what they need from large jars. Many of the versions available in cans or jars from China (Pearl River Bridge brand) or Hong Kong are quite good, especially the Koon Chun Sauce Factory's bean sauce.

Storage Notes

If you buy the sauce in cans, transfer it to a glass jar. It will keep indefinitely in the refrigerator.

Useful Hints

Bean sauce is a good foundation for making a favorite sauce: combine it with hoisin sauce and chilli bean paste.

BIRD'S NEST

A truly exotic food, bird's nest is one of the most sought-after delicacies of China. Historically, it was most popular in southern China, though served in other parts of China also. But it is now much sought-after in affluent Hong Kong and Taiwan, as well as throughout Southeast Asia. It is literally a bird's nest, made of regurgitated spittle of a certain breed of swallow, the Collacallia, from the East Asian tropics: Thailand, Vietnam, Java, and the Philippines. Their nests are found in large caverns where workers climb on long bamboo scaffolding to retrieve them – certainly dangerous work. The gelatinous substance (spittle) of the nest is believed to possess powerful medicinal and youth-restoring virtues. Bird's nest is also said to be good for the complexion and is prescribed for convalescing patients. There are shops in Hong Kong and Taiwan specializing in this delicacy, which comes in various grades. The best ones are the 'white nests' and 'pink or blood nests', which are shaped like cups.

The nests are expensive and are usually sold pre-cleaned, that is, feathers and other bits are hand-plucked from the nests. Bird's nest is sold dried and must be soaked before using. The result, like shark's fin, is a flavorless, soft, crunchy jelly that relies for flavor on a rich sauce or broth, which may be either savory or sweet. Bird's nest is also used in extravagant stuffings.

Shopping Tips

Buy the best quality your budget can afford.

Storage Notes

Since it is dried, it will keep in a dry place indefinitely.

Useful Hints

● Soak overnight in cold water. Then simmer it for 20 minutes in fresh water. Finally rinse in cold water and squeeze dry before proceeding with the recipe.
● This is by no means an ordinary household food. Beginners will need some expert guidance in gaining an appreciation of the virtues of this gelatinous, exotic delicacy.

BITTER MELON

MOMORDICA CHARANTIA

This unusual vegetable is very much an acquired taste. It has as many detractors as it has fans, even among the Chinese, but those who love it insist it is worth the effort to appreciate its taste. Bitter melon has a bumpy, dark to pale green skin, and a slightly bitter quinine flavor that has a cooling effect in the mouth. Not surprisingly, it was originally prized for its supposed medicinal qualities: something so bitter had to be good medicine. This tropical fruit's fibrous seed core is usually cut away, leaving a thin ring of flesh. It is used in soups as well as stir-fried, steamed and quick braised. A popular preparation, which reduces its bitterness, is to stuff it with seasoned pork and steam it. It is often paired with strong, pungent ingredients, such as black beans, garlic, or chilli, that tone down the melon's bitterness. In some parts of China it is often dried and used as medicine. It is also thought to purify blood and to cool the digestive system.

Shopping Tips

Canned bitter melon is less appealing than fresh, as it tends to be overcooked and without flavor, so buy only the fresh variety, which can be found at Chinese markets or grocers. The greener, firmer melons tend to be stronger and more bitter, while the yellowish varieties tend to be milder.

Storage Notes

Store in the bottom of your refrigerator in a loose plastic or paper bag. It can keep there for about 3–5 days, depending on the condition in which it was bought.

Useful Hints

To use, cut in half, seed, and discard interior membrane. Then, to lessen its bitter taste, either blanch in boiling water or salt it, according to the instructions in the recipe.

17

BLACK BEANS

FERMENTED BLACK BEANS, SALTED BEANS, PRESERVED BEANS

These small black soybeans are pre-served by being cooked and fermented with salt and spices. They have a distinctive, salty taste and pleasantly rich aroma and are often used as a seasoning, usually in conjunction with garlic, fresh ginger, or chillies. They are among the most popular flavors of southern China, but are used less in other parts of the country. Black beans are especially good in steamed, braised, and stir-fried dishes, imparting a rich flavor to them. They should not be confused with the dried black beans used in Western cooking.

Shopping Tips

Black beans are readily available in the West; I see them often in supermarkets. Although you can find them in cans marked 'Black Bean Sauce', I would avoid these. Instead, buy the ones that come packed in plastic bags. The best packaged variety is the Pearl River Bridge brand, labeled 'Yang Jiang Preserved Beans (with Ginger)', from southern China. This brand has a rich, aromatic flavor that is inviting and assertive at the same time.

Storage Notes

The beans will keep indefinitely if stored in the refrigerator or in a cool place. Take the beans from the package and transfer them to a clean covered jar. Store away from light and heat.

Useful Hints

Depending on the recipe, the black beans should be lightly chopped or crushed to release their tangy aromas. Although some recipes say to rinse them before using, I find this unnecessary, as the salt adds to the flavor of the dish without overpowering the other flavors.

CAUL FAT

Caul fat is the lacy membrane that surrounds the organs in the abdominal cavity of the pig. The membrane is used by French and Chinese cooks to encase stuffings and to keep food moist while cooking. The caul fat itself melts entirely away during cooking and imparts richness to the ingredients. Because it concurrently keeps foods moist and adds to their flavor, it is especially useful as a wrapping for delicate chicken, fish, and seafood.

Shopping Tips

You can order fresh or frozen caul fat from your local butcher.

Storage Notes

Caul fat is highly perishable so buy it in small quantities and use quickly. For longer storage, wrap the caul fat carefully and freeze. It can be kept 3 weeks at the most.

Useful Hints

● I find that soaking caul fat in cold water helps to separate the sheet of fat without tearing its lacy and fragile webs.

● It is useful for wrapping foods to be grilled.

CHILLI BEAN PASTE OR SAUCE

CHILLI PASTE WITH GARLIC, SICHUAN CHILLI SAUCE

C hilli peppers, both sweet and hot, were introduced into China scarcely 100 years ago. Their popularity was immediate and, along with the tomato, they transformed Chinese cooking. There are many varieties of chilli pastes and sauces. The basic ingredients, which include ground chillies, oil, salt, and garlic, are fermented into a rich paste that ranges in taste from mild to very hot. Chinese cooks will also mix into the basic version such ingredients as ground soybeans, black beans, ginger, preserved vegetables, and other condiments. In the so-called 'hot bean pastes' soybeans predominate. Every chef in every region of China has his or her own special recipe for chilli bean paste.

Shopping Tips

The brand you buy will greatly influence the taste of the dish that calls for this paste. Unfortunately, the labels never indicate whether the paste is hot or mild. However, one of the best is the Lan Chi brand from Taiwan. It is a high quality paste that is well balanced in seasoning. There are many good brands from China, but, unfortunately, their availability is rather unreliable; they should be purchased whenever possible, especially the ones from Sichuan province. Brands from Hong Kong tend to be of high quality and are generally milder; however, there may be one or two very hot ones. It is best to try a few and decide what suits your palate. I would avoid many of the Singapore brands, which vary from bland to very hot without any balancing seasonings.

Storage Notes

Be sure to seal the jar tightly after use and store in the refrigerator where the paste will keep indefinitely.

Useful Hints

● When using a chilli bean paste or sauce for the first time, temper your usage until you are familiar with the flavor, then adjust the amount according to your taste. Combine chilli bean paste with other sauces, such as soy sauce, or with Shaoxing rice wine, to create your own personal flavors.

● *Note:* There is a chilli sauce that is used mainly as a dipping sauce. It is a hot, reddish, thin sauce made without any added beans and should not be confused with this thicker, more complex chilli bean paste or sauce.

CHILLIES, DRIED RED

D ried red chillies are used extensively in some regions of China. Drying is done for practical purposes so that chilli is always available. In the southwest region of Sichuan province and in Hunan, one may see long strings of dried red chillies hanging in kitchens of homes and restaurants. The drying process concentrates the power of the chilli, which then adds vigor and complexity to spicy dishes. Chillies are often combined with other ingredients, such as peppercorns and garlic, to make a rather fiery concoction.

Shopping Tips

Look for good dried chillies with a bright red color. They should also have a pungent aroma.

Storage Notes

Dried chillies will keep indefinitely in a tightly covered jar in a cool place.

Useful Hints

Large dried chillies tend to be milder than the smaller ones. Dried chillies are used to make chilli oil. They are most suited for use in stir-fried dishes; split and chopped, they are excellent in sauces and for braising. They are normally left whole or cut in half lengthways, or finely ground. The seeds may be left in or discarded, depending on your taste. Remember the seeds increase the intensity, or hotness, of the chilli flavor.

CHILLIES, FRESH

CAPSICUM FRUTESCENS

Archaeological records suggest that peppers were eaten in Mexico 9,000 years ago and were cultivated 2,000 years later. They were introduced to Asia around 100-150 years ago from the Americas. There are two varieties: sweet or bell peppers, which are very mild, and hot peppers, known as chillies. There are many different types of hot chillies, varying in size, shape, color, and intensity or 'hotness'. In Chinese cuisine, fresh chillies are stuffed or eaten whole. They are used to make sauce or paste and are dried as well as being pickled and preserved for use in stir-fried and braised dishes. Chillies are also dry-roasted to add a special pungent, smoky flavor. In China, fresh chillies are small and generally red, but there are also green varieties. Their taste is mildly spicy and pungent. Smaller varieties can be found, but the larger, longer ones are the ones most widely available. They are popular not only for their color and presentation as garnishes but also for the zest they add to many dishes and sauces.

Shopping Tips

Try the varieties available in your local markets. People's tastes vary, so it is important that you find the chillies that best suit your palate as some are very hot. Look for firm, bright chillies without blemishes or dark spots.

Storage Notes

Store in the vegetable crisper of your refrigerator. Fresh chillies should keep for at least 1 week.

Useful Hints

Use red chillies wherever possible; they are generally milder than green ones because peppers sweeten as they ripen. To prepare fresh chillies, first rinse them in cold water. Then, using a small sharp knife, slit them lengthways. Remove and discard the seed (unless you want a very hot flavor). Rinse the chillies well under cold running water and then prepare them according to the instructions in the recipe. Wash your hands, knife, and chopping board before preparing other foods, and be careful not to touch your eyes or lips until you have washed your hands thoroughly with soap and water.

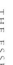

CHILLI OIL, CHILLI DIPPING SAUCE

C hilli oil is used extensively in Chinese cooking, to impart a sharp, hot flavor. It is sometimes served as a dipping condiment as well as being used as a seasoning. It is made from crushed dried chillies or small whole chillies, depending on the flavor you are seeking.

Shopping Tips

It is better to make your own chilli oil, as many store-bought versions can easily go rancid. The Chinese versions of commercially made chilli oil tend to be milder and certainly are never as hot as the chilli oils from Southeast Asia. Of course, as chillies vary, so do the oils vary in strength and flavor. You can purchase chilli oil from Chinese markets. The Thai and Malaysian versions are especially hot; the Taiwanese and Chinese versions are more subtle.

Storage Notes

It is easy to make your own chilli oil. Once made, put it in a tightly sealed glass jar and store in a cool, dark place where it will keep for months.

Useful Hints

Commercial products are quite acceptable, but I include the following recipe because the homemade version is the best. Remember that chilli oil is too dramatic to be used directly as the sole cooking oil; it is best used as part of a dipping sauce or as a condiment, or combined with other mild oils. I include spices (pepper and black beans) for additional flavors because then I can also use the oil as a dipping sauce.

Chilli Oil/Chilli Dipping Sauce

250ml/8floz/1 cup groundnut oil [US peanut oil]
30g/1oz/1¼ cups coarsely chopped dried
    red chillies
4tbsp whole unroasted Sichuan peppercorns
3tbsp whole black beans

Heat a wok over a high heat and add the oil. When the oil is very hot, add the rest of the ingredients. Stir for 1 minute over a low heat. Remove from the heat and allow the mixture to cool undisturbed. Let the mixture sit overnight. The next day, strain the oil and keep it in a cool, dry, dark place.

THE ESSENTIAL INGREDIENTS

23

CHINESE BROCCOLI

BRASSICA ALBOGLABRA

This very nutritious green leafy plant with smooth round stems and small white flowers is sometimes called Chinese kale. That name should tell you that it is not quite the same thing as broccoli but resembles Swiss chard. It is a delicious vegetable but earthy in taste and slightly bitter, perhaps the price to pay for its being so rich in calcium, iron, and vitamins A and C.

Chinese broccoli is usually prepared by blanching in boiling salted water and then is served with oyster sauce – it has character enough to go well with that distinctively flavored condiment. It also works well in stir-fries with meats, to be served with noodles and soups.

Shopping Tips
Look for stems that are firm and leaves that look fresh and are deep olive green.

Storage Notes
Store in a plastic bag in the vegetable crisper of the refrigerator. It will keep for several days.

Useful Hints
Use Chinese broccoli the way you would use regular broccoli, kale, Swiss chard, and rape greens (broccoli di rape). It is one of the world's most nutritious vegetables, with one of the highest calcium contents of any food.

CHINESE CHIVES

ALLIUM TUBEROSUM

hives, garlic, and shallots are closely allied to onions. Each has its own distinctive flavor that makes it a valued addition to many recipes, especially to stir-fried dishes. Chives are mild, small versions of the onion. Having no bulb, only the green shoots are eaten. In China, which has relatively few food herbs (medicinal herbs are abundant), garlic chives are very popular as a flavoring herb. With their stronger flavor they are preferred in stuffings as well as in stir-fried dishes and soups.

There are several variations of this chive:

Yellow chives are distinctly, if mildly, onion-flavored. Their yellow color and mild taste come from their being grown out of direct sunlight.

Flowering chives have hollow stems topped by a flower bud. The tough ends are chopped off and the remainder is consumed as a vegetable.

Green chives have a distinctive pungency that adds richness to stir-fried dishes.

Shopping Tips
Buy them fresh at Chinese markets or grocers. They should be fresh-looking, not wilted and tired. Flowering chives will be stiff and aromatic. Yellow chives *are* limp and should not have brown edges. Garlic and green chives should be deep green and fresh-looking.

Storage Notes
Wash and dry thoroughly and store, between paper towels, in a plastic bag in the lower part of your refrigerator. They are highly perishable. Most will remain fresh for 2 days; however, yellow chives are extremely fragile and will only keep for 1 day.

Useful Hints
To prepare, select the freshest leaves possible and trim any decaying parts, then proceed with your recipe.

CHINESE DRIED BLACK MUSHROOMS

LENTINUS EDODES

These 'black' mushrooms actually range from light brown to dark brown in color. The most popular are the larger sized, light brown ones with a highly cracked surface. These are, predictably, the most expensive ones. But all versions and grades of this mushroom add a most desirable flavor and aroma to Chinese recipes. It is interesting to note that these mushrooms grow on fallen, decaying trees; the Chinese have been gathering them for over a thousand years. The Japanese cultivate them by growing them on the *shii* tree, hence the familiar *shiitake* mushrooms.

The Chinese rarely eat the mushrooms fresh. Rather, they prefer the dried version because this process concentrates the smoky flavors of the mushrooms and allows them to absorb sauces and spices, imparting an even more succulent texture. This makes them most appropriate for use as seasonings, finely chopped and combined with meats, fish, or poultry. These dried black mushrooms are prescribed for respiratory and other problems.

Shopping Tips

Depending on your budget, the lighter and more expensive grade is the best to buy. These should be reserved for special occasions. However, for normal everyday fare, a moderately priced good quality mushroom is fine.

Storage Notes

In an air-tight container, they will keep indefinitely in a cool dry place. If they are not to be used often, store them in the freezer.

Useful Hints

• *To use Chinese dried mushrooms:* Soak them in a bowl of warm water for about 20 minutes or until they are soft and pliable. Squeeze out the excess water and cut off and discard the woody stems. Only the caps are used.

• The soaking water can be saved and used in soups and as rice water, as a base for a vegetarian stock, or added to sauces or braised dishes. Strain through a fine sieve to remove any sand or residue from the dried mushrooms.

CHINESE FLOWERING CABBAGE

BRASSICACAE CHINENSIS VAR. PARACHINENSIS

In their marvelously successful effort to provide themselves with nutritious sustenance, the Chinese people have gladly and imaginatively exploited every food resource available to them. Among the most beneficial means to that end is their broad reliance on a vast number of different vegetable greens, the unique source of so many essential vitamins, minerals, and trace elements. Chinese flowering cabbage is but one, albeit very important, example of this dietary proclivity.

The cabbage family of vegetables in China is actually almost unrepresented in the rest of the world, except as it has spread from China. It would be tedious to list all of the types that are cultivated and consumed in enormous quantities every day in China. It is safe to say, however, that the Chinese flowering cabbage is among the most popular. A relative of another favorite green, pak choi, this cabbage is slimmer, with yellow flowers to complement its green leaves. Its attributes make it more desirable and more expensive than pak choi.

Stir-frying is the preferred cooking method, the cabbage leaves requiring little cooking to bring out their delicate, sweet, mustard flavor.

Shopping Tips

Look for firm stalks and check the stems to make sure they are not old and fibrous. The leaves should look fresh without brown spots.

Storage Notes

Store in the vegetable crisper of the refrigerator. Like pak choi, it should keep for about 1 week.

Useful Hints

This vegetable is delicious stir-fried with olive oil and garlic. Use it in fillings and with pasta. It also makes a mustardy salad green; however, it needs to be washed well. The best way to prepare it is to trim and cut according to recipe instructions and then wash it in several changes of cold water.

CHINESE LONG BEANS

VIGNA SESQUIPEDALIS

A lso known as Chinese pea, snake bean, and asparagus pea or bean, these beans either originated in China or were introduced there in prehistoric times. Sometimes they are called yard-long beans as they grow as long as 3 feet. They are very popular and, in season, may be found in great abundance in every market. They provide significant calories and vegetable protein to the Chinese diet.

Quite unrelated to the familiar Western green beans, they are neither crisp nor sweet. They do have a crunchy texture, but their taste is mild and subtle and they are best when combined with more assertively flavored foods. There are two varieties: pale green ones and dark green, thinner types. In China, the beans are chopped and then stir-fried with meats or fermented bean curd. They cook rapidly and this makes them very suitable for stir-fry recipes.

Shopping Tips

Buy beans that are fresh and bright, light green or deep, dark green, with no dark marks. Although they are not crisp, they should nevertheless not be soft. You will usually find long beans sold in looped bunches.

Storage Notes

Store the fresh beans in a plastic bag in the refrigerator and use within 4 days.

Useful Hints

● There is no need to string Chinese long beans before cooking them.

● Paired with assertive seasonings, the beans are very tasty when simply stir-fried, with or without meats. The Cantonese often cook them with black beans or fermented bean curd. In Sichuan, they are deep-fried and then paired with chillies and garlic.

CHINESE MUSTARD CABBAGE OR GAAI CHOY

BRASSICA JUNCEA

Mustard plants are not the same thing as cabbages but they are very close in terms of appearance, nutrition and popularity. With rice and soybeans, mustard plants and cabbage have been the poor people's basic diet for many centuries. Preserved with chillies or pickled in brine or sugar, mustard cabbages are eaten throughout the year. When in season and fresh, they can be simply stir-fried with ginger and salt. They are also used in soups, to which they impart flavor and astringency. Young, fresh mustard cabbages are tender throughout and are consumed in their entirety. They are a good source of vitamins and of minerals such as calcium.

Shopping Tips
Choose mustard cabbage that has firm, broad leaves without discoloration. Avoid limp and tired-looking cabbage. Stems should be firm without holes, which indicate age and a fibrous texture.

Storage Notes
Stored in the vegetable crisper of your refrigerator, Chinese mustard cabbage should last for at least 5 days.

Useful Hints
Cut the mustard cabbage into pieces before washing in several changes of cold water.

CHINESE WHITE CABBAGE

PAK CHOI, BOK CHOY

BRASSICA CHINENSIS

C hinese white cabbage, popularly known as pak choi or bok choy, is a nutritious and versatile vegetable. It has been grown in China since ancient times. Although there are many varieties – in Hong Kong alone 20 kinds are available – the most common, best known and most popular is the one with a long, smooth, milky-white stem and large, crinkly, dark green leaves, found in many supermarkets today. Pak choi has a light, fresh, slightly mustardy taste and requires little cooking. In China, it is used in soup, stir-fried with meats, or simply blanched. When cooked, the leaves have a robust, almost spinach-like flavor, while the stalks are sweet and mild with a refreshing taste. Pak choi is often said to resemble Swiss chard in taste; however, in fact, it is milder and juicier – and much more popular – than chard!

Shopping Tips

Look for firm, crisp stalks and unblemished leaves. The size of the plant indicates how tender it is: the smaller the better, especially in the summer, when the hot weather toughens the stalks. Look at the bottom of the stalk; if it has a hole, it means that the pak choi is old and fibrous, and best avoided.

Storage Notes

Store pak choi, wrapped tightly in paper towels, in the vegetable crisper of your refrigerator. It will keep for up to 1 week.

Useful Hints

• The best way to rinse pak choi is to cut it according to the recipe, then rinse in at least two or three changes of cold water. Drain thoroughly before cooking.

Other Notes

• Pak choi is delicious cooked in olive oil and garlic. Use it as you would spinach or cabbage in fillings or stuffings.

• A close relative is Shanghai pak choi, often called baby pak choi. Use it in the same way as pak choi.

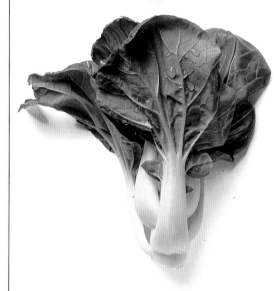

CHINESE WHITE RADISH

MOOLI, DAIKEN

RAPHANUS SATIVUS

C hinese white radish is also known as Chinese icicle radish, as mooli, or by its Japanese name, daikon. It is long and white and rather like a carrot in shape but usually much larger. It is a winter radish or root and can withstand long cooking without disintegrating. It thus absorbs the flavors of the food it is cooked with and yet retains its distinctive radish taste and texture. In China, these radishes are usually found in homemade dishes, treated as Western cooks use potatoes or carrots, and the texture is crisp and tender after cooking. They are never used without being peeled. In addition to being cooked they are also pickled or salted and dried to preserve them.

White radishes vary in flavor from sweet and mild to hot and pungent. The stronger flavored variety is used for pickles, the milder for cooking. The hot flavor is in the skin so, when peeled, the radish is mild tasting. Like turnips, these radishes are most often stir-fried, braised, boiled, or steamed and then combined with pork or beef. The milder radish can even be made into a savory pudding for dim sum in southern China. Unlike most root vegetables, these radishes are light and refreshing, not heavy and starchy.

In ancient times, the white radish was valued both as a food and as a medicine – although some avoided it because it allegedly induced hiccups.

Shopping Tips

Look for firm, heavy, solid, unblemished radishes. They should be slightly translucent inside, with smooth skin. Avoid very large ones which tend to be fibrous. You can find them in some supermarkets and almost always at Chinese or Asian markets.

Storage Notes

Store in a plastic bag in the vegetable crisper of your refrigerator. They will keep for at least 1 week.

Useful Hints

Use as you would turnips, carrots, or potatoes. White radishes absorb the sauces in which they are cooked as they become tender.

31

CINNAMON BARK

CINNAMONMUM ZEYLANICUM, C. CASSIA

lso known as Chinese cinnamon or cassia, cinnamon is produced in China exclusively from the bark of a type of laurel tree. It is one of the most ancient and widely known spices in the world. Believed to have been used in Egypt around 3000 B.C., it was mentioned in Exodus (1700 B.C.), and was already popular in China by 1000 B.C.

In Chinese cuisine its aromatic properties are exploited particularly well in braised dishes. Cinnamon sticks – curled paper-thin strips – have a more concentrated and, therefore, more assertive spiciness and are preferred in recipes that involve robust flavors. The famous five spice powder would be terribly lacking without its cinnamon element.

Incidentally, 'cassia' is derived from the bark of a different type of laurel tree. It is more strongly scented than true cinnamon. Most of the 'cinna-mon' sold in Europe and North America is actually cassia. True cinnamon is tan in color; cassia is darker reddish-brown.

Shopping Tips
Look for thin rolled cinnamon sticks or barks in Chinese markets or grocers. They are usually found in plastic bags and are inexpensive and very fresh. If you find barks, look for firm, aromatic ones. Avoid packages of cinnamon broken up into small bits.

Storage Notes
Store cinnamon sticks or bark in a tightly sealed jar to preserve their aroma and flavor.

Useful Hints
Ground cinnamon is not a satisfactory substitute for cinnamon bark or stick.

Left *cinnamon bark*; right *cinnamon sticks*

CITRUS PEEL

CITRUS RETICULATA

 his ingredient is also known as dried tangerine peel or dried orange peel.

Until this century, fresh fruits were relatively expensive and, therefore, an infrequent part of the diet of all but the very rich. Understandably, the orange and tangerine peels which were so unthinkingly tossed out were highly valued by the less fortunate. The concentrated essence of these golden fruits served to enliven many prosaic dishes and to recall to people the warm glow of summertime. In China, by the year 1200 A.D., citrus peel already featured in the dishes of better restaurants. In a single orange-growing area as many as 80,000 pounds of citrus peel were produced each year.

As with many acidic foods, the peels have been used as a medicine in China for centuries. Today, they serve mainly as a seasoning ingredient. The most cherished are the peels of Chinese tangerines, which have a rich aroma and flavor. Citrus peels are often used in braised or simmered dishes, their fruity essence suffusing the entire dish. Occasionally, the peels are used in 'master sauces', providing them with a contrasting flavor dimension.

More rarely, they are used in stir-fry dishes.

Shopping Tips

Dried citrus peel is sold in Asian or Chinese grocery stores or can be easily made at home.

Storage Notes

Stored in an airtight jar, the dried peel will last for months or years. When you are ready to use the peel, rehydrate it in a bowl of warm water for 20 minutes or until it is soft.

Useful Hints

● Citrus peel can also be rehydrated in Shaoxing rice wine, with the hydrating wine then used in the dish too.

● *To make citrus peel at home:* Wash and rinse the fruit well (ideally, use organic fruit that has not been sprayed or given a wax coating). Use a good vegetable peeler to peel off the skin carefully. Then, using a sharp knife, carefully separate any white pith from the peel. Dry the peel on a rack in a warm place or in direct sunlight until it is hard. When dried, store as instructed above. These peels *improve* with age.

CLOUD EARS, TREE EARS, WOOD EARS

These edible fungi are variously known as tree ears, black fungus, black tree fungus, mu-er, and wood fungus. As the name indicates, they grow on trees, deriving the growth chemicals they lack from the wood of either live or decaying trees. They have been used in Chinese cooking since the sixth century A.D. and have always been highly regarded for their supposed medicinal properties, particularly as purifiers of the blood.

To speak of the flavor of these mushrooms is rather contradictory. Most of them have little or no discernible taste. Rather, their virtue lies in the fact that they readily take on the flavors of the foods with which they are cooked, flavors they mysteriously help to bring out, and their distinctive and pleasing texture adds by contrast to the enjoyment of other ingredients.

There are two main types and sizes of these fungi. The small black, dried, flaky variety are known as cloud ears because, when soaked, they puff up like fleecy little clouds. The larger variety of tree fungi have a slightly tougher but still pleasantly crunchy texture.

Shopping Tips

You can find them at Chinese markets, usually wrapped in plastic or cellophane bags. There are no particular name brands that can be recommended. Many are from China and are usually repackaged by the grocer who is selling them. They should be hard and dry.

Storage Notes

They keep indefinitely in a jar in a cool, dry place.

Useful Hints

• *To prepare cloud ears:* Soak them in hot water for about 15 minutes or until they are soft. They should then be rinsed several times to remove any sand.

• *To prepare tree ears and wood ears:* Soak them in hot water for about 15 minutes or until they are soft. Then they should be rinsed several times to remove any sand. Trim their hard stems before using. Once soaked, they will swell up to four or five times their original size.

Left *cloud ears;* middle and right *tree or wood ears*

COCONUT MILK

C oconut milk was known to the Chinese as early as 800 A.D., but it never became a staple in their diet. Elsewhere in Southeast Asia coconut milk is widely used. It has some of the properties of cow's milk: the 'cream' (fatty globules) rises to the top when the milk sits; it must be stirred as it comes to a boil; and its fat is closer in chemical composition to butterfat than to vegetable fat. The milk itself is the liquid wrung from the grated and pressed coconut meat combined with water. Coconut milk is not unknown in southern China. That region has for centuries been open to the influences emanating from Southeast Asia, from places, that is, where curries and stews made with coconut milk are common. The milk is used as a popular cooling beverage and in puddings and candies. In Hong Kong and parts of southern China today one will find many coconut milk dishes and desserts, directly inspired by Thai and other Southeast Asian cuisines.

Shopping Tips

In some Chinese markets, it may be possible to find freshly made coconut milk, especially near areas where there is a large Southeast Asian population. Fortunately, however, inexpensive canned versions can be found. Many of the available brands are high quality and quite acceptable and can be recommended. Look for the ones from Thailand or Malaysia. You can find them at most Asian specialty markets. They are usually sold in 400 or 450ml/14 or 15 floz cans. Be sure to shake the cans before opening in order to mix the liquid thoroughly.

Storage Notes

Place any fresh or left-over canned coconut milk in a glass jar and store it in the refrigerator for no longer than 2 days.

Useful Hints

You can make your own coconut milk according to this recipe:

Coconut Milk

1 small coconut
500ml/16 floz/2 cups boiling water

To prepare the coconut, pierce two of the 'eyes' in the shell and drain off and discard the liquid inside. Place the drained coconut in a preheated 180°C/350°F/gas mark 4 oven and bake for about 20 minutes. If this does not crack the shell, split it by rapping it with a hammer along the center until the coconut breaks apart. (Wrap the coconut in a towel while cracking to prevent the small pieces from flying about.) Pry off any meat that sticks to the shell using a knife. Cut the coconut meat into small pieces and place in a medium-sized saucepan. Cover the coconut meat with the boiling water and simmer for 5 minutes. Remove the mixture from the heat, allow it to cool, and then process it in a blender on high speed for 1 minute. Let the coconut 'milk' stand for 15 minutes and then strain into a bowl. Using the back of a wooden spoon, press well to squeeze all the liquid from the chopped coconut meat. Allow the liquid to cool, and refrigerate until you are ready to use it.

CORIANDER

CHINESE PARSLEY, CILANTRO

CORIANDRUM SATIVUM

Fresh coriander is one of the relatively few food herbs in the Chinese lexicon. It is a standard in southern China and has been used in China since 200 B.C. It looks like flat parsley, but its pungent, musky, citrus-like character gives it an unmistakable flavor. Again, with such properties, it was also valued as a medicinal agent. Its feathery leaves are often used as a garnish or it is chopped and then mixed into sauces and stuffings. It helps moderate rich flavors, its own flavor being strong, earthy and fresh.

Shopping Tips

When buying fresh coriander, look for deep green, fresh-looking leaves. Yellow and limp leaves indicate age and should be avoided.

Storage Notes

If you buy fresh coriander with roots, stand them in water. Otherwise, to store fresh coriander, wash it in cold water, drain it thoroughly or spin dry in a salad spinner, and put it in a clean plastic bag with a couple of sheets of moist paper towel. Store it in the vegetable crisper of your refrigerator; it will keep for several days.

Useful Hints

You may mix it with basil for an Asian pesto-style flavoring for noodles.

CURRY PASTE/CURRY POWDER

Curry is derived from the leaves of a plant native to Southwest Asia. Like chutney, 'curry' itself does not define one particular flavor. All curry powders and pastes are, in fact, different combinations of spices and seasonings. In India, most noted for its curries, it is a generic term for a great number of possible sauces.

All curries are pungent, but they range in taste from hot to mild. There are no all-purpose curry pastes or powders. In the West, most consist mainly of turmeric, with the presence of other spices determined more by economic than culinary factors. Curry pastes and powders need careful consideration if they are to be used appropriately.

Curries were brought to southern China centuries ago by Chinese merchants returning from India. Because they are pungent, they never really caught on, their strength being perceived as an interference with the enjoyment of the undiluted flavors of fresh foods. Curries are used in China – but sparingly and cautiously.

Shopping Tips

Many of the brands from India have an authentic taste. Buy the Madras curry paste variety, which has a rich, spicy, hot but complex taste, for Chinese dishes.

Storage Notes

In the refrigerator, it will keep indefinitely.

Useful Hints

Do not confuse Indian curry paste with Thai curry paste which is quite different.

FISH SAUCE

F ish sauce, the product of salted and fermented fish, has long been a staple in Southeast Asia, where it is used like soy sauce. Fish sauce is used occasionally in southern China, perhaps brought back by Chinese returning from Southeast Asia. A fish sauce is usually a clear, brownish, salty liquid that is rich in protein. The sauce, in fact, was originally concocted as a means of preserving fish protein. Also known as fish gravy, *nước mắm* in Vietnam, or *nam pla* in Thailand, fish sauce has a strong odor and a taste to match. Cooking or mixing with other ingredients, however, diminishes the 'fishy' flavor and the sauce adds a special richness, fragrance, and quality to dishes. It is also used as a dipping sauce, usually combined with other ingredients to mitigate its strength.

Shopping Tips

It is said that the best brands come from Vietnam and Thailand. However, Vietnamese brands are not always readily available. Fortunately, many of the Thai brands can easily be found in Chinese markets or grocers. Viet Huong 'Three Crab Brand Fish Sauce' and Flying Lion Brand 'Phy Quoc', both from Thailand, are highly recommended.

Storage Notes

Fish sauce in bottles will keep indefinitely. Store it in a cool, dry place.

FIVE SPICE POWDER

This ancient spice formula harmonizes star anise, Sichuan peppercorn, fennel, clove, and cinnamon or the stronger-scented cassia. But why stop at five spices? The answer perhaps lies not in cookery but in cosmology. In ancient Chinese lore, the universe is composed of five elements – wood, metal, water, fire, earth – some combinations of which were harmonious, others disharmonious, so care had to be taken in mixing them together. This five-fold categorization was carried over into daily life. Thus, just as the elements of the universe had to be carefully balanced, so, too, had the elements of civil life to be harmonized. In the preparation of food especially, the proper five-fold relationships had to be created and maintained. One result was five spice powder, which traditionally had powerful medicinal as well as culinary potency. On the other hand, it might have been just an accidental concatenation that worked to perfection.

Whatever its provenance, this spice is pungent, fragrant, hot, mild, and slightly sweet – all at once. Its distinctive fragrance and flavor make even the most prosaic dish something special.

Shopping Tips

Spices are always better freshly ground. There are no 'brand name' five spice powders, and, given our new cosmology, sometimes there are more or less than five spices in the package. The mixture is sold in good Chinese supermarkets and Asian specialty shops and comes in plastic bags or small glass jars. You should experiment with a number of them to find the one that suits your taste. They are all inexpensive.

Storage Notes

Store in a tightly closed glass jar in a cool, dry place.

Useful Hints

- Five spice is wonderful mixed with salt for a dipping condiment. It should be used in small quantities as a little goes a long way.
  - Try it with grilled meats.

FLOURS AND STARCHES

I n China and throughout Asia there are many flours and types of starch, such as water chestnut powder, taro starch and arrowroot, which are used to bind and thicken sauces and to make batter.

CORNFLOUR, CORNSTARCH

Cornflour is among the most commonly used in Chinese cooking, although many traditional cooks prefer a bean flour because it thickens faster and holds longer. In China, sauces are light and must barely coat the food, which never 'swims' in thick sauces. As part of a marinade, cornflour helps to coat food properly and to give dishes a velvety texture. It also protects food during deep-frying by helping to seal in the juices, producing a crisper coating than does wheat flour. It can also be used as a binder for minced stuffings. Cornflour is blended with cold water until it forms a smooth paste and is then added at the last moment to sauces. The mixture will look milky at first, but when the dish is properly prepared, the cornflour turns clear and shiny as it thickens the sauce. This translucent, glossy effect appeals to Chinese aesthetics. It results from the lack of gluten proteins in corn-flour which in wheat flour glazes produce an opaque effect.

Shopping Tips

All brands available at supermarkets are recommended.

Storage Notes

Store cornflour as you would wheat flour, in a clean glass jar or canister, tightly closed, and keep it in a cool, dry place.

Useful Hints

Mix two parts liquid to one part cornflour before adding to a sauce.

GLUTINOUS RICE FLOUR

Also known as sweet rice flour or sweet rice powder, this flour is made from short-grain rice that becomes moist, firm and sticky when cooked, a result of its higher proportion of waxy starch molecules. Because of its chewy texture, glutinous rice flour is a favorite base for dumplings, buns and pastries. Sweets made with glutinous rice flour are popular and widely available throughout Southeast Asia.

Glutinuous rice flour; cornflour; rice flour; potato starch

Shopping Tips

Most of the brands from China and Hong Kong are quite good and all are recommended.

Storage Notes

Store like flour in a cool, dry place.

Left potato starch; *right* wheat starch

Useful Hints

Regular rice flour cannot be substituted in recipes that call for glutinous or sweet rice flour.

RICE FLOUR

This flour, sometimes called rice powder, is made from finely milled white raw rice and is used to make fresh rice noodles, pastries and sweets. Rice flour is a staple food item throughout China and Southeast Asia.

Shopping Tips

All brands are recommended. Do not confuse it with glutinous rice flour, which is sometimes labeled sweet rice flour.

Storage Notes

Store in a cool, dry place.

Useful Hints

Substitute rice flour for wheat flour in crêpes or pancakes. Rice flour is lighter.

POTATO STARCH

Usually used in the making of a batter or for dusting food before frying, this starch is less commonly used as a binder. It is more glutinous in texture than cornflour [US cornstarch]. Potato starch is used more commonly in Japan than in China.

Shopping Tips

Available in Chinese markets and grocers, it is often labelled potato powder. All commonly available brands can be recommended.

Storage Notes

Store in a cool, dry place.

Useful Hints

It makes for a very crispy batter and holds better than cornflour for deep-frying.

WHEAT STARCH

Wheat starch is the fine, flour-like white powder left after the protein is removed from wheat flour. Although it is sometimes used to thicken sauces, it is more commonly made into a wrapping for dim sum dumplings in China. When steamed, this ingredient lends a soft, translucent, opaque sheen to the delicate pastry wrapping.

Shopping Tips

Wheat starch is available in 450g/llb sacks at Chinese markets and grocers. All brands can be recommended.

Storage Notes

It will keep indefinitely, tightly sealed, in a cool, dry place.

41

GARLIC

ALLIUM SATIVUM

The English word 'garlic' comes from the Anglo-Saxon word for 'spear plant'. This is an apt description of the straight, branchless stems characteristic of the subfamily of the lily to which garlic belongs, along with leeks, spring onions or scallions, shallots and onions. In terms of pungent flavor, raw garlic is the most potent member of the family, but cooking tones its flavor down to the level of merely delightful. True garlic is not found in the wild, the plant having been domesticated thousands of years ago in central Asia. The Chinese have been cultivating garlic since at least 3000 B.C., and Chinese cuisine is inconceivable without its distinct, sweet, pungent, aromatic contribution. Cooks often smash a clove of garlic into hot cooking oil; this 'sweetens' the oil and gives it a bracing aroma. Once its essence is captured by the oil, the garlic husk is removed and discarded. Garlic, whether whole, chopped, minced, crushed, pickled, boiled or smoked, used in flavored oils and spicy sauces, by itself or with other robust ingredients such as black beans, curry, shrimp paste, spring onions or ginger, is an essential and revered element in the Chinese diet.

Shopping Tips

Select fresh garlic that is firm and heavy. Cloves that are pinkish in color seem to have better flavor.

Storage Notes

It should be stored in a cool, dry place, but not in the refrigerator where it can easily become mildewed or begin sprouting.

Useful Hints

● The true garlic flavor is released by chemical reactions that occur when the garlic cells are broken. Garlic flavor is thus strongest when the cloves are squeezed and their juice extracted, slightly less strong when the cloves are grated or finely chopped, even less strong when the cloves are merely sliced, and mildest when whole unbroken cloves are used. In addition, the longer garlic is cooked, the milder it becomes.

● Peeling garlic cloves is laborious. However, the skin will come off quite easily if you use the Chinese technique of quickly boiling the garlic cloves with the skin on for 2 minutes and then leaving them in the hot water for 5 minutes. The cooking also mutes the intensity of the garlic. Another trick is to bruise the cloves with the side of a Chinese cleaver or heavy kitchen knife; the skin then tends to break away.

● If the garlic has begun to sprout, cut the clove in half and remove the central greenish core before proceeding with the preparation.

● Keep chopped garlic in oil to prevent it from oxidizing and growing bitter.

Other Notes

Scientists have recently begun to take seriously the alleged magical and medicinal qualities of garlic. Herbalists and traditional folk healers have always maintained that garlic is both a preventer and a healer of disease. Recent scientific studies now indicate that there may be a factual basis to their beliefs. Controlled experiments have led many researchers to conclude that the consumption of garlic lowers the risk of stomach cancer, fights off harmful cholesterol, lowers blood pressure, and reduces the incidence of unhealthy blood clotting. Garlic consists of over 200 chemical compounds in unstable balance and such chemicals may readily perform therapeutic func-tions. We now know, for example, that the compound diallyl disulfide, which is the major source of garlic's odor, is also one of the most active chemopreventive agents known to science. All of these claims need further scientific analysis; in the meantime, we should simply enjoy the culinary virtues of one of nature's greatest gifts to our palates.

GARLIC SHOOTS

As the name indicates, these are young shoots of garlic that precede the formation of the garlic bulb. And, as might be expected, garlic shoots have a mild and refreshing flavor with a delicate aroma, a combination that is highly prized among discerning gourmets. The shoots look like and are used in the manner of spring onions [US scallions], with their green tops serving as a garnish or flavoring.

Shopping Tips

Like spring onions, they should be firm and green-looking without any brown spots. Their fragrance indicates their freshness. They are available for a brief time each year, usually in the spring or before each garlic harvest.

Storage Notes

Keep in the bottom part of your refrigerator. They should be used within 2 days.

Useful Hints

Use them like spring onions. Their stem and every part of the green can be used.

GINGER

ZINGIBER OFFICINALE

G inger belongs to the small subfamily of spices that also includes cardamom and turmeric, all of which are native to southern Asia. The name ginger derives from a Sanskrit term that means 'horn-shaped', a reference to one of the common natural shapes of this rhizome or underground stem. Ginger is one of the five 'ancient' spices of Chinese cookery, along with red chillies, spring onions [US scallions], garlic, and cinnamon. The Chinese have been exploiting its virtues since 600 B.C., both as a spice and as a medicinal food. In its latter role ginger is believed to soothe the intestines, ward off the common cold, and do wonders for the sexual and gustatorial appetites. It appears that ginger was introduced to Western Europe early in the Middle Ages and it soon became one of the most popular or, at least, abundant spices in use.

Ginger is golden beige in color, with a thin dry skin. Whether whole, sliced, or ground into a powder, or pickled or candied, ginger preserves its peculiar fragrance and taste, giving a rich dimension to any recipe of which it is a part. It has a 'clean' taste that adds subtlety to delicate dishes, such as fried seafood, and that counterbalances the stronger flavors of more robust foods, such as beef and pork. Local boosters claim that the most aromatic and potent ginger is to be found in Guangzhou (Canton), but throughout China ginger is used in all sorts of recipes including soups, sauces, and flavored beverages. In China, fresh ginger is often shredded into light soups and added to marinades. Small wonder it is as ubiquitous in Chinese cuisine as garlic.

In India and Pakistan, and throughout southern Asia, ginger is an essential element in almost every traditional dish, whether soups, vegetables, fish and seafood, meats, curries, sauces, or rice. In Europe, ginger has most often been used in pastries, cookies, and other sweet treats. In recent years, however, European chefs, influenced by their Asian colleagues, have been utilizing this versatile spice in main-course recipes with great effectiveness.

Shopping Tips

Fortunately, fresh ginger is now widely available even in supermarkets. Look for ginger that is firm and not at all shriveled (older, more shriveled ginger is used for medicinal broths); it should be solid, heavy, and clear-skinned. Avoid large, fibrous ginger.

Storage Notes

Very young, almost pale yellow ginger should be used within 2 days of purchase. Ordinary ginger, wrapped in a paper towel and then in plastic wrap, will keep in the refrigerator for up to 2 weeks. Peeled ginger covered in Shaoxing rice wine or dry sherry and refrigerated in a glass jar will last for several months. This has the added benefit of producing a flavored wine that can be substituted in recipes. Ginger should never be frozen.

Useful Hints

● *Ginger juice* is made from fresh ginger and is used in marinades to give a subtle ginger taste without the bite of the fresh chopped pieces. Here is a simple method of extracting ginger juice: cut unpeeled fresh ginger into 2.5cm/1in chunks and drop them into a running food processor. When the ginger is finely chopped, squeeze out the juice by hand through a cotton or linen towel. Or, mash the ginger with a kitchen mallet or the side of a cleaver or knife until most of the fibers are exposed. Then simply squeeze out the juice by hand through a cotton or linen towel. Alternatively, place a piece of fresh ginger together with 2tbsp of water in a blender and liquidize, then strain the juice.
● Ginger should be peeled before using. Use the peel to flavor oil before stir-frying.

Other Notes

Fresh young stem ginger often makes a seasonal appearance in the markets of China, but is hard to find in the West. These are knobby and moist pink, looking rather naked in appearance. This is the newest spring growth of ginger. It is usually stir-fried and eaten in various dishes; it is also commonly pickled. Because it is so tender, it does not need peeling and can be eaten as a vegetable. A popular way to enjoy pickled young ginger is with preserved 'thousand-year-old' duck eggs as a snack. It is often served in restaurants or private homes as an *hors d'oeuvre*.

HAM

YUNNAN AND JINHUA HAM

T he pig was domesticated in Neolithic China more than 7,000 years ago and has lived symbiotically with the Chinese people ever since. It is a revered animal, not only because it is China's 'red meat'. Its contributions to Chinese life and diet come at little or no cost to the people who benefit from its virtues. Remember, nothing that is edible by humans is ever wasted in China. The pig, however, not only eats everything that humans can eat but much that humans cannot, so it does not compete with humans at the basic nutritional level. It is a clear net gain.

Nonetheless, given the natural and demographic constraints on the Chinese food supply, pigs never became plentiful and inexpensive. Every part of the pig was valued and consumed, from the snout to the trotters. The most valued parts, understandably, are the hams or hind legs. These were, and are, accorded special care in preparation. Before refrigeration, salting, drying, and smoking were essential procedures in preserving foods. Hams are 'cured', that is salted, variously seasoned, dried, and smoked in regionally distinct ways. They can remain edible and flavorful for as long as 3 years.

The most famous and highly valued Chinese hams are those from southwestern Yunan and eastern Jinhua provinces. Specialists in both regions breed particular types of pigs; they follow their own secret and elaborate curing processes; and they insist that a special diet must be fed to pigs destined to provide hams. Chinese gourmands have always applied this principle to their foodstuffs. There is, for example, an ancient recipe for Peking duck in which care and feeding of the duck from hatching to preparation for the pot were integral aspects of the prescribed method.

So with these hams. The Jinhua version has a succulence and a natural sweet flavor and aroma that, it is claimed, the curing process does not create but only captures. And those virtues are ascribed to the carefully controlled diet that these favored pigs enjoy before their destiny unfolds. The hams have a rich red color – in Chinese, the word for hams is 'fire legs' – and are justly popular everywhere.

Hams of all regions are available at specialty shops in China. They may be seen hanging in the windows of such shops, which happily serve them by the slice. They have a firm, slightly dry texture with well-developed flavors. Because they are expensive, such hams are used mainly as seasonings or as savory garnishes. As such, they are a standard in the ancient canon of Chinese cuisine.

Unfortunately still rare outside China, they are well worth the price of a tasty morsel if you ever come across them, for example in Chinese communities in Hong Kong, Singapore, Taiwan, etc.

Shopping Tips
Unfortunately, the cured Yunnan and Jinhua hams are not obtainable in the West. However, on rare occasions, Yunnan ham can be found in cans. Italian prosciutto (Parma ham) and American Smithfield hams are acceptable substitutes for the wonderfully rich, smoky-flavored Chinese hams.

Storage Notes
Smithfield ham sold in some Chinese grocers in slices or large pieces will keep for months, tightly wrapped, in the refrigerator. If a small amount of mold appears on the skin, simply scrape or cut it off.

CHINESE HAM

JINHUA

金華火腿

HAM

上海永隆食品商店

上海淮海中路1324号 电话：370393

HOISIN SAUCE

Hoisin sauce is part of the bean sauce family. It is a rich, thick, dark, brownish-red sauce that is made from soybean paste, garlic, vinegar, sugar, spices, and other flavorings. It is at once sweet and spicy. The texture ranges from creamy thick to thin. It is used in China as a condiment and as a glaze for roasted meats. In the West, it is often used as a sauce (mixed with sesame oil) for Peking Duck instead of the traditional bean sauce. Hoisin sauce is sold in cans and jars (it is sometimes also labeled 'barbecue sauce with hoisin sauce'; however, check carefully as there are barbecue sauces available which are quite different from hoisin sauce).

Shopping Tips

The best hoisin sauce comes from China under the brand name Pearl River Bridge. Another good one from China is under the Ma Ling label. Other good brands are from Hong Kong, under the Amoy and Koon Chun Sauce Factory's labels.

Storage Notes

Chee Hou Sauce is a slightly stronger version of hoisin sauce and can be used as a substitute for hoisin sauce.

LEEKS

ALLIUM RAMOSUM

T his vegetable is grown and used primarily in northern China. It is treated as an onion and stir-fried with meats. In the West, except among the Welsh, the leek is often regarded as the poor relative of its cousins, asparagus and onions. This is both unfair and incorrect because the leek possesses notable dietary riches.

One clarification: the European leek, of Mediterranean origin and already a standard by the time of Richard II, is rather larger and more fibrous than the Chinese leek. The Chinese leek, being smaller and thinner, has a finer texture; its pungent and slightly acidic flavor sweetens with cooking. To quote one authority, 'It has a warm character', and its nutritional virtues are matched by its medicinal potency. One Ming dynasty herbalist listed it first among important vegetable medicines, noting that, 'It restores the spirit and calms the five viscera'. No one has ever claimed as much for asparagus and onions.

Shopping Tips
The young leeks available in season at organic food stores and in some Chinese markets are a good substitute for Chinese leeks which are currently not available outside of China. Look for firm stalks without brown or yellow spots.

Storage Notes
Wrap them in paper towels and store them in plastic bags in the vegetable crisper of your refrigerator where they should keep for at least 5 days.

Useful Hints
To use, cut off and discard the green tops and roots and slice the leek in half lengthwise. Wash them well.

49

LEMONGRASS

CYMBOPOGON CITRATUS

This Southeast Asian original is little used in China and then usually only in dried form for making tea. Its subtle lemony fragrance and flavor impart a very special cachet to delicate foods and it is a standard ingredient in Thai and Vietnamese dishes. As is typical in Asian cuisine, the herb is considered a medicinal agent as well as a flavoring and is often prescribed for digestive disorders.

Lemongrass is closely related to Citronella grass. The latter plant has a stronger oil content and is used commercially in perfumes and as a mosquito repellent. The two should not be confused.

Fresh lemongrass is sold in stalks that can be 60cm/2 feet long – it looks like a very long spring onion [US scallion]. It is a fibrous plant but this is no problem because what is wanted is its fragrance and taste. Lemongrass pieces are almost always removed after the dish is cooked. Some recipes may call for lemongrass to be finely chopped or pounded into a paste, in which cases it becomes an integral part of the dish.

Shopping Tips

Get the freshest possible, usually found in Chinese or other Asian markets. Avoid dried lemongrass, which is mostly used for herbal teas.

Storage Notes

It can be kept, loosely wrapped, in the bottom part of your refrigerator for up to 1 week.

Useful Hints

• Pound the bulb end of the stalk. Outer leaves should be trimmed. For dishes calling for lemongrass, use only the tender core in the center.

• Lemon is not a substitute for the unique flavors of lemongrass.

LILY BUDS

HEMEROCALLIS SPP.

lso known as tiger lily buds, golden needles, or lily stems, dried lily buds are the unopened flowers, not buds, of a type of day lily. About 5cm/2in in length, they have a slightly furry texture and an earthy fragrance that is special. The buds serve well as an ingredient in muxi (mu shu) dishes of stir-fried pork with cloud ears and in hot and sour soup, providing texture as well as an additional flavor dimension.

Shopping Tips

Buy lily buds that are bright golden yellow in color. Avoid dark, brittle ones, as they are too old. Available in plastic or cellophane bags from Chinese grocers or supermarkets, they are very inexpensive.

Storage Notes

Transfer the lily buds to a jar and store in a cool, dry place. They will keep indefinitely.

Useful Hints

Before use, soak the buds in hot water for about 20 minutes or until soft. Cut off the hard ends and shred or cut in half according to the recipe directions.

LOTUS ROOT

NELUMBO NUCIFERA

This well-known, perennial aquatic plant with its beautiful white and pink water-lily flowers, is a native of Asia. Although all the plant is edible, the root or stems are the parts most commonly available. The buff-color, wooden-looking roots are quite long and are normally divided into sausage-like segments, each up to 12.5cm/5in long. Air passages run the length of the root, giving them a beautiful, paper chain cross-section. They have a crispy fibrous texture with a mild, distinctive flavor (some say they resemble artichokes). They may be cooked in many ways: stir-fried, mixed with other vegetables, used in vegetarian dishes, dried, steamed in soup, fried, or candied. They are also used raw in salads, cut into slices for a most attractive appearance. In addition, they also provide a specialty starch.

Shopping Tips
Look for lotus roots that are firm and free of bruises.

Storage Notes
Uncut, they can be kept in the bottom part of your refrigerator for up to 3 weeks.

Useful Hints
Deep-fried, they make a wonderful-looking garnish for many dishes.

MALTOSE SUGAR, MALT SUGAR

This thick, syrupy liquid is made by fermenting germinated cereal grains, such as barley, wheat or millet, in a process that converts the grain's starch into the maltose sugar. It is used to give the lacquered look to Peking duck. It is also used in preparing other roast meats, particularly in northern China. Recipes often call for its use with vinegar and soy sauce, the maltose first being diluted with water into a lighter syrup. Maltose sugar is not as cloyingly sweet as refined sugar so it can serve well in many dishes.

Shopping Tips

Found only in Chinese grocers or supermarkets, it comes in a small plastic tub or ceramic crock from China, the brand most often available.

Storage Notes

It can be stored at room temperature and keeps indefinitely.

Useful Hints

- Honey can be used as a substitute.
- Maltose sugar is hard and sticky. I have found that the best way to use it is to dip a spoon in very hot water and then scoop out what sugar you need.

53

MANGETOUTS

Snow Peas, Sugar Peas, Pea Pod

Pisum sativum, var. sacharatum

These delicacies are the early or spring variety of the common green pea. Native to the Middle East, peas were introduced into China by Europeans, hence their literal Chinese name 'Holland peas'. I would guess that the name 'snow peas' derives from their being picked while some snow still remained on the ground, as is the case with 'red cabbage in the snow'. The type available in the West is slightly larger than that to be found in China.

In any event, they need only be washed, topped, and tailed to be ready to be cooked and eaten, pods and all: hence their French name mangetouts. Many people who don't particularly like green peas in general find mangetouts deli-

cious – no doubt because the younger peas are sweeter and less starchy. I enjoy eating mangetouts raw, and in any event their tender, sweet crispiness needs little cooking. Thus, they are perfect for quick stir-fry dishes using a little oil, garlic, and ginger or in combination with seasoned poultry or meat.

Shopping Tips

Look for pods that are firm with very small peas. This indicates they are tender and young.

Storage Notes

Mangetouts are readily available at supermarkets, and should be eaten as quickly as possible after purchase. However, they will keep for at least 3 days in the vegetable crisper of the refrigerator.

MONOSODIUM GLUTAMATE

A void this ingredient. That it was originally derived from a naturally occurring salt in no way mitigates its perniciousness. It is at once unnecessary, undesirable, and destructive to authentic Chinese cuisine. In the words of the peerless authority on Chinese food, E.N. Anderson, MSG 'wrecks the subtle and complex blending of flavors essential to fine cuisine'. It also produces in susceptible people an allergic reaction – a burning sensation in the torso, a feeling of pressure behind the forehead and eyes, and chest pain – known as 'Chinese restaurant syndrome'.

Traditional Chinese cooking uses sugar but sparingly, salt only in pickled and preserved dishes, and MSG not at all, because that additive was only discovered in 1908. Sad to say, it has entered into Chinese restaurant fare and even into modern cookbooks, along with overdoses of oil, sugar, cornflour [US cornstarch] and salt. To be blunt about it: MSG is used only by lazy cooks and fast food providers who rely upon cheap ingredients and use watery stocks that require sugared, salted, and 'enhanced' additives to satisfy the consumers who have never tasted the real thing. The best food, Chinese or otherwise, relies only upon the freshest natural ingredients, carefully prepared and pleasingly combined and served. It is all worth the effort. I am happy to report that more and more restaurants are proclaiming 'No MSG' on their doorfronts and menus. Keep it out of your kitchen too.

NOODLES

Dried egg and wheat noodles

It has been said that pasta noodles originated in northern China around 100 B.C., and they are without doubt an important element of the Chinese diet. Noodles are rarely made in the home in China, as commerical noodle-making is an ancient craft. It is common to find fresh noodles of all types available throughout China and in many parts of the world where there is a substantial Chinese-speaking community.

WHEAT NOODLES AND EGG NOODLES

There are many types of noodles. One of the most important is the egg noodle, made from wheat flour and egg, a bit like Italian pasta. Most common are the thin, round strands that are sold both fresh and dry. They tend to be yellowish in color. Occasionally, they are flavored with fish or shrimp. Egg noodles are used in stir-fried dishes, as well as in soups. Wheat noodles contain no eggs: they are made simply from wheat flour, water, and salt, and are whiter in appearance. They are available both fresh and dried. Like egg noodles, they are used in soups as well as in stir-fried dishes.

Shopping Tips

Although many types of fresh noodles are now available in supermarkets, they tend to be more starchy than Chinese-made noodles. Fresh egg or wheat noodles in Chinese markets or grocers

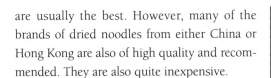
are usually the best. However, many of the brands of dried noodles from either China or Hong Kong are also of high quality and recommended. They are also quite inexpensive.

Storage Notes

Fresh noodles will keep in the bottom part of your refrigerator for at least 2 or 3 days. Dried noodles keep indefinitely.

Useful Hints

● If using noodles in a stir-fried dish or soup, pre-cook dried noodles in simmering salted water for 3–5 minutes, and fresh noodles for slightly less time. It is best to give the fresh noodles a quick rinse and drain before stir-frying them or putting them in soups.

● Fresh noodles freeze well but should be thawed thoroughly before pre-cooking in simmering salted water.

● If you are cooking noodles ahead of time or before stir-frying them, after draining toss the noodles in 2tsp sesame oil and put them into a bowl. Cover this with plastic wrap and refrigerate. The cooked noodles will remain usable for about 2 hours.

Other Notes

● Noodles are very good served with main dishes instead of plain rice. I think dried wheat or fresh egg noodles are best for this. Use 225g/8oz fresh or dried Chinese egg or wheat noodles to serve 2–4. If you are using fresh noodles, immerse them in a pot of boiling water and cook them for 3–5 minutes or until you find their texture to your taste.

● If you are using dried noodles, either cook them according to the instructions on the package, or cook them in boiling water for 4–5 minutes. Drain and serve.

RICE NOODLES

Fresh rice noodles are very popular in southern China where they are widely known as *Sha He* noodles. The name derives from that of a small village outside of Guangzhou (Canton). The villagers proudly claim that their ancestors discovered the process of fresh noodle-making; they have so far refrained from demanding royalties on every noodle consumed.

Fresh rice, or *fen*, noodles are made from a mixture of rice flour, wheat starch (not flour), and water. This 'pasta' is steamed into large sheets and then, when cooked, is cut into noodles to be eaten immediately. Restaurants and street food stalls in southern Chinese cities specialize in offering this nutritious and tasty treat, most often serving the noodles in a broth or sauce.

Dried rice noodles are made from a dough of finely ground rice flour and water. This pasta is then extruded into opaque white noodles of varying thicknesses and sizes. One of the most common types is rice stick noodles which are flat and about the length of a chopstick; very thin rice stick noodles are sometimes called rice vermicelli. Deep-fried, they puff up instantly and become delicately crisp and light. Because they are absorbent and have little flavor of their own, they readily take on the taste and fragrance qualities of the foods with which they are cooked. They are a basic and extremely versatile food.

Shopping Tips

All brands can be recommended, especially the ones from China and Thailand. They come attractively wrapped in paper or cellophane and often tied with red ribbon. Fresh rice noodles can be found almost exclusively in Chinese markets or grocery stores.

Storage Notes

Dried rice noodles stored in a cool, dry place will last indefinitely. Fresh rice noodles are best eaten on the day they are purchased. They can be refrigerated for 2 days, but you should let them soften at room temperature before stir-frying or preparing them.

Useful Hints

Dried rice noodles are very easy to use. Simply soak them in warm water for 20 minutes, until they are soft. Drain them in a colander or sieve, and they are ready to use, for example, in soups or stir-fries. Dried rice noodles are perfect for quick, easy cooking as they take little time to soften and can be cooked with almost any vegetable, meat, fish or seafood.

BEAN THREAD NOODLES
CELLOPHANE NOODLES
TRANSPARENT NOODLES
MUNG BEAN THREADS

These noodles are not made from a grain flour but from ground mung beans, which are also the source of the more familiar bean sprouts. Freshly made noodles can sometimes be seen in

Fresh and dry rice noodles

Bean thread noodles

China, fluttering on lines in the breeze like long thread-like skeins. They are available dried, and are very fine and white. Easy to recognize, packed in their neat, plastic-wrapped bundles, they are stocked by most Chinese markets and some supermarkets. They are never served on their own, but are added to soups or braised dishes or are deep-fried and used as a garnish. Once they are soaked they become soft and slippery, springy and translucent. Since they are a vegetable product, they are popularly used in vegetarian dishes. When fried, they puff up immediately and become very white and crispy.

Shopping Tips

There are only a few brands available; all are recommended. They come in packages from 28g/1oz to 450g/1lb. I recommend the smaller packages, as these are easier to handle as well as to measure. The ones most widely available are from China and are quite inexpensive.

Storage Notes

Stored in a dry place, they will last indefinitely.

Useful Hints

They should be soaked in hot water, rather than boiled, for about 5 minutes before use. As they are rather long, you might find it easier to cut them into shorter lengths after soaking. If you are frying them, omit the soaking but make sure to separate them first. A good technique for separating the strands is to put them into a large paper bag before pulling them apart; this stops them from flying all over the place.

Other Notes

Once fried they make a light, airy bed for stir-fried dishes.

OILS AND FATS

Many different types of oils and fats are used in Chinese cooking. Edible oils obtained from seeds of oil-bearing plants are featured in recipes that are 2,000 years old. Before that time, lard from pigs and fat from chickens and ducks were used. Vegetable oils pressed from soybeans, rapeseed, sunflower seeds, corn, cotton seeds and peanuts are now all in use. Unlike animal fats, they do not burn until a high temperature is reached, and they impart a crispier texture to foods. Though oils may be more expensive than fats, they are more versatile to use.

GROUNDNUT OIL, PEANUT OIL

Peanuts, or groundnuts, a New World legume (not a nut), were introduced into China over 400 years ago and were immediately adopted into the culinary canon. They are eaten boiled, roasted, and even, although rarely, raw; they are used in pastries, candies, and sweets and as the basis of a sweet soup. Like the soybean, peanuts are an anomaly among the legumes in that they store oil instead of starch. This feature was immediately noted and exploited by the Chinese. Groundnut oil quickly became the most popular cooking oil because of its mild, unobtrusive taste and because it heats to a high temperature without burning. It is thus perfect for stir-frying and deep-frying. The semi-refined groundnut oils in China are cold-pressed, retain the fragrance of fresh nuts, and possess a distinctive flavor preferred by many cooks. It is an excellent cooking oil.

Shopping Tips

Some Chinese supermarkets stock the Chinese brands of semi-refined groundnut oil from either Hong Kong or China; often their names are written in Chinese characters. The Lion and Globe brand from Hong Kong is highly recommended. However, the best, if you can get it, is the one from China with the Chinese characters for 'double happiness'. It comes in a gold and red can and is well worth the search. If you cannot find it, use the best quality local groundnut oil from your supermarket; look for semi-refined oil.

Storage Notes

Store in a cool, dry place, away from light.

Useful Hints

After deep-frying, groundnut oil can be re-used at least once (unless used to fry fish or other strong-flavored foods). Simply cool the oil after use and filter it through muslin, or through a sieve or fine strainer, into a jar. Cover it tightly and keep it in a cool, dry place. If kept in the refrigerator it will become cloudy but it will clarify again when the oil returns to room temperature. Never use oils more than twice: constantly re-used oils increase in saturated fat content. For clarity of flavors, I use them only once. The best Chinese cooking requires that only fresh oil be used.

CORN OIL

Corn oil is a light, healthful, mostly polyunsaturated oil that is good for cooking and also has a high burning temperature. Being thus similar to groundnut oil, I find it an adequate substitute and ideal for Chinese stir-frying or deep-frying. It has a heavier, distinct flavor and is an easily acquired taste.

Shopping Tips

The highest quality corn oil you can find at your local supermarket is recommended.

Storage Notes

Store in a cool, dry place, away from light.

Corn oil

OTHER VEGETABLE OILS

Some of the cheaper vegetable oils are available in China: these include rapeseed or canola, cottonseed, soybean, safflower, and sunflower oils. They are light in color and taste and can be used in cooking, although they tend to burn rather quickly. In China, they are used mainly by food stalls and the cheaper restaurants. They are quite edible and serviceable but not as good or as effective as groundnut oil.

Shopping Tips

Most brands available at supermarkets are perfectly acceptable.

Storage Notes

Store in a cool, dry place, away from light.

SESAME OIL

In China, sesame oil is used only as a flavoring oil. A native of India and one of the world's oldest spices and oil seed crops, sesame seeds produce an aromatic oil that is golden or dark brown in color, thick, rich and strong-flavored. This latter quality explains why in China it is not used as a cooking oil. Chinese cooks prefer lighter, more subtly flavored oils for cooking. However, sesame oil is highly regarded as a flavoring and

is, therefore, used, though sparingly, in marinades or as a final seasoning in small amounts. In Sichuan and in northern China, cooks will sometimes use it for cooking, alone or in combination with other cooking oils, but this is an exceptional practice. Sesame oil is favored in many cold dishes, as part of a dressing, or as an element of a dipping sauce.

Shopping Tips

The purest and best sesame oil is the Kadoya brand of Japan. It has a clean, fresh, aromatic flavor. Brands from China, Hong Kong, and Taiwan can be very good, although you may occasionally stumble upon a bottle that is rancid. This is due to storage and shipping time. Buy sesame oil only in glass bottles. Avoid any of the sesame oils that come in plastic bottles, as the chances of these turning rancid are great.

Storage Notes

Store in a cool, dry place, away from direct light.

Useful Hints

Sesame oil is a wonderful aromatic addition to marinades, whether Chinese or otherwise. Use it like walnut oil, adding a few drops to your salad dressing.

OYSTERS, DRIED

ried oysters are a standard item in the coastal parts of southern China. Like many dried seafood preparations in China, these oysters are frequently used in finely minced form to enhance dishes. They come in all grades and sizes and add a strong, distinctive sea-flavor to a variety of braised dishes and soups. They are naturally sun-dried, usually without salting.

Shopping Tips

The best dried oysters are usually the most expensive. There are no particular brands: however, reject any darkish ones that are too shriveled.

Storage Notes

Store them in a jar in a cool, dry place.

Useful Hints

Use dried oysters carefully because they can overwhelm a dish with their assertive flavors. Soak them in a bowl of warm water for at least 1 hour, or even as long as overnight.

OYSTER SAUCE

rich and distinctive savory flavor, one that goes nicely with the preferred subtleties of southern Chinese cuisine. It is also used as a condiment, diluted with a little oil, for vegetables, poultry, and meats. It is a very popular southern Chinese sauce.

Shopping Tips

It is usually sold in bottles and can be bought in Chinese markets and some supermarkets. Search out the most expensive ones; they tend to be less salty, have more flavor, and contain less cornflour [US cornstarch] – their higher quality is worth the price. Cheaper oyster sauces tend to have MSG, as well as other additives, to make up for the lack of oysters used. I have found two especially good brands from China and Hong Kong: Sa Cheng, labeled 'Oyster Flavored Sauce from China', and the more widely available Hop Sing Lung's 'Oyster Flavored Sauce'.

Storage Notes

Oyster sauce is best kept in the refrigerator where it will last indefinitely.

Useful Hints

● Oyster sauce is delicious as a dipping sauce. Dilute it with a bit of water or oil.
● It can be used directly from the bottle over blanched vegetables.

T his very popular and versatile southern Chinese sauce is a thick, brown, richly flavored concoction and is one of the most ancient sauces in the culinary canon. Fresh oysters are boiled in large vats, the whole being seasoned with soy sauce, salt, spices, and seasonings and made into a viscous substance. The original version contained bits of dried fermented oysters, but these are no longer included.

The salty taste of oyster sauce largely dissipates during the cooking process; it doesn't even taste 'fishy' after it has been cooked. But it retains its

KEN HOM'S CHINESE KITCHEN

64

PEANUTS

ARACHIS HYPOGAEA

P eanuts are a wonderfully successful transplant. Introduced by way of the Portuguese – from the New World to Manila to Macao to China and elsewhere in Asia – the peanut has been enthusiastically adopted everywhere and immediately absorbed into local cuisines. It grows well in soils unsuited for other crops and is a source of cooking oil as well. As I noted elsewhere (see page 60), the Chinese eat peanuts in almost every way. Being legumes, peanuts have a significant amount of vegetable protein and are high in calories, thus making a substantial contribution to the Chinese diet. Their flavor is distinctive but does not overpower other foods. Peanuts are consequently valued as a versatile and congenial element in many recipes. They are usually stir-fried or boiled before being added to recipes. They are also eaten as salted snacks or ground into a peanut sauce.

Shopping Tips

They can be found at health food shops, good supermarkets, and Chinese markets. Make sure they are well packed so they remain fresh and do not go rancid.

Storage

Store them in a glass jar in a cool, dry place.

Useful Hints

● The thin red skins need to be removed before you use the nuts. To do this, simply immerse them in a pot of boiling water for about 2 minutes. Drain them and let them cool, and the skins will come off easily.

● Stir-fry or roast the peanuts just before using.

PEKING CABBAGE

CHINESE LEAVES, NAPA CABBAGE

BRASSICA PEKINENSIS

T he Chinese have no word that corresponds to our word 'vegetable'. The word 'cai', however, which means 'greens' (or leaf and stem of vegetables), is generalized to cover all plant dishes. There are four other words for root and tuber plants and for fruits and nuts. But cai is the most important category because it includes the vegetables that comprise the greater part of the Chinese diet, except for rice and other grain starches. Preeminent among the cai foods are cabbages, which with grains and soybeans are the most characteristic and abundant foods in the Chinese diet.

All types of cabbages cultivated in China are more nutritious than the common European varieties. All of them have a mild taste, but Peking cabbages are the most mild. They have been cultivated for over 1,500 years because they are very rich in vitamins, minerals, and fiber, and, in the aggregate, provide many calories as well. They are in these vital matters more like broccoli than Western cabbages. Peking cabbages have delightfully crisp, fibrous leaves, leading them to be called 'celery cabbages'.

Because of the regional and climatic differences in China, these cabbages come in various shapes and sizes, from long, barrel-shaped specimens to fat, squat types. Their leaves are firm and tightly packed and pale green (sometimes slightly yellow) in color. They look most like cos or romaine lettuce.

This versatile cai is used in soups and in stir-fried meat dishes. Its leaves, which readily absorb flavors, and its sweet, pleasant taste make it a favorite as a match for foods that have rich flavors. It is also enjoyed pickled with salt and chilli.

Shopping Tips

Look for fresh cabbage that is not wilted. It should have a crisp look with no yellow or brown spots.

Storage Notes

Wrapped loosely in paper towels and kept in the lower part of your refrigerator, it should last up to one week.

Useful Hints

- It can be used as a green for salads.
- Do not boil this cabbage: it is rather delicate and fragile. Light cooking is best.
- Every part of the cabbage can be used.

PLUM SAUCE

P lums have been grown in China since ancient times. The fresh fruits spoil quickly, so, in order to capture their juicy richness, the Chinese hit upon the idea of preserving them with ginger, chilli, spices, vinegar, and sugar. The result is a sweet, tart, jam-like condiment that is used as a cooking ingredient in recipes that call for assertive flavors. It is a popular item in Chinese restaurants where it is sometimes used, unauthentically, with Beijing (or Peking) duck.

Shopping tips

Some of the best brands are from Hong Kong. Especially recommended is the Koon Chun Sauce Factory's plum sauce. Brands from China are quite good, although they are harder to find and only available occasionally.

Storage Notes

If purchased in a can, transfer plum sauce to a glass jar and keep it in the refrigerator where it will last indefinitely.

PRESERVED MUSTARD GREENS OR CABBAGE

BRASSICA JUNCEA

Mustard greens are known in Chinese as 'greens heart' because only the heart of the plant is eaten, that is the stem, buds and young leaf. They are unrelated to and quite unlike the mustard greens of the American south. These greens are a vital part of the Chinese diet, being rich in vitamins and minerals and easy to cultivate. As such, they are enjoyed year-round, either fresh or preserved. The leaves are pickled with salt, water, vinegar and sugar, making a true sweet and sour food that is used as a vegetable or as a flavoring ingredient, especially in soups. Mustard greens can be served as a snack or used in stir-fries with meats, poultry, or fish.

Shopping Tips

The best preserved mustard greens can be found in large crocks in Chinese markets, which usually means they are locally made. The next best alternative is the ones available in small cans, labeled 'Preserved Vegetable', from Hong Kong, Taiwan, or China. All are recommended.

Storage Notes

Remove from the crock or can and store in a glass jar. They will keep indefinitely in the refrigerator.

RED IN SNOW CABBAGE

AMARANTH

AMARANTHUS TRICOLOR

A relative of spinach with a similar flavor, this leafy vegetable has a long history, being mentioned in ancient Chinese culinary records. There are two varieties. The green one is most similiar to spinach, with a watercress-like, mild and slightly tart flavor. The other variety has red stems with a red coloration that is prominent throughout the leaves also. It is a hardy vegetable and arrives in early spring when it peeks through snow that is still on the ground. Hence, its name is most apt as its crimson leaves contrast with the snowy fields. It is salt-pickled as well as eaten fresh. The pickled variety adds a pungent, slightly sour but not unpleasant taste to dishes when used as a flavoring. It can also be used as an interestingly textured vegetable ingredient in stir-fried and braised dishes. The fresh variety has a wonderful pungent, green, earthy taste and flavor.

Shopping Tips

The pickled version can be purchased in cans at Chinese markets or grocers. The best brands are from China and Taiwan. All are recommended. When purchasing the fresh version, look for the variety with green leaves. These should be fresh, not wilted.

Storage Notes

The canned variety will last indefinitely in the refrigerator. The fresh version should be consumed within 2 days of purchase. Store the fresh variety in the bottom part of your refrigerator, wrapped in paper towels in a plastic bag.

RICE

R ice is the staple food for one half of the world's population, including the Chinese. It was first cultivated in prehistoric times in either India or China. In southern China, the phrase chi fan (literally, 'to eat rice') also means simply 'to eat', while the word fan (cooked rice, cooked grains) also means simply 'food'. Northern Chinese consume other grains as well, such as wheat, millet, and corn.

Rice is the most useful plant known to humans. It is a source not only of food but of wine and vinegar and of straw used for fodder, thatch, sandals and other commercial purposes. Among the virtues of rice, beyond its unquestionable nutritional value, is its warm congeniality with so many other foods and with so many spices and seasonings. Moreover, by changing the cooking time, rice can be made into baby food, porridge (congee), and other nutritious dishes. Even the water that remains after the rice is done is

White and black glutinous rice

saved and made into a cooling drink. Rice flour, of course, serves a myriad of purposes. It is no wonder that there can be no true meal in China without a serving of rice.

LONG-GRAIN AND SHORT-GRAIN RICE

The favored variety in China is the long-grain type that cooks up relatively dry with easily separated grains.

Short-grain white rice is slightly stickier than long-grain rice, making it easier to eat with chopsticks. However, this non-glutinous rice is more frequently eaten in Japan than China. Although occasionally available in northern China in areas bordering Korea and Japan, it is not as popular with the Chinese. Some, however, find it useful for making rice porridge, a popular southern Chinese morning dish.

Shopping Tips

Many of the brands of long-grain white rice available in local supermarkets are highly recommended. Especially good in Chinese grocers or supermarkets is the fragrant Thai long-grain rice. All the best recommended brands of short-grain rice are Japanese, which can be found in Chinese grocers or supermarkets.

Storage Notes

Keep rice in a cool, dry place.

Useful Hints

● Although the Chinese go through the ritual of washing it, rice purchased at supermarkets doesn't require this step.
● The best method to cook white rice the Chinese way is to steam it, which is simple, direct and efficient. I prefer to use long-grain white rice which is drier and fluffier when cooked. The secret of preparing rice without it being sticky is to cook it first in an uncovered pot at a high heat until most of the water has evaporated. Then the heat should be turned very low, the pot covered and the rice cooked slowly in the remaining steam. As a child I was always instructed never to peek into the rice pot during this stage or else precious steam would escape and the rice would not be cooked properly, thus bringing bad luck.

● Here is a good trick to remember: if you make sure that you cover long-grain rice with about 2.5cm/1in of water it should always cook properly without sticking (use slightly less water for short-grain rice). Many recipes on rice packages use too much water and result in a gluey mess. Follow my method and you will have perfect steamed rice, the easy Chinese way. So, follow these rules for perfect rice:
● For the most authentic Chinese cooking, the preferred variety of rice is simple long-grain white rice, of which there are many varieties.
● The water should be at a level 2.5cm/1in above the surface of the rice; too much water means gummy rice. Recipes on packages of rice generally recommend too much water.
● Never uncover the pot once the simmering process has begun; time the process and wait.

GLUTINOUS RICE

There are some 2,500 different varieties of rice, but for cooking purposes only one distinction is crucial: glutinous rice has proteins that do not dissolve in water, and it absorbs twice its weight in water when cooked.

Round and pearly white, glutinous rice cooks into a sticky mass that makes it suitable for use in stuffings, puddings and pastries. After being

71

ground into flour, it is used for other pastries, sweet dumplings and cakes. It is featured in special dinner dishes, such as rice wrapped in lotus leaves, or combined with sausages or dried shrimp. Glutinous rice lends itself to exotic treats and is, thus, a common banquet food. Fermented, it is the basis of Shaoxing rice wine and rice vinegar.

Shopping Tips

Most Chinese markets and grocers stock glutinous rice. All brands from Taiwan, Hong Kong, or Thailand are recommended.

Storage Notes

Keep in a cool, dry place.

Useful Hints

Glutinous rice must be soaked for at least 8 hours or overnight. It should then be rinsed and drained before cooking. To cook: line the bottom of a steamer with a damp piece of muslin or cheesecloth and steam the rice gently for 1–1½ hours. Taste to see that it is cooked through. Alternatively you can cook it on top of the stove in water.

Outside *long-grain rice*; inside *short-grain rice*

Rice Papers, Rice Paper Wrappers

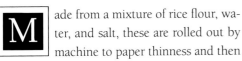

Made from a mixture of rice flour, water, and salt, these are rolled out by machine to paper thinness and then dried on bamboo mats in the sun, which gives them their beautiful cross-hatch imprint or pattern. Rice papers (bánh tráng) are available only in dry form, semi-transparent, thin, and hard. They may be round or triangular. Rice papers are used extensively for wrapping Vietnamese spring rolls of pork and seafood, which are then fried and wrapped with crispy fresh lettuce and herbs and finally dipped in a sweet, sour hot sauce. Although more identified with Vietnamese cooking, rice papers have nevertheless become quite popular elsewhere and are often used by restaurants in Hong Kong, Taiwan and parts of southern China.

Shopping Tips

Available in many Chinese grocers and supermarkets, they come in packages of 50–100 sheets. They are very inexpensive. All brands are good, especially the ones from Vietnam and Thailand. Look for white papers, avoid yellowish ones, which may be too old. Broken pieces in the package may also indicate age.

Storage Notes

Store them in a cool, dry place. After use, wrap left-over rice papers carefully in the package they came in, put this in another plastic bag, and seal well before storing.

Useful Hints

• Rice papers must be softened before use. Simply immerse them, one or two sheets at a time, in a warm sugar-water solution or in beer. Soak them until they are soft, approximately 1 or 2 minutes. Using a sugar-water solution or beer will result in a golden, crispy spring roll.
• Handle them carefully as the sheets are brittle.
• Drain them on a linen towel before rolling.

RICE VINEGAR

Vinegars used in Asian cooking are usually made from fermented rice and grains such as wheat, millet and sorghum. They should not be confused with Western wine vinegars which are much more acidic. Vinegar is one of the oldest seasonings used in Asian cuisine; its name appears in documents from the 12th century B.C. It is used directly as a seasoning in dishes or in dipping sauces. There are several main types. Western-style wine vinegars cannot serve as a substitute. Nor should rice vinegar be confused with Shaoxing rice wine – which is a wine not a vinegar.

BLACK RICE VINEGAR

Black rice vinegar is very dark in color with a rich but mild taste and an appealing depth of flavor, similar to Italian balsamic vinegar. It is usually made from glutinous rice, which imparts its mildness and taste. Really good black rice vinegar has a rich, impressive complexity of flavors and aromas. In northern China, it is used for braised dishes, noodles, and sauces.

Shopping Tips
Gold Plum's Chinkiang vinegar from China is the best.

Storage Notes
Kept at room temperature, it will last indefinitely.

RED RICE VINEGAR

Red rice vinegar is a clear, pale red. It has a delicate, tart, slightly sweet and salty taste and is usually used as a dipping sauce for seafood or shark's fin soup.

Shopping Tips
Koon Chun brand from Hong Kong is the best.

Storage Notes
Kept at room temperature, it will last indefinitely.

WHITE RICE VINEGAR

White rice vinegar is clear and mild in flavor. It has a faint taste of glutinous rice and is used for sweet and sour dishes. Western cider vinegar can be substituted.

Shopping Tips
China's Pearl River Bridge brand is the best.

Storage Notes
Kept at room temperature, it will last indefinitely.

SWEET RICE VINEGAR

This vinegar is a brownish-black and thicker than plain rice vinegar. It is processed with sugar and star anise, and the result is an aromatic, caramel taste. It is used in large quantities for braised pork dishes.

Shopping Tips
China's Pearl River Bridge brand is the best.

Storage Notes
Kept at room temperature, it will last indefinitely.

SHAOXING RICE WINE

R ice wine has been an integral part of Chinese cuisine for over 2,000 years. At banquets and special feasts it is an essential element. I should note that the Chinese also know how to make wine from wheat, millet, and other grains. About 1,000 years ago, wines made from grapes were popular, but they eventually lost out to the ever-popular rice wine. It is made from a blend of glutinous rice, millet, yeast, and spring water.

Shaoxing rice wine is China's most famous wine. It is known in Chinese as *hua tiao*, or 'carved flower', from the name given to the pattern carved on the urns in which the wine is stored. The wine is kept in cellars until it matures, usually for 10 years, although some have been aged for as long as 100 years. With its amber color, bouquet, and alcohol content, it more resembles sherry than grape wine. The wine is drunk warm or at room temperature. And it is always consumed in the context of a meal. Rice wine is an indispensable ingredient in many recipes, imparting a rich flavor and aroma to all sorts of dishes. It is also used in marinades and sauces.

Storage Notes

It should be kept tightly corked at room temperature and it will last indefinitely.

Useful Hints

● Do not confuse Shaoxing rice wine with Japanese *sake*, which is a Japanese version of rice wine and quite different. Nor should one confuse it with Chinese rice vinegar.

● A good quality, pale, dry sherry can be substituted but cannot equal the rich, mellow taste of rice wine. Western grape wines are not an adequate substitute.

75

SALT

S alt is composed of two mineral elements, sodium and chlorine, that are essential in our diet. It is one of the oldest known food seasonings in both the East and the West. We have a natural, specialized ability to detect salt in foods, and even though we don't need much of it (perhaps 2 or 3 grams a day), our bodies seem ready to absorb a great deal more. Until this century it was relatively expensive, being either rare or heavily taxed. This was beneficial because too much salt apparently does play a role in hypertension. Use salt sparingly and avoid processed foods, which are almost always heavily laced with sodium.

In China, natural salt deposits provided both a necessary ingredient in cooking and the basis for a thriving trade in the commodity. Again, salt was used to preserve foods, and these salted, dried, and pickled foods were an important part of the diet. Today, free salt is still rarely used; instead, salt is found in soy sauce, salted soybeans, pickled vegetables, and salted seafood. In the Guangdong region, instead of adding free salt, cooks will add very salty fermented soybeans ('black beans') when they wish to make a dish saltier.

While salt is chemically the same, there are variations which many people believe make for different tastes. Sea salt allegedly has a different taste from that of ordinary refined table salt. Rock salt has large, coarse crystals which make better heat conductors in cooking; they do dissolve readily, however. I myself am not aware of any taste benefits that flow from any special salts, but I do like to work with the coarser crystals.

Shopping Tips

Kosher salt, available in specialty sections of some supermarkets, is highly recommended. Another salt that is delicious to use is Maldon sea salt. Some of the French sea salts, such as the *fleur de sel*, have a distinctive flavor and are highly recommended.

Storage Notes

Store in a cool, dry place.

Clockwise from bottom left *fine ground sea salt; rock salt; Maldon sea salt; coarse ground sea salt*

SEAFOOD, DRIED

By the time of the Sung Dynasty (960–1289 A.D.), fish and seafood had become so popular in Chinese cuisine that poets began to wax lyrical over them, dropping their conceits concerning the previous favorite, chicken, which disappeared as a poetic theme. This emergence of seafood and fish reflected a movement of both politics and ecology. The center of gravity, as it were, shifted to southern China where fish and seafood had long been favorites and where there are thousands of species, both wild and pond-reared.

Before the age of refrigeration and rapid transport of goods, drying, salting and pickling were the only ways to preserve foods for any length of time, allowing it to retain much of its nutritional value and, as such, to become a year-round part of the diet. The drawback of preserving food by drying and salting (and pickling too) is that flavors and aromas become concentrated and often strong. The remedy is to use the foods sparingly, as a condiment or flavoring ingredient, and with the knowledge that in the cooking process the wilder flavors are usually domesticated.

Dried shrimp; dried squid;
dried scallops

Fish are the most prevalent dried seafood in China. All types and sizes are thus preserved, often in a semi-moist state that is a great favorite with southern Chinese. The dried fish are cut up and fried or steamed, sometimes alone but more often in combination with other foods. Today, fresh fish are available, but the dried versions still retain their place in the cuisine as providers of a special taste and aroma.

Other dried seafood includes: abalone, squid, scallops, jellyfish, and shrimp.

Shopping Tips

There are many varieties of dried fish and seafood. The quality is very simply based on price. The more exotic and desirable varieties cost more than the lesser and more abundant ones. Some dried fish also come packed in oil and are very good; look for the brands from Hong Kong or China. These all tend to be of high quality.

Storage Notes

Dried seafood will keep indefinitely whether simply dried or in oil. Store in a cool, dry place, away from light.

Useful Hints

• Soak dried fish or seafood in warm water for 30 minutes. When it has softened, remove any bones and chop.

• Some dried seafood, like abalone and squid, needs to be soaked for up to 24 hours before using.

SESAME PASTE

T his rich, creamy, light brown paste is made from toasted sesame seeds. Sesame was introduced into China over 2,000 years ago. Chinese sesame paste is quite different from the Mediteranean *tahini*, whose seeds are raw when ground, producing a much lighter color and taste.

The Chinese use the paste either as part of a sauce or as an integral ingredient in both hot and cold dishes. Sesame paste is most popular in northern and western China, the hotter, wet-ter climate of eastern and southern China being uncongenial to the sesame plant.

Shopping Tips

Sesame paste is sold in jars at Chinese markets.

I highly recommend all brands from China (par-ticularly the Pearl River Bridge brand), Hong Kong, and Taiwan (Lan Chi brand).

Storage Notes

Kept in the refrigerator, it will last indefinitely.

Useful Hints

If the paste has separated in the jar, empty the contents into a blender or food processor and blend or process well. Always stir well before using.

Other Notes

If you have a recipe that calls for sesame paste, and you can't locate any, use a smooth peanut butter instead.

SESAME SEEDS

SESAMUM INDICUM

T he sesame plant is native to Central Asia, Indonesia, or East Africa. It is cultivated today in the Middle East, Africa, China, and Japan. The seeds are highly valued, being rich in protein and in polyunsaturated oil. They are usually pressed into oils or made into pastes to use as flavoring agents or in sauces. Some seeds may be toasted and used as a garnish for foods, sweets and breads. In China, there are sweeter varieties that are used in dessert soups. Toasted, they make a good snack food.

Shopping Tips

Purchase them in small plastic bags or in glass jars from supermarkets or Chinese grocers.

Storage Notes

Keep them in a glass jar in a dry, cool place. They should last indefinitely. Some people prefer to keep them in the freezer to prevent them from getting rancid.

Useful Hints

If you don't use them often, check the sesame seeds to ensure they are fresh. Toss them out if they have a rancid smell.

Other Notes

To toast sesame seeds: Heat a frying pan or skillet over a burner until hot. Add the sesame seeds and stir occasionally. Watch them closely and, when they begin to brown lightly, about 3–5 minutes, stir them again and pour them onto a plate. When they are completely cold, store them in a glass jar in a cool, dark place. Alternatively, you could roast them in a preheated 160°C/ 325°F/gas mark 3 oven: spread the sesame seeds on a baking sheet and roast for about 10–15 minutes until they are nicely toasted and lightly browned. Allow them to cool and keep in a glass jar until you are ready to use them.

SHALLOTS

ALLIUM ASCALONICUM

S hallots are mild-flavored members of the onion family. Used extensively in Southeast Asian cooking and to a lesser extent in Chinese cooking, they range from small to medium size, with thin copper-red skins. They have a distinctive onion taste without being as strong or tear-inducing as ordinary onions. Readily available, they make an excellent substitute for the small onion cultivated in China. These small onions grow wild in the mountains in Kiangsi and are often confused with shallots. In China, you will find shallots, fresh or pickled, to go with preserved eggs as a snack.

Shopping Tips

Similar to onions, look for firm shallots with no soft or brown spots.

Storage Notes

Keep them in a cool, dry place (not the refrigerator). Peel, slice, or chop them as you would an onion.

SHARK'S FIN

Although shark meat has been eaten for a long time, it is the fin that is a rare delicacy in China. As with bird's nest, it is an exotic food and, thus, is one of the most expensive ingredients in Chinese cooking. It is served in soup or braised in a rich stock, or sometimes stir-fried. Chinese restaurants occasionally offer a long list of shark's fin dishes. Perhaps more than anything else, it is a blatant symbol of extravagance.

Shark's fin is available dried and sold whole, in pieces, or in cleaned strands, in many dry food shops in China. The fin refers to the dorsal 'comb fin' or the two ventral fins of any of a variety of sharks. Indeed, in China, fins are imported from all over the world. Preparation usually involves an elaborate process of soaking and boiling in several changes of water and stock. However, thanks to modern technology, one can now purchase prepared shark's fin in the freezer section of the Chinese market. This convenience brings shark's fin within the scope of today's adventurous home cook.

Like bird's nest, the other extravagant Chinese delicacy, shark's fin has little flavor of its own. However, cooked in a rich flavorful stock, it is

prized for its absorbency, its clear gelatinous strands, and its texture which makes for an enjoyable combination. It is usually served with a rich stock, as in shark's fin soup, or stuffed with poultry, or scrambled with eggs and crab. It also holds high status as a general medicinal tonic.

Shopping Tips

● Quality is based on price: the higher the price, the better the quality.

● High quality shark's fin can sometimes be found already prepared and frozen, and this is a good buy because all the preparation work has been done and freezing does not affect the quality or texture of the shark's fin.

Storage Notes

If dried, store in a cool, dry place. If frozen, keep in the freezer until ready to use.

Useful Hints

Dried shark's fin must be softened before use: Put it in a large pot of cold water with spring onions [US scallions] and slices of ginger, bring slowly to a boil, and simmer for at least 2 hours, then allow to cool in the liquid. Drain carefully, cover in fresh cold water and refrigerate. The next day, repeat the process. When the shark's fin is soft, it is ready to be paired with a rich stock.

SHRIMP, DRIED

S mall, peeled shrimp, dehydrated by the sun or air-dried, are used as a seasoning to perk up fried rice and other dishes. Dried shrimp also give an added dimension to soups and stuffings. When cooked, the dried shrimp impart a delicate taste to sauces; cooking moderates their strong odors.

Shopping Tips
Dried shrimp are sold in packages and may be found in Chinese grocers or markets. Look for the brands with the brightest orange-pink color; avoid grayish ones as this indicates age.

Storage Notes:
Dried shrimp will keep indefinitely in a glass container in the refrigerator. Or, if you plan to use them within a month, they can be stored in a cool, dry place.

Useful Hints
● Soak them in warm water or Shaoxing rice wine, or steam them, to soften them before using.
● The liquid they have been soaked in may be used in the dish.

SHRIMP ROE, DRIED
Shrimp roe are minuscule orange-red eggs taken from female shrimp. They are dried and salted, which transforms them into tiny, red, hard grains. Like other dried seafood used in Chinese cooking, they have a strong odor and flavor. They are usually sprinkled sparingly over soups, or vegetable dishes, egg dishes, or dumplings. Such a garnish highlights by contrast the flavors of other foods.

Shopping Tips
A rather rare and expensive ingredient, dried shrimp roe is found on occasion at some Chinese grocers.

Storage Notes
Dried shrimp roe should be stored in a glass jar in the refrigerator.

83

Shrimp Sauce/Shrimp Paste

T his sauce is made from salted shrimp that are pulverized and then allowed to ferment. It is packed in a thick, moist state directly in jars. Once packed, the light pink shrimp sauce slowly turns a grayish shade, acquiring a pungent flavor as it matures. For shrimp paste, the mixture is dried in the sun and then cut into cakes. Popular in southern Chinese cooking, both shrimp sauce and paste add a distinctive flavor and fragrance to dishes. Although their odour takes getting used to, remember that the cooking process quickly tones down the aroma and taste. Shrimp sauce is similar to anchovy paste in texture, though stronger in taste and odor.

Shopping Tips

Available in Chinese supermarkets and grocers, the best brands are from Hong Kong or China (Pearl River Bridge brand).

Storage Notes

Kept in the refrigerator, it will last indefinitely.

Useful Hints

Don't confuse Chinese shrimp paste with that from Thailand or Malaysia, where a milder and different version of shrimp paste is also used.

SICHUAN PEPPERCORNS

ZANTHOXYLUM SIMULANS

Also known as fagara, wild pepper, Chinese pepper, and anise pepper, Sichuan peppercorns are an ancient spice known throughout China as 'flower peppers' because they look like flower buds opening. Used originally and extensively in Sichuan cooking (hence their popular name), they are enjoyed in other parts of China as well. They are a rusty reddish-brown in color and have a strong, pungent odour, which distinguishes them from the hotter black peppercorns with which they may be used interchangeably. Not related to peppers at all, they are the dried berries of a shrub that is a member of the prickly ash tree family known as *fagara*. Their smell reminds me of lavender, while their taste is sharp and slightly numbing to the tongue, with a clean, lemon-like wood spiciness and fragrance. It is not the peppercorns that make Sichuan cooking so hot; rather it is the chilli pepper that gives it its fieriness. These peppercorns are one of the components of five-spice powder. They can be ground in a conventional peppermill but should be roasted (see below) before grinding to bring out their full flavor.

Shopping Tips
An inexpensive item, they are sold wrapped in cellophane or plastic bags in Chinese stores. Avoid packets with dark seeds: they should be a vibrant, rusty reddish-brown color.

They are best if vacuum-packed, as they quickly lose their special aroma if left out too long.

Storage Notes
They will keep indefinitely if stored in a well-sealed container.

Useful Hints
● *To roast and grind Sichuan peppercorns*: Heat a wok or heavy frying pan to a medium heat. Add the peppercorns (you can cook up to about 110g/4oz or ¼ cup at a time) and stir-fry them for about 5 minutes until they brown slightly and start to smoke. Remove the pan from the heat and let them cool. Grind the peppercorns in a peppermill or clean coffee grinder, or with a mortar and pestle. Sift the ground peppercorns through a fine mesh and discard the hard hulls. Seal the mixture tightly in a screw-top jar to store. Alternatively, keep the whole roasted peppercorns in a well-sealed container and grind them when required.
● *To make Seasoned Salt & Pepper*: Roast Sichuan peppercorns with a little bit more sea salt and grind coarsely together. Keep in a glass jar for future use.

Other Hints
Combine them with other peppercorns for additional flavors. They can be used as part of a dry marinade with salt for grilled meats.

SICHUAN PRESERVED VEGETABLE

Also known as Sichuan preserved mustard stem or Sichuan preserved radish, this is one of the most popular of the large variety of pickled and preserved cabbages in China, a specialty of Sichuan province. This is the root of the mustard green, pickled in salt with hot chillies and garlic. It is then fermented in large pottery tubs and the result is a strikingly piquant pickled vegetable. It is used to give a pleasantly crunchy texture and spicy, strong taste to stir-fried, braised, or simmered dishes and to soups. It is also used in stuffings or may be thinly sliced and served as a cold appetizer.

Incidentally, the hot, humid climate of Sichuan makes food spoil very quickly. Making a virtue of necessity, Sichuan chefs have concocted a great variety of spicy pickled and fermented foods that are at once delightful to eat and preserved against spoilage.

Shopping Tips

It is sold in cans or pottery crocks in Chinese grocery stores or supermarkets. The best brand is May Ling from China.

Storage Notes

Any left-over vegetable should be transferred to a tightly covered glass jar and stored in the refrigerator where it will keep indefinitely.

Useful Hints

Before using it, rinse in cold water and then slice or chop as required.

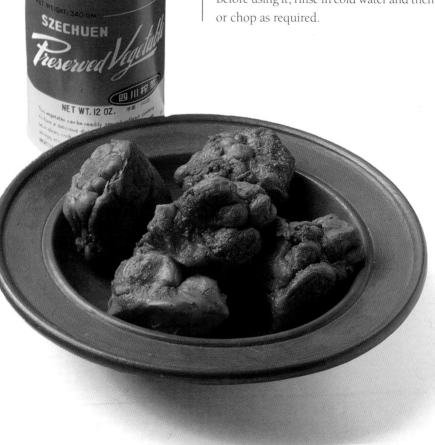

SILK SQUASH

ANGLES LUFFA, CHINESE OKRA

LUFFA ACUTANGULA

 popular vegetable frequently found in markets throughout China, this is a long, thin, cylindrical squash (or melon), tapering at one end, with deep narrow ridges. Silk squash is eaten when young, as it grows bitter with age. It is very similar to a courgette [US zucchini] in texture, with a wonderful earthy flavor. Some people find a similiarity in taste and texture to okra, hence another of its names. The inside flesh turns soft and tender as it cooks, tasting finally like a cross between a cucumber and a courgette. Absorbent, it readily picks up flavors of the sauce or food with which it is cooked. It is usually stir-fried or deep-fried.

Shopping Tips

Choose firm young squash with unblemished skin. They are available at Chinese supermarkets or grocers.

Storage Notes

Good, firm silk squash should keep at the bottom of the refrigerator for at least 1 week.

Useful Hints

You must peel away the tough ridge before use. You can leave on some of the green.

Soy Sauces

An ancient seasoning, soy sauce was first used in China more than 3,000 years ago, when it was a thin, salty liquid in which fragments of fermented soybean floated. Its use has been documented throughout Chinese history and the process by which it is made has changed many times over the years. One thousand years ago in China, soy sauce was one of the 'seven essentials' of daily life, the others being firewood, rice, oil, salt, vinegar and tea. Today, the type of soy sauce we use is strained to remove all traces of the bean solids. Soy sauce is an essential ingredient in Chinese as well as other types of Asian cooking. It is made from a mixture of soybeans, flour, and water, which is then naturally fermented and aged for some months. The distilled liquid is soy sauce. There are two main types:

Light Soy Sauce: As the name implies, this is light in color, but it is full of flavor and is the best one to use for cooking, as well as dipping. It is known in Chinese markets as 'superior soy' or 'light soy sauce' and is saltier than dark soy sauce.

Dark Soy Sauce: This sauce is aged for much longer than light soy sauce, hence its darker, almost black color. It is slightly thicker and stronger than light soy sauce and is more suitable for stews. I prefer it to light soy as a dipping sauce. It is known in Chinese markets as 'soy superior sauce' or 'dark soy sauce' and, although used less than light soy, it is important to have some on hand.

Shopping Tips

• The type of soy sauce you buy will make a great difference to the way a dish will taste. Avoid any soy sauces from Singapore, as they are synthetically or chemically manufactured and, although they are inexpensive, they tend to have a metallic taste. I highly recommend the Koon Chun and Amoy brands from Hong Kong and the Pearl River Bridge brand from China. The soy sauces from Hong Kong tend to be more consistent than the ones from China, which can vary in quality. The naturally brewed Japanese soy sauces are quite popular, have a more complex flavor, and can be substituted for light soy sauce in Chinese cooking. Kikkoman is delicious and is highly recommended.

• Although the light and dark soy sauce brands from China have similar names, which leads to a lot of confusion, the best way I have found to distinguish between the two is to shake the bottle. If the sauce is thin, then it is light soy. If the sauce heavily coats the bottle's sides and is dark in color, you can be sure that it is dark soy sauce.

Storage Notes

Soy sauce will last for quite a long time without refrigeration. However, it is best to keep it tightly sealed and away from light. Since it is already fermented, you don't have to worry about spoilage.

Useful Hints

Often light and dark soy sauces are used together in Chinese cooking. They are also wonderful taste additions for sauces and marinades.

Other Notes

• *Mushroom soy sauce* is a delicious type of dark soy sauce that is infused with dried straw mushrooms. The recommended brand is Pearl River Bridge, produced in mainland China.

• *Shrimp-flavored soy sauce*, primarily an eastern Chinese favorite, is infused with briny, dried shrimp for a sharp interesting accent.

STAR ANISE

ILLICIUM VERUM

S tar anise is the hard, star-shaped seed-pod of a small tree that grows in south-western China. It is also known as Chinese anise or whole anise. It is similar in flavor and fragrance to common anise seed but is more robust and licorice-like. Star anise is an essential ingredient of five spice powder and, like cinnamon bark, is widely used in braised dishes to which it imparts a rich taste and fragrance. Star anise has been popular in Europe since the early 1600s.

Shopping Tips

Buy whole pods, not broken pieces. Sold in plastic packs at Chinese markets and groceries, they are quite inexpensive.

Storage Notes

Stored in a tightly covered jar in a cool, dry place, away from light, the spice should keep for many months.

SUGAR

S ugar has been used – sparingly – in the cooking of savory dishes in China for a thousand years. Excessive sugar destroys the palate, but when it is properly employed, sugar helps balance the various flavors of sauces and other dishes. There are many different types of sugar used. They include:

Rock or yellow lump sugar: I particularly like to use rock sugar which I find to have a richer, more subtle flavor than that of refined granulated sugar. It also gives a good luster or glaze to braised 'red-cooked' Chinese dishes. It imparts translucence to glazes and sauces. You may need to break the lumps into smaller pieces with a wooden mallet or rolling pin.

Brown sugar slabs: This type of sugar is layered and semi-refined, having been compressed into flat slabs and cut to resemble caramel candy. It has the flavor of good brown sugar. See also maltose sugar (page 53).

Shopping Tips

Buy brown sugar slabs and rock or yellow lump sugar in Chinese markets, where it is usually sold very inexpensively in packages. If you cannot find it, you can use ordinary granulated sugar or coffee sugar crystals (the amber, chunky kind) instead.

Storage Notes

It will keep indefinitely if stored in a dry, cool place.

Useful Hints

Rock sugar reduced with water makes a good syrup.

WATER CHESTNUTS

ELEOCHARIS DULCIS

There are many water vegetables eaten in China. In a land tiered by rice fields the cultivation of aquatic vegetables has been a natural development. The vegetables are sometimes rotated with the rice crop or are grown alongside the rice. This is why fresh water chesnuts are often muddy. Most of these vegetables are grown in tropical or semi-tropical areas as they require a long summer to develop. Water chestnuts do not actually belong to the chestnut family, although they look as though they should: they are mahogany-colored and shaped like a chestnut, with papery layers attached to the skin that come to a tufted point in the center. In fact the water chestnut is a perennial reed-like plant, with long, thin hollow leaves over 60cm/2 feet high. It is a sweet, white, crunchy and juicy vegetable that is eaten raw as well as cooked. Water chestnuts have been enjoyed in China for centuries. They are a popular snack, having first been boiled in their skins, or peeled and simmered in a rock sugar syrup. They need only light cooking and are often added to cooked dishes, chopped or sliced. They are also the source of water chestnut flour or powder which is used to thicken sauces or to coat food. Another water vegetable that is also sometimes known as water chestnut is the two-horned water caltrop, with a shiny black skin; however, this is rarely available in the West. Canned water chestnuts have a good texture but little taste because both crispness and flavour are lost in the canning process.

Shopping Tips

In the West, fresh water chestnuts can be obtained from Chinese markets or some supermarkets. When buying fresh ones, look for a firm, hard texture. The skin should be tight and taut, not wrinkled. If they are mushy, they are too old. Feel them all over for soft, rotten spots. Canned water chestnuts are sold in many supermarkets and Chinese markets. Those from China (the May Ling brand) tend to be less bland than those from Taiwan.

Storage Notes

If you peel fresh water chestnuts in advance, cover them with cold water to prevent browning and store them in the refrigerator. They will keep, unpeeled, in a paper bag in the refrigerator for up to 2 weeks. Store any left-over canned water chestnuts in a jar of cold water. They will keep for several weeks in the refrigerator if you change the water daily.

Useful Hints

Fresh water chestnuts must be peeled before eating. Rinse canned water chestnuts well in cold water before use.

Other Notes

Jicama is a suitable substitute for fresh water chestnuts, and is preferable to using canned ones. This crisp tuber, brought from South America to Asia by the Spanish, is crunchy and juicy with the texture of water chestnuts. It is available throughout most of the year, especially in Chinese markets.

WHEAT GLUTEN

T his is made from washing out the starch from wheat dough until only the adhesive, glutinous substance remains. It is usually boiled or deep-fried and then cooked with other ingredients. Dried, spongy cakes of gluten dough are often used in Chinese cuisine, but especially so in vegetarian cooking where wheat gluten forms the basis of many 'mock meat' dishes. Gluten itself has very little taste, but its virtue is that it readily absorbs the flavors of seasonings and other ingredients that are cooked with it.

Shopping Tips

Wheat gluten can be found in the refrigerated section of Chinese grocers or supermarkets. Canned varieties are available. All brands are good, but I prefer those from Taiwan and China.

Storage Notes

If purchased fresh from Chinese grocers or supermarkets, it should be used within 1 week. Keep in water, changing the water every day.

WONTON WRAPPERS, WONTON SKINS

I n China, wonton wrappers and other such doughs were traditionally made painstakingly by hand, with the entire extended family engaging in the process of wrapping each dumpling with filling while sitting around the main table of the house. Today, fortunately, there is no need to summon the extended family from the four corners of the earth. There are very good commercially produced wonton wrappers, made from egg and flour, that can be bought fresh or frozen not only at Chinese markets but increasingly at ordinary supermarkets. They range from very thin to medium-thick pastry-like squares, stretched like freshly-made noodles. They can be stuffed with minced meat and then fried, steamed, or used in soups.

Shopping Tips

Wonton wrappers are sold in little piles of 7.5cm/3in squares (or sometimes a bit larger), wrapped in plastic. The number of squares in a package varies, depending upon the supplier. Buy the very thin ones.

Storage Notes

Wonton wrappers freeze very well; however, they should be well wrapped before freezing. Fresh wonton wrappers will keep for about 5 days if stored in cling film [US plastic wrap] or a plastic bag in the refrigerator. If you are using frozen wonton wrappers, just peel off the number you require, leaving the remainder in the freezer; thaw them thoroughly before use.

Useful Hints

● Use your imagination for the filling, which, of course, does not have to be strictly Chinese.
● Deep-fried, they make a wonderful snack with drinks.

SOUPS

STUFFED CUCUMBER SOUP

———————— SHOPPING LIST ————————

700g/1¹/₂lb cucumbers, 225g/8oz boneless fatty pork, spring onions [US scallions], fresh ginger, egg

———————— STAPLES ————————

Cornflour [US cornstarch], Chicken Stock, Shaoxing rice wine or dry sherry, light soy sauce, sugar, sesame oil, salt and black pepper

———————— PREPARATION TIME ————————

30–45 minutes

———————— COOKING TIME ————————

15 minutes

SERVES 4

The Chinese are masters at combining what seem to be unrelated elements into a delicious recipe. For example, this light soup is complemented by cucumbers with a savory filling. The stuffing in this recipe uses seasoned chopped pork. It is the type of soup that is rich and light at the same time. It makes a perfect one-dish meal.

700g/1¹/₂lb cucumbers
2 tbsp cornflour [US cornstarch]
900ml/1¹/₂pints/3³/₄cups Chicken Stock (page 128)
2 tbsp Shaoxing rice wine or dry sherry
Salt and freshly ground black pepper to taste

———————— STUFFING ————————

225g/8oz boneless fatty pork, finely chopped
1 egg white
1¹/₂ tbsp finely chopped spring onions [US scallions]
1 tbsp finely chopped fresh ginger
2 tsp Shaoxing rice wine or dry sherry
2 tsp light soy sauce
2 tsp sugar
1 tsp salt
¹/₂ tsp freshly ground black pepper
1 tsp sesame oil

———————— GARNISH ————————

2 tsp sesame oil
2 tbsp finely chopped spring onions [US scallions]

Cut the cucumbers into 2.5cm/1in slices without peeling them. Remove the seeds and pulp from the center of each cucumber slice using a small, sharp knife. Hollow the cucumber so that you have no less than a 5mm/¹/₄in-thick shell. Lightly dust the hollow interior of each cucumber slice with a little cornflour. Mix all the stuffing ingredients together in a large bowl. Stuff each cucumber ring with this mixture.

Next set up a steamer or put a rack into a wok or deep pan and add 5cm/2in of water. Bring the water to the boil over a high heat. Put the stuffed cucumbers onto a heatproof plate and then carefully lower it into the steamer or onto the rack. Turn the heat to low and cover the wok or pan tightly. Steam gently for 10 minutes. You will have to cook this in two batches. When done reserve the juices. (You can do this part ahead of time.)

Bring the chicken stock to a simmer in a medium-sized pan. Add the rice wine and season with salt and pepper. Add the steamed stuffed cucumbers and reserved juices and simmer for 2 minutes. Ladle the mixture into a soup bowl. Garnish with the sesame oil and spring onions and serve at once.

VEGETABLE EGG FLOWER SOUP

———————— SHOPPING LIST ————————

1 small onion, 175g/6oz mangetouts [US snow peas], Chinese dried black mushrooms, eggs

———————— STAPLES ————————

Groundnut oil [US peanut oil], Shaoxing rice wine or dry sherry, Chicken Stock, sesame oil

———————— PREPARATION TIME ————————

15 minutes

———————— COOKING TIME ————————

10 minutes

SERVES 4

This is characteristic of soups served during meals in China. The name derives from the pattern made by the eggs when they are added. The soup is clear, light, refreshing, and nutritious and it serves as a beverage. An easy-to-make soup, you may substitute vegetables in season or your favorite vegetables. A quick stir-fry of the vegetables added to the soup gives it new, smoky flavors and more substance.

50g/2oz Chinese dried black mushrooms (page 26)
1¹/₂ tbsp groundnut oil [US peanut oil]
1 small onion, finely sliced
175g/6oz trimmed mangetouts [US snow peas]
1 tsp salt
¹/₂ tsp freshly ground white pepper
2 tbsp Shaoxing rice wine or dry sherry
1.1 litres/2 pints/5 cups Chicken Stock (page 128)
2 eggs, beaten
1 tsp sesame oil

Remove and discard the mushroom stems and finely shred the caps into thin strips.

Heat a wok or large frying pan over high heat until it is hot. Add the oil and, when it is very hot and slightly smoking, add the onion and mushroom. Stir-fry for 1 minute. Add the mangetouts, salt, pepper, and Shaoxing rice wine or dry sherry and continue to stir-fry for 2 minutes. Remove from the heat and set aside.

In a large pot, bring the stock to a simmer. In a small bowl, combine the eggs with the sesame oil. Add the contents of the wok to the stock and simmer for 2 minutes. Next, stir in the egg mixture in a very slow, thin stream. Using a chopstick or fork, pull the egg gently into strands. Turn into a tureen or bowl and serve at once.

CHINESE CABBAGE SOUP

SHOPPING LIST

450g/1lb Peking cabbage (Chinese leaves or Napa cabbage), Chinese dried black mushrooms, dried shrimp

STAPLES

Shaoxing rice wine or dry sherry, Chicken Stock

PREPARATION TIME

25 minutes

COOKING TIME

15 minutes

SERVES 4

Peking cabbage is now available in most supermarkets. Unlike the Western variety, the Chinese cabbage is easier to cook and simmering results in a sweet broth that lingers on the palate. This is one of those simple, clear soups that are the hallmark of fine Chinese cooking. It would make an excellent opening course for a special meal, or, by itself, it is an ideal light and satisfying meal.

450g/1lb Peking cabbage (Chinese leaves or Napa cabbage)
50g/2oz Chinese dried black mushrooms (page 26)
50g/2oz dried shrimp
3 tbsp Shaoxing rice wine or dry sherry
1.2 litres/2 pints/5 cups Chicken Stock (page 128)
1 tsp salt
¹/₂ tsp freshly ground white pepper

Cut the cabbage into strips 2.5cm/1in x 4cm/1¹/₂in.

Remove and discard the mushroom stems and finely shred the caps into thin strips.

Mix the dried shrimp with the Shaoxing rice wine or dry sherry and let the mixture sit for 10 minutes.

Bring the stock to a simmer in a large pot. Add the cabbage, mushrooms and shrimp mixture and simmer together for 10 minutes. Add the salt and pepper and stir to mix well. Serve the soup at once.

OXTAIL-CHICKEN SOUP

──────── SHOPPING LIST ────────

900g/2lb oxtails, 1.35–1.75kg/3–4lb cornfed chicken, 900g/2lb Peking cabbage (Chinese leaves or Napa cabbage), fresh ginger, spring onions [US scallions]

──────── STAPLES ────────

Shaoxing rice wine or dry sherry, Sichuan peppercorns

──────── PREPARATION TIME ────────

30 minutes

──────── COOKING TIME ────────

3¹/₂-4 hours

SERVES 4

Chinese soups, as I often remember from my childhood, are full of intense flavor, rich in aroma, but light in taste. I would describe them as deliciously tonic in nature: when you drink them, you instinctively know they are good for you. Some of these soups are made with Chinese medicinal herbs and roots, while others are simply made using a long-simmered stock, with a touch of Shaoxing rice wine to give an added richness. This soup is simple to make. However, it requires a long cooking time to bring out its full potential of taste and flavors. Your patience will be rewarded by a satisfying soup that can serve as a first course or even as a main course on a cold wintry night.

2 litres/6 pints/15 cups water
900g/2lb oxtail, cut in sections
1.35–1.75kg/3–4lb cornfed chicken
6 slices fresh ginger
6 spring onions [US scallions]

2 tbsp Sichuan peppercorns
4 tbsp Shaoxing rice wine or dry sherry
1 tbsp salt
900g/2lb Peking cabbage (Chinese leaves or Napa cabbage)

Bring the water to the boil in a large pot. Add the oxtail and simmer for 20 minutes, skimming all the while. Cut the chicken into quarters and add it to the pot. Wrap the ginger, spring onions, and peppercorns in a piece of muslin or cheesecloth. Add this with the Shaoxing rice wine or dry sherry and salt. Reduce the heat to a simmer, partly cover, and cook for 3 hours.

Cut the Peking cabbage into 4cm/1¹/₂in strips across the leaves.

Skim all the excess fat from the soup with a spoon. Add the cabbage and cook for another 30 minutes. Test the meat of a piece of oxtail to be sure it is tender enough. If not, continue to simmer for another 30 minutes.

When the soup is done, remove and discard the chicken and bag of ginger, spring onions, and peppercorns. Adjust the seasoning by adding more salt to taste, if necessary. Serve the soup with the oxtail and cabbage still in it.

DOUBLE STEAMED MUSHROOM SOUP

──────── SHOPPING LIST ────────

50g/2oz finest quality Chinese dried black mushrooms

──────── STAPLES ────────

Chicken Stock, salt

──────── PREPARATION TIME ────────

15 minutes

──────── COOKING TIME ────────

10 minutes + 3 hours steaming time

SERVES 4

Double steaming involves an unusual method of making a rich but clear soup. You must first prepare the soup in its own covered pot, so that it is producing its own steam. Then you place it on a rack over boiling water in another pot, cover the pot tightly, and steam the soup for 3 hours. This technique is usually reserved for the finest ingredients with the most delicate flavors and textures. Steaming is a gentle cooking method that works best with such foods. In this soup, the highest quality dried mushrooms that money can buy are used. They should be thick so they can absorb all the flavors from the long steaming process. The result is a clear but concentrated and therefore rich consommé, redolent of the essence of mushroom.

All the work can be done in advance. In fact, the soup can even be frozen and reheated. This soup would make an earthy and elegant opener for any meal.

50g/2oz finest quality Chinese dried black mushrooms (page 26)
900ml/1¹/₂ pints/3³/₄ cups Chicken Stock (page 128)
salt, to taste

Bring the chicken stock to a boil in a large pot. Pour the stock and the mushrooms into a heatproof soup tureen. (This is the first steaming process.)

Cover the tureen and set it on a rack inside a large steamer, over simmering water. Cover the steamer tightly. Steam for 3 hours. Replenish the hot water from time to time as necessary.

Adjust the seasoning with salt to taste and serve at once.

CHICKEN WONTON SOUP

SHOPPING LIST

225g/8oz peeled raw prawns [US shrimp], 225g/8oz boneless, skinless chicken thighs, 225g/8oz wonton wrappers [US wonton skins], fresh or canned water chestnuts, tree ears, spring onions [US scallions], egg

STAPLES

light soy sauce, Shaoxing rice wine or dry sherry, sesame oil, sugar, Chicken Stock

PREPARATION TIME

30 minutes

COOKING TIME

15 minutes

SERVES 4

This is a variation of the classic wonton soup using chicken instead of the traditional pork. It is, thus, a lighter dish while the use of tree ears adds subtlety and texture to the filling. You must poach the wonton dumplings before adding them to the soup. Otherwise, the soup will be clouded by the starch from the wonton wrappers. Wonton wrappers are now available in many supermarkets. Once the wontons are filled, the soup cooks in minutes. It makes a hearty, delicious, one-dish meal or an elegant first course for a dinner party.

225g/8oz wonton wrappers [US wonton skins]

FILLING

225g/8oz peeled raw prawns [US shrimp], deveined and coarsely chopped
225g/8oz boneless, skinless chicken thighs, coarsely chopped
1 tsp salt
¹/₂ tsp freshly ground white pepper
110g/4oz peeled fresh or canned water chestnuts, coarsely chopped (page 92)
50g/2oz tree ears, soaked, rinsed, and finely shredded (page 34)

101

1¹/₂ tbsp light soy sauce

3 tbsp finely chopped spring onions [US scallions],
white part only

1¹/₂ tbsp Shaoxing rice wine or dry sherry

1 tsp sugar

2 tsp sesame oil

1 egg white, beaten lightly

——————— STOCK ———————

1.7 litres/3 pints/7¹/₂ cups Chicken Stock (page 128)

1 tbsp light soy sauce

1 tsp sesame oil

——————— GARNISH ———————

chopped spring onions [US scallions]

For the wonton filling, put the prawns and chicken in a large bowl, add the salt and pepper, and mix well, either by kneading with your hand or by stirring with a wooden spoon. Then add all the other filling ingredients and stir them well into the prawn and chicken mixture. Cover tightly and chill for at least 20 minutes.

When you are ready to stuff the wontons, put 1 tbsp of the filling in the center of the first wonton wrapper. Dampen the edges with a little water and bring up the sides of the wrapper around and over the filling. Pinch the edges together at the top so that the wonton is sealed; it should look like a small, filled bag.

When the wontons are ready, bring the stock, soy sauce, and sesame oil to a simmer in a large cooking pot.

In another large pot, bring salted water to a boil and poach the wontons for 1 minute or until they float to the top. With a slotted spoon, remove them immediately and transfer them to the stock. Continue to simmer them in the stock for 2 minutes. Transfer to either a large soup bowl or to individual bowls. Garnish and serve immediately.

CHICKEN SICHUAN VEGETABLE SOUP

——————— SHOPPING LIST ———————

225g/8oz boneless, skinless chicken breasts,
Sichuan preserved vegetable, spring onions [US
scallions]

——————— STAPLES ———————

Shaoxing rice wine or dry sherry, sugar, Chicken
Stock, light soy sauce, sesame oil

——————— PREPARATION TIME ———————

15 minutes

——————— COOKING TIME ———————

15 minutes

SERVES 4

This is a quick and very satisfying soup I often make when I am in a hurry and have guests coming for dinner. It is easy to make, but requires that you have good chicken stock – the foundation of any good soup – on hand. The Sichuan preserved vegetable provides unusual texture and sparkling flavor to the soup. Add freshly blanched noodles for a complete one-dish winter meal.

900ml/1¹/₂ pints/3³/₄ cups Chicken Stock (page 128)

225g/8oz boneless, skinless chicken breasts, finely
shredded

50g/2oz/¹/₈ cup Sichuan preserved vegetable,
rinsed and finely shredded

¹/₂ tsp freshly ground white pepper

1¹/₂ tbsp Shaoxing rice wine or dry sherry

1 tsp sugar

1 tbsp light soy sauce

2 tsp sesame oil

3 tbsp finely chopped spring onions [US scallions],
white part only

In a large pot, bring the stock to a simmer. Add the chicken, vegetable, pepper, Shaoxing rice wine or dry sherry, sugar, and soy sauce. Simmer for 2 minutes. Then add the sesame oil and spring onions. Transfer to a large soup bowl or to individual bowls and serve immediately.

BEEF SOUP WITH FRESH CORIANDER

SHOPPING LIST

225g/8oz minced beef [US ground beef], egg, fresh coriander [US cilantro], spring onions [US scallions]

STAPLES

Shaoxing rice wine or dry sherry, light and dark soy sauces, Chicken Stock, sesame oil, sugar, cornflour [US cornstarch]

PREPARATION TIME

15 minutes

COOKING TIME

15 minutes

SERVES 4

Beef is relatively uncommon in classical Chinese cuisine, but the new Hong Kong style restaurants have popularized it in many recipes such as this one. Note, however, that but a small amount of beef is used. It is a simple but satisfying and refreshing soup, rich and flavorful. As with all delicious soups, good stock is essential, and, although this is called beef soup, as is usual in Chinese cookery, chicken stock is used. This is an easily prepared soup and is perfect as a first course or, with the addition of some quickly blanched noodles, as a light meal.

225g/8oz minced beef [US ground beef]
1 tbsp + 2 tsp dark soy sauce
2 tsp Shaoxing rice wine or dry sherry
1 tsp cornflour [US cornstarch]
2 eggs, beaten
2 tsp sesame oil
3 tsp sugar
900ml/1¹/₂ pints/3³/₄ cups Chicken Stock (page 128)
2 tsp cornflour [US cornstarch] blended with
1 tbsp water
2 tsp salt
2 tsp light soy sauce
¹/₂ tsp freshly ground white pepper

GARNISH

4 tbsp finely chopped spring onions [US scallions]
3 tbsp finely chopped fresh coriander [US cilantro]

Combine the beef with 1 tbsp dark soy sauce, the rice wine or dry sherry and cornflour. In a small bowl, combine the eggs with the sesame oil. In a large pot, bring the stock to a simmer. Add the beef, 1 tsp sugar, and the cornflour mixture and stir for 1 minute, breaking up any clumps of meat. Then add the salt, remaining dark soy sauce, the light soy sauce, remaining sugar, and the pepper and simmer for 2 minutes. Next stir in the egg mixture in a very slow, thin stream. Using a chopstick or fork, pull the egg gently into strands. Turn into a soup tureen or bowl, garnish with the spring onions and fresh coriander, and serve at once.

WATERCRESS FISH SOUP

SHOPPING LIST

350g/12oz firm white fish fillets, such as cod, seabass, or halibut, watercress leaves, fresh ginger, spring onions [US scallions]

STAPLES

Shaoxing rice wine or dry sherry, Chicken Stock light soy sauce, sugar, sesame oil

PREPARATION TIME

15 minutes

COOKING TIME

8 minutes

SERVES 4

This is an unassuming but very delicious fish soup. The fish steeps gently in the soup, a process which cooks it perfectly. However, only the freshest fish will do. The watercress adds color and, with the other seasonings, a spicy bite to the soup. Much of the preparation can be done well in advance while the cooking can be done quickly and at the last minute. This makes it ideal for a special dinner party.

350g/12oz firm white skinned fish fillets, such as
haddock, halibut, cod, seabass, etc.
1 tsp salt
2 tsp ginger juice (page 45)
2 tsp + 1 tbsp Shaoxing rice wine or dry sherry
175g/6oz watercress leaves, about 1 bunch
900ml/1¹/₂ pints/3³/₄ cups Chicken Stock (page 128)
1 tbsp light soy sauce
¹/₄ tsp freshly ground white pepper
1 tsp sugar
2 tsp sesame oil
2 tbsp finely chopped spring onions [US scallions]

Sprinkle the fish fillets evenly on both sides with
the salt. Cut the fish into thin slices about 3mm/
¹/₈in thick. Combine the slices with the ginger
juice and 2 tsp rice wine or sherry and let these
sit for 20 minutes.

Remove the stems from the watercress, leaving
only the leaves.

Bring the stock to a simmer in a large pot. Add
the remaining Shaoxing rice wine or dry sherry,
the soy sauce, pepper, and sugar and simmer
for 3 minutes.

Place the watercress leaves on the bottom of a
soup tureen or large bowl. Place the fish on top.
Bring the stock to a boil and pour it over the
fish and watercress. Allow it to sit undisturbed
for 5 minutes. Stir in the sesame oil and spring
onions and serve at once.

PRAWN DUMPLING SOUP

—————— SHOPPING LIST ——————
450g/1lb raw prawns [US shrimp], 225g/8oz
spinach, pork fat or very fatty boneless pork, egg,
spring onions [US scallions], fresh ginger

—————— STAPLES ——————
Shaoxing rice wine or dry sherry, sesame oil,
Chicken Stock

—————— PREPARATION TIME ——————
20 minutes

—————— COOKING TIME ——————
10 minutes
SERVES 4

I remember seeing in my uncle's restaurant how
laborious it was to chop the prawns until they
were smooth and like a paste. Now, thanks to
modern kitchen equipment, this dish can be
easily prepared at home in minutes. There has
been some progress in the twentieth century!
The prawn dumplings are tasty and light. The
pork fat gives them a special richness, resulting
in a soup that is at once subtly delicate and richly
delicious.

450g/1lb raw prawns [US shrimp], peeled and
deveined
25g/1oz pork fat or very fatty boneless pork
1 egg white
1 tsp salt
¹/₄ tsp freshly ground white pepper
2 tsp finely chopped spring onions [US scallions]
1 tsp finely chopped fresh ginger
225g/8oz spinach
900ml/1¹/₂ pints/3³/₄ cups Chicken Stock (page 128)
2 tbsp Shaoxing rice wine or dry sherry
1 tsp salt
1 tsp sesame oil

Combine the prawns, pork fat, egg white, salt,
pepper, spring onions, and ginger in a food processor and process the mixture until you have a
smooth paste. If you are using an electric blender,
pulse by turning the blender on and off until
the mixture is well mixed; otherwise the paste
will turn out rubbery.

Bring a large pot of salted water to simmering
point. Take spoonfuls of the prawn paste and
form it into balls about 2.5cm/1in in diameter.
Poach the balls in the boiling water until they

float to the top. (This should take about 3–4 minutes.) Remove them with a slotted spoon and drain them on paper towels.

Remove the stems of the spinach and wash the leaves well.

In a large pot, bring the stock to a simmer. Add the rice wine or sherry and salt and simmer for 2 minutes. Then add the spinach and prawn dumplings and continue to simmer for a further 2 minutes.

Stir in the sesame oil. Turn the soup into a large bowl or soup tureen and serve at once.

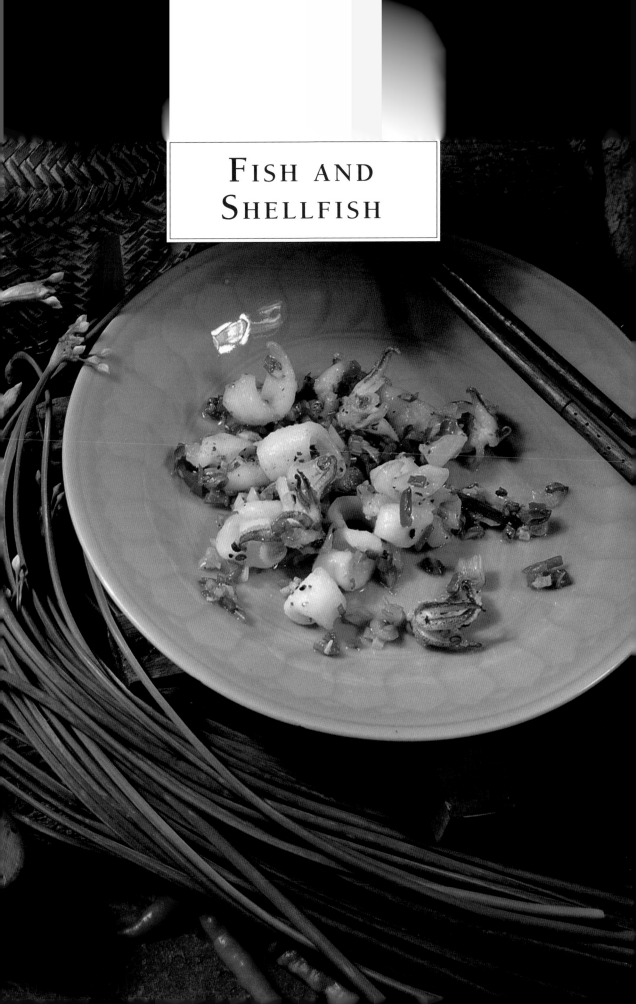

FISH AND
SHELLFISH

RED COOKED FISH

SHOPPING LIST

450g/1lb firm white fish fillets, such as haddock, halibut, cod, seabass, etc, garlic, fresh ginger, spring onions [US scallions]

STAPLES

groundnut oil [US peanut oil], Shaoxing rice wine or dry sherry, hoisin sauce, dark soy sauce, ground bean sauce, rock or ordinary sugar, Chicken Stock, cornflour [US cornstarch]

PREPARATION TIME

25 minutes

COOKING TIME

10 minutes

SERVES 4

'Red-cooked' usually means dishes that are braised for a long time so that the food takes on the reddish tones of the soy sauce mixture. This is more difficult to do with fish, as quick cooking is usually the rule for fish and does not allow time for absorption of color. However, in this case, the fish is pan-fried beforehand, and then it is braised briefly in the sauce. The result is indeed colorful and the delicious taste of the fish is enhanced and its texture preserved. Serve this with a fried rice and another vegetable dish.

2 firm white fish fillets such as haddock, halibut, cod, seabass, etc. weighing 225g/8oz each
2 tsp salt
cornflour [US cornstarch], for dusting
3 tbsp groundnut oil [US peanut oil] or vegetable oil

SAUCE

1¹/₂ tbsp groundnut oil [US peanut oil] or vegetable oil
1 tbsp finely chopped garlic
1 tbsp finely chopped fresh ginger
2 tbsp Shaoxing rice wine or dry sherry
1¹/₂ tbsp hoisin sauce
1 tbsp dark soy sauce
2 tsp ground bean sauce
1 tbsp rock sugar or ordinary sugar
175ml/6fl oz/³/₄ cup Chicken Stock (page 128)
2 tsp cornflour [US cornstarch] blended with 1 tbsp water
2 tsp sesame oil

GARNISH

chopped spring onions [US scallions]

Put the fish fillets on a baking tray. Sprinkle the salt and cornflour evenly over both sides of each fillet. Shake off any excess cornflour.

Heat a wok over high heat until it is hot, then add the 3 tbsp oil. When the oil is slightly smoking, slide the fish in and pan-fry for 2 minutes or until the fillets are golden brown. Then carefully turn the fish over and fry the other side. Remove the fish and drain on paper towels.

Reheat the wok over high heat until it is hot, then add the 1¹/₂ tbsp of oil for the sauce. When the oil is hot and slightly smoking, add the garlic and ginger and stir-fry for 20 seconds. Then add the rest of the sauce ingredients except the cornflour mixture and sesame oil. Stir-fry this mixture for 1 minute. Add the cornflour mixture and, when the sauce boils, turn the heat to low. Carefully slide the fillets into the sauce, and cook for 3–5 minutes, basting constantly.

Carefully remove the fish and arrange on a platter. Add the sesame oil to the sauce. Pour the sauce over the fish and garnish with spring onions. Serve at once.

SPICY BRAISED FISH

SHOPPING LIST

1 whole firm white fish, such as haddock, halibut, cod, seabass, etc., 1.35–1.5kg/3–3¹/₂lb or 2 fillets, 450g/1lb each, 2 eggs, garlic, fresh ginger, shallots, spring onions [US scallions], fresh coriander [US cilantro]

Previous page: *Prawns with Broad Beans; Salt and Pepper Squid*

───── STAPLES ─────

cornflour [US cornstarch], groundnut oil [US peanut oil], Shoaxing rice wine or dry sherry, whole bean sauce, light and dark soy sauces, chilli bean paste, sugar, Chicken Stock, sesame oil

───── PREPARATION TIME ─────

15 minutes

───── COOKING TIME ─────

20 minutes

SERVES 4–6

I always enjoy the experience of whole fish being served at family banquets and on special occasions such as Chinese New Years. Whole fish is a symbol of prosperity and good luck and, thus, reserved for special occasions. One of my favorites is this spicy braised fish which is as delicious as it is elegant. It goes well with plain rice and another vegetable dish. If you are unable to get a whole fish, the recipe works equally well with fish fillets – but fillets carry no guarantees of good luck or prosperity, only wonderful eating.

1 whole fish, weighing 1.35–1.5kg/3–3¹/₂lb, or 2 haddock or halibut skinned fillets, weighing 450g/ 1lb each
2 tsp salt
cornflour [US cornstarch], for dusting
2 eggs, beaten
600ml/1 pint/2¹/₂ cups groundnut oil [US peanut oil] or vegetable oil

───── SAUCE ─────

1¹/₂ tbsp groundnut oil [US peanut oil] or vegetable oil
2 tbsp finely chopped garlic
2 tbsp finely chopped fresh ginger
2 tbsp finely chopped shallots
2 tbsp Shaoxing rice wine or dry sherry
2 tbsp whole bean sauce
1¹/₂ tbsp dark soy sauce
1 tbsp light soy sauce
1 tbsp chilli bean paste
2 tsp sugar
450ml/15fl oz/1⁵/₈ cups Chicken Stock (page 128)
2 tsp cornflour [US cornstarch] blended with 1 tbsp water
3 tbsp finely chopped spring onions [US scallions]
2 tsp sesame oil

───── GARNISH ─────

chopped fresh coriander [US cilantro]

Put the fish on a baking tray. Make three slanted cuts on each side of the fish or fillets; this will help the fish to cook evenly. Sprinkle the salt and cornflour evenly over both sides of the fish. Shake off any excess cornflour. Then baste the fish with the beaten egg and again coat both sides with cornflour, shaking off any excess.

Heat a wok over high heat until it is hot, then add the 600ml/1 pint/2¹/₂ cups oil. When the oil is slightly smoking, slide the fish in and deep-fry for 4 minutes (fillets will take a little less time) or until golden brown. Then carefully turn the fish over and fry the other side. Remove the fish and drain on paper towels. Discard the oil and wash out the wok.

Reheat the wok over high heat, then add the 1¹/₂ tbsp of oil for the sauce. When the oil is hot and slightly smoking, add the garlic, ginger and shallots and stir-fry for 20 seconds. Add the rest of the sauce ingredients except the stock, cornflour mixture, spring onions, and sesame oil. Stir-fry for 1 minute. Add the stock and cornflour mixture and, when it boils, turn the heat down. Carefully slide the fish into the sauce and continue to cook for 5 minutes or until the fish is cooked, basting constantly.

Carefully remove the fish and arrange on a platter. Add the spring onions and sesame oil to the sauce. Pour the sauce over the fish and garnish with coriander. Serve at once.

HONG KONG STYLE BAKED FISH

——————— SHOPPING LIST ———————

450g/1lb firm white fish steaks, such as haddock, halibut, cod, seabass, etc., Japanese miso

——————— STAPLES ———————

Shaoxing rice wine or dry sherry, sugar

——————— PREPARATION TIME ———————

8 hours or overnight, marinating time

——————— COOKING TIME ———————

10 minutes

SERVES 4

This is a delicious recipe for fish and is popular in Hong Kong as well as in Taiwan. It is unusual because it uses *miso* which is a Japanese sweet bean paste. The influence of Japanese ingredients in Chinese cooking is slight; however, in this case it makes for a quick and appetizing fish dish. Unlike many Chinese dishes, this recipe uses the oven instead of the wok, which makes it ideal if you are planning a dinner party.

450g/1lb firm white fish steaks, such as haddock, halibut, cod, seabass, etc.

——————— MARINADE ———————

225g/8oz/1 cup miso
2 tbsp sugar
3 tbsp Shaoxing rice wine or dry sherry
2 tbsp water

Wipe the fish dry with paper towels. Combine the *miso*, sugar, rice wine, and water. Rub this mixture over both sides of the fish steak. Leave to marinate for 8 hours or overnight in the refrigerator.

Preheat the oven to 230°C/450°F/gas mark 8. Remove the excess marinade. Arrange the fish steaks in a baking dish and bake for 10 minutes or until slightly firm to the touch. Remove the steaks, arrange on a platter, and serve at once.

STIR-FRIED FISH IN TOMATO SAUCE

——————— SHOPPING LIST ———————

450g/1lb firm white fish fillets, such as haddock, halibut, cod, seabass, etc., small onion, small tomatoes, egg, fresh or frozen peas

——————— STAPLES ———————

cornflour [US cornstarch], groundnut oil [US peanut oil], Chicken Stock, Shaoxing rice wine or sherry, light soy sauce, sugar, sesame oil

——————— PREPARATION TIME ———————

25 minutes

——————— COOKING TIME ———————

10 minutes

SERVES 4

Although the tomato is a recent entry into the Chinese culinary repertoire (less than 100 years), it has become a favorite throughout China. It pairs well with firm-textured fish that will not fall apart during the stir-frying process. The tang of the tomato complements the more delicate taste of the fish.

450g/1lb firm, skinned white fish fillets, such as haddock, halibut, cod, seabass, etc.
2 tsp salt
1 egg white
2 tsp cornflour [US cornstarch]
300ml/10fl oz/1¼ cups groundnut oil [US peanut oil] or water

——————— SAUCE ———————

1 small onion, sliced
3 small tomatoes, quartered
150ml/5fl oz/⅝ cup Chicken Stock (page 128)
1 tbsp Shaoxing rice wine or dry sherry
1 tbsp light soy sauce
1 tsp salt, ½ tsp freshly ground white pepper
2 tsp sugar
2 tsp cornflour [US cornstarch] blended with 2 tsp water
2 tsp sesame oil
110g/4oz/½ cup fresh or frozen peas, thawed

Cut the fish fillets into 2.5cm/1in cubes. In a medium-sized bowl, combine the fish with the salt, egg white and cornflour. Put the mixture in the refrigerator to chill for 20 minutes. Heat a wok until it is very hot and then add the oil. When the oil is very hot, remove the wok from the heat and immediately add the fish pieces, stirring gently to keep them from sticking. When the fish pieces turn white, about 2 minutes, quickly drain the fish and discard all but 1¹/₂ tbsp of the oil.

If you choose to use water instead of oil, bring it to a boil in a saucepan. Remove the saucepan from the heat and immediately add the fish pieces, stirring gently to keep them from sticking. When the fish pieces turn white, about 2 minutes, quickly drain the fish in a stainless steel colander set in a bowl to drain well. Discard the water.

Reheat the wok and the reserved oil (add 1¹/₂ tbsp of oil if you used the water method). When it is hot and slightly smoking, add the onion and stir-fry for 2 minutes. Then add the tomatoes, stock, rice wine, soy sauce, salt, pepper, and sugar. Bring the mixture to a boil. Add the cornflour mixture and when the sauce begins to thicken, return the drained fish to the wok together with the peas and add the sesame oil. Cook at high heat for 1 minute. Turn on to a serving platter and serve at once.

CRISPY FISH FILLETS

──── SHOPPING LIST ────
450g/1lb firm white fish fillets such as haddock, halibut, cod, seabass, etc., egg, breadcrumbs, fresh ginger, lemon

──── STAPLES ────
groundnut oil [US peanut oil], cornflour [US cornstarch], Sichuan peppercorns

──── PREPARATION TIME ────
35 minutes

──── COOKING TIME ────
5 minutes
SERVES 4

This is the Chinese version of fried fish without the chips, 'french fries' being one dish the Chinese really cannot claim to have created.

450g/1lb firm, skinned white fish fillets, such as haddock, halibut, cod, seabass, etc.

──── MARINADE ────
1 tsp salt
¹/₂ tsp freshly ground black pepper
2 tbsp ginger juice (page 45)

──── FOR COATING ────
cornflour [US cornstarch], for dusting
1 egg, beaten
dry breadcrumbs
450ml/15fl oz/1⁵/₈ cups groundnut oil [US peanut oil]

──── GARNISH ────
1 lemon, cut into wedges
Seasoned Salt & Pepper Mixture (page 85)

Combine the fish fillets with the marinade ingredients and allow them to sit for 30 minutes in the refrigerator.

Dip the fillets in the cornflour, shaking off any excess. Then put them in the egg and finally roll them in breadcrumbs.

Heat a wok or large frying pan over high heat until it is hot (200°C/400°F). Add the oil and, when it is very hot and slightly smoking, turn the heat to medium. Deep-fry the fish fillets, turning once, for about 1¹/₂ minutes or until they are golden brown. Drain well on paper towels.

Gently slice the fillets and arrange on a platter. Serve immediately, with lemon wedges and the Seasoned Salt & Pepper.

CRISPY SOLE

SHOPPING LIST

700–900g/1¹/₂-2lb Dover sole or other flat fish such as plaice or flounder, spring onions [US scallions]

STAPLES

groundnut oil [US peanut oil], Shaoxing rice wine or dry sherry, light soy sauce

PREPARATION TIME

25 minutes

COOKING TIME

15 minutes

SERVES 4

Sole has been a favorite fish in southern China for over a thousand years. As with fish in general, whether in restaurants or home kitchens, the simplest cooking method with the most straightforward seasonings is the preferred way to prepare sole. My mother made sole this way often, and it is a childhood favorite of mine which I enjoy to this day.

In this recipe, you must closely monitor the frying process so as not to overcook the delicate flesh of the sole. Paradoxically, you might burn it on the outside but undercook it within. The oil must be very hot to begin with, but after the first minute, the heat must be reduced. Properly done, you can enjoy a clean, crispy sole without a hint of grease. This makes a delectable main course.

700–900g/1¹/₂-2lb Dover sole, plaice or flounder, cleaned
1 tsp salt
1 tbsp Shaoxing rice wine or dry sherry
900ml/1¹/₂ pints/3³/₄ cups groundnut oil [US peanut oil]
3 tbsp finely chopped spring onions [US scallions]
1 tbsp light soy sauce

Put the fish on a baking tray. Make three diagonal slashes on both sides of the fish; this will help the fish to cook evenly. Rub the fish with the salt and 1 tbsp Shaoxing rice wine or sherry and let it sit for 20 minutes. Pat the fish dry with paper towels.

Heat a wok or large frying-pan over high heat until it is hot. Add the oil and, when it is very hot and slightly smoking, carefully lower in the fish. Turn the temperature down to moderate and continue to fry the fish for 8–10 minutes or until it is crispy and brown. Remove it from the oil and drain well on paper towels.

Pour off most of the oil, leaving 2 tsp. Re-heat the wok, add the spring onions, rice wine, and light soy sauce. Pour this over the fish and place on a warm platter. Serve at once.

FISH WITH MEAT SAUCE

SHOPPING LIST

700–900g/1¹/₂-2lb whole, firm white fish, such as haddoc, halibut, cod, seabass, etc., 225g/8oz minced [US ground] pork, garlic, fresh ginger, spring onions [US scallions]

STAPLES

cornflour [US cornstarch], groundnut oil [US peanut oil], chilli bean sauce, sugar, light and dark soy sauces, Chicken Stock, sesame oil

PREPARATION TIME

50 minutes

COOKING TIME

20 minutes

SERVES 4

The Chinese are masters at combining two apparently contradictory main ingredients into a delicious and harmonious dish. Here, fish is extended with a rich meat sauce, which at the same time flavors the fish. Pork, of course, while distinctly flavored, is not an aggressive food.

Redolent with garlic and spices, the sauce makes the fish a perfect centerpiece with plain rice and vegetables for a complete meal.

Although you can use fish fillets, it is much more spectacular with a whole fish. Get fresh fish from your fishmonger or local fish store.

700–900g/1¹/2-2lb whole, firm white fish, such as
haddock, halibut, cod, seabass, etc.
1 tbsp salt
cornflour [US cornstarch], for dusting
240ml/8fl oz/1 cup groundnut oil [US peanut oil]
3 slices fresh ginger

─────── MEAT SAUCE ───────

225g/8oz minced pork [US ground pork]
3 tbsp coarsely chopped garlic
2 tbsp finely shredded fresh ginger
6 tbsp spring onions (US scallions)
1¹/2 tbsp chilli bean paste
2 tsp sugar
2 tsp light soy sauce
1 tbsp dark soy sauce
240ml/8floz/1 cup Chicken Stock (page 128)
2 tsp cornflour [US cornstarch] blended with 1¹/2
tbsp water
2 tsp sesame oil

Score the fish by making diagonal slashes at 2.5cm/1in intervals on both sides. Sprinkle the salt evenly on both sides and allow the fish to sit for 30 minutes. Blot any moisture with paper towels. Dust evenly with cornflour, shaking off any excess.

Heat a wok or large frying-pan over high heat until it is hot. Add the oil and ginger slices and, when the oil is very hot and slightly smoking, add the fish. Lower the heat slightly and cook for 5 minutes or until it is crispy. Carefully turn it over and allow the other side to brown and cook for another 5 minutes. Remove the fish and drain well on paper towels. Pour all but 2 tbsp of oil from the wok and discard.

Re-heat the wok and when it is hot, add the pork and stir-fry for 1 minute. Add the garlic, ginger and spring onions and continue to stir-fry for 3 minutes. Finally, add the chilli bean paste, sugar, light and dark soy sauce, and chicken stock. Bring the mixture to a boil, turn the heat down to a simmer, and add the cornflour mixture. Then stir in the sesame oil.

Add the fish and baste it with the meat sauce until it is hot. Carefully put on a warm platter and serve at once.

SPICY STEAMED FISH

─────── SHOPPING LIST ───────

450–700g/1–1¹/2lb firm white fish fillets, such as
cod or sole, or a whole fish such as sole or turbot,
fresh ginger, garlic, fresh coriander [US cilantro],
spring onions [US scallions], fresh red chillies

─────── STAPLES ───────

black beans, Shaoxing rice wine or dry sherry, light
soy sauce

─────── PREPARATION TIME ───────
15 minutes

─────── COOKING TIME ───────
5–15 minutes, depending on the type of fish you use
SERVES 4

Steaming is perhaps the best method of cooking fish as it preserves the purest flavors. Nevertheless, one may add a spicy sauce so long as the fish is not overwhelmed. In this recipe, the fish remains moist, tender, and flavorful while still allowing you to savor the sauce. This contrast in taste and texture is a favorite technique in Chinese cuisine. It is an easy dish to make and is quite dramatic if you use a whole fish.

450–700g/1–1¹/2lb firm, white skinned fish fillets,
such as cod or sole, or a whole fish such as sole or
turbot, cleaned
1 tsp salt ¹/2 tsp freshly ground white pepper

113

—————— SAUCE ——————

1¹/₂ tbsp finely chopped fresh ginger
1 tbsp finely chopped garlic
2 tbsp finely chopped black beans
1¹/₂ tbsp Shaoxing rice wine or dry sherry
2 tbsp light soy sauce
2 fresh red chillies, seeded and chopped
3 tbsp finely shredded spring onions [US scallions]

—————— GARNISH ——————

1¹/₂ tbsp groundnut oil [US peanut oil]
2 tbsp finely chopped fresh coriander [US cilantro]

If you are using a whole fish, remove the gills. Pat the fish or fish fillets dry with paper towels. Rub with the salt and pepper on both sides, then set aside. This helps the flesh to firm up and draws out any excess moisture. After 30 minutes, pat fish dry again with paper towels. In a small bowl, combine the ginger, garlic, black beans, Shaoxing rice wine or dry sherry, and soy sauce and mix well. Place the fish on a heatproof plate. Pour the sauce over the fish and scatter the chillies and spring onions evenly on top.

Set up a steamer or put a rack into a wok or deep pan and add 5cm/2in of water. Bring the water to the boil over a high heat. Put the fish, on its heatproof plate, into the steamer or onto the rack. Cover the pan tightly and gently steam the fish until it is just cooked: flat fish will take about 5 minutes to cook; thicker fish or fillets such as sea bass will take 12–14 minutes. Remove the plate of cooked fish. Heat the oil in a small saucepan and when it is very hot, pour it over the top of the fish. Sprinkle with the fresh coriander and serve at once.

SMOKED FISH

—————— SHOPPING LIST ——————

450–700g/1–1¹/₂lb firm white fish fillets, such as cod or sole, or a whole fish such as sole or turbot, fresh ginger, spring onions [US scallions], black tea leaves, raw long-grain white rice, brown sugar

—————— STAPLES ——————

Shaoxing rice wine or dry sherry, light soy sauce, black beans, star anise, cinnamon bark or sticks, Sichuan peppercorns, five spice powder

—————— PREPARATION TIME ——————

15 minutes

—————— COOKING TIME ——————

5 minutes steaming + 10 minutes smoking

SERVES 4

The smoking process gives delicate fish a subtle dimension that makes you forget that the fish is not perfectly fresh. This Shanghai-inspired recipe requires no great expertise. It makes a wonderful cold dish but is equally tasty when served warm.

450–700g/1–1¹/₂lb firm white skinned fish fillets, such as cod or sole, or a whole fish such as sole or turbot, cleaned
1¹/₂ tbsp finely chopped fresh ginger
1¹/₂ tbsp Shaoxing rice wine or dry sherry
2 tbsp light soy sauce
3 tbsp finely chopped spring onions [US scallions]

—————— FOR SMOKING ——————

50g/2oz/¹/₄ cup brown sugar
50g/2oz/¹/₄ cup long-grain white rice
50g/2oz/¹/₄ cup black tea
3 star anise, broken into sections
2 cinnamon bark or cinnamon sticks, broken into sections
2 tbsp Sichuan peppercorns
2 tsp five spice powder

If you are using a whole fish, remove the gills. Pat the fish or fish fillets dry with kitchen paper. In a small bowl, mix the ginger, rice wine or sherry, soy sauce, and spring onions thoroughly until they form almost a paste. You can use the food blender for this. Rub this mixture evenly on both sides of the fish, and then set aside for 30 minutes.

Next, set up a steamer or put a rack into a wok or deep pan and add 5cm/2in of water. Bring the water to the boil over a high heat. Put the fish on a heatproof plate and put the plate of fish into the steamer or onto the rack. Cover the pan tightly and gently steam the fish for 5 minutes, fillets for 3 minutes.

Remove the plate of semi-cooked fish and allow it to cool slightly.

Line the inside of a wok with aluminum foil. Place the sugar, rice, tea, star anise, cinnamon bark, Sichuan peppercorns, and five spice powder in the wok. Rub a rack with oil and place it over the smoking ingredients. Place the fish on top of the rack.

Now heat the wok over high heat until the mixture begins to burn.

Turn the heat down to moderate, cover, and let it smoke for 5 minutes. Turn off the heat and allow it to sit, covered, for another 5 minutes. Remove the fish and discard the smoking ingredients with the aluminum foil. Serve at once.

BRAISED CATFISH CASSEROLE

──────────── SHOPPING LIST ────────────

40g/1¹/₂oz small package of bean thread noodles, 700–900g/1¹/₂–2lb whole fresh catfish or sea bass, 225g/8oz minced [US ground] pork, garlic, fresh ginger, spring onions [US scallions], fresh red chillies

──────────── STAPLES ────────────

groundnut oil [US peanut oil], light and dark soy sauces, Shaoxing rice wine or dry sherry, sugar, Chicken Stock, sesame oil

──────────── PREPARATION TIME ────────────

30 minutes

──────────── COOKING TIME ────────────

30 minutes

SERVES 4

Fish farming has been practiced in China for over 2,000 years. Originally an inland people who clustered along China's many rivers, the Chinese learned to love the carp, bream and other freshwater fish available to them. They soon learned as well that it was better to 'harvest' the fish than to throw lines and nets randomly into the water to catch them. They, thus, perfected a system of freshwater ponds in which they placed the fish, seeing to it that there was ample food, fresh clean water, and, in fact, an ecologically sound environment in which the fish prospered. Such pond-reared fish never taste 'muddy' unless they are raised improperly or their water is allowed to stagnate. In China, proper procedures are always followed, and after each harvest, the ponds are dried off and then carefully refilled and restocked.

The Chinese also selectively breed the fish to enhance their most desirable natural attributes – firm, white flesh with delicate taste – and, in the case of carp especially, to create aesthetically pleasing, ornamental fish, of which the various 'goldfish' are the most widely known.

Other than carp, which is the most popular variety, farmed fish include mullet, bream, eels, and catfish. In this recipe, which is quite popular in Hong Kong, the catfish is deep-fried to seal in its flavor; it is then combined with bean thread noodles, which, while providing a textural contrast, also absorb all of the delicious tastes and aromas characteristic of this recipe. It is an easy-to-make one-pot dish, perfect when served with plain steamed rice and an accompanying vegetable.

40g/1¹/₂oz package of bean thread noodles
700–900g/1¹/₂–2lb whole fresh catfish or
sea bass, cleaned
350ml/12fl oz/1¹/₂ cups groundnut oil [US peanut oil]
225g/8oz minced [US ground] pork, chopped
3 tbsp coarsely chopped garlic

115

2 tbsp finely shredded fresh ginger
6 tbsp finely chopped spring onions [US scallions]
3 tbsp seeded and finely shredded fresh red chillies
2 tsp salt
2 tbsp light soy sauce
2 tbsp dark soy sauce
3 tbsp Shaoxing rice wine or dry sherry
2 tsp sugar
175ml/6fl oz/³/₄ cups Chicken Stock (page 128)
1 tbsp sesame oil

Soak the bean thread noodles in a large bowl of warm water for 15 minutes. When they are soft, drain them. Cut them into more manageable lengths using scissors or a knife.

Dry the fish thoroughly with paper towels. Cut the fish into 4cm/1¹/₂in pieces.

Heat a wok or large frying pan over high heat until it is hot. Add all but 2 tbsp of the groundnut oil and, when it is very hot and slightly smoking, add the catfish. Deep-fry for 8 minutes or until the pieces are golden brown. Remove and drain well on paper towels. Discard all the oil. Wipe the wok clean. Reheat the wok and add the reserved 2 tbsp of groundnut oil. When it is hot, add the pork, garlic, ginger, spring onions and chillies and stir-fry for 3 minutes. Then add the salt, soy sauces, rice wine or sherry, sugar, and chicken stock and cook for 2 minutes.

Quickly pour the pork mixture into a clay pot or a large casserole. Add the drained noodles and pieces of catfish. Cover and cook over high heat for 10 minutes. Add the sesame oil. Turn onto a large, warm serving platter and serve. Or, if you are using the clay pot, serve directly from the pot.

STIR-FRIED PRAWNS WITH BROAD BEANS

SHOPPING LIST
450g/1lb large raw prawns [US shrimp], egg, frozen broad beans [US frozen lima beans], garlic

STAPLES
cornflour [US cornstarch], groundnut oil [US peanut oil], Chicken Stock, Shaoxing rice wine or dry sherry, light soy sauce, sugar, sesame oil

PREPARATION TIME
20 minutes

COOKING TIME
10 minutes

SERVES 2–4

Fresh prawns are a popular shellfish in eastern China, especially as prepared in this Shanghai-inspired dish with broad beans. It is simple to make. Raw prawns must be used or else you will lose much of the taste and texture of the dish. Washing them first in salt cleans and firms the flesh. The sweetness of the broad beans is a nice foil for the richness of the prawns.

PRAWNS
2 tsp salt
300ml/10fl oz/1¹/₄ cups water
450g/1lb large raw prawns [US shrimp], peeled and deveined
1 small egg white
1 tsp cornflour [US cornstarch]
150ml/5fl oz/ ⁵/₈ cup groundnut oil [US peanut oil] or vegetable oil

SAUCE
1 tbsp finely chopped garlic
110g/4oz/¹/₄ cup thawed frozen broad beans [US frozen lima beans]
3 tbsp Chicken Stock (page 128)
1 tbsp Shaoxing rice wine or dry sherry
1 tsp sugar
2 tsp light soy sauce
¹/₂ tsp salt

¼ tsp freshly ground white pepper
1 tsp cornflour [US cornstarch] blended
with 2 tsp water
1 tsp sesame oil

Mix the salt with the water and wash the prawns in this mixture. Rinse well and pat dry with paper towels. Mix the prawns with the egg white and cornflour. Refrigerate for at least 15 minutes.

Heat a wok until it is hot, then add the oil. When the oil is hot and slightly smoking, remove from the heat. Add the prawns, and quickly stir to separate them. Let them sit in the oil for 2 minutes. Drain in a colander and discard all but 1 tbsp of the oil.

Reheat the wok and add the reserved oil. When it is hot, add the garlic and stir-fry for 10 seconds. Then add the broad beans and stir-fry for 1 minute. Add the chicken stock, rice wine, sugar, soy sauce, salt and pepper. Stir to mix well and cook for 30 seconds. Stir in the cornflour mixture and cook for 10 seconds. Return the prawns to the wok and stir the mixture to coat them thoroughly. When the prawns are heated through, stir in the sesame oil and serve at once.

DEEP-FRIED PRAWN BALLS

SHOPPING LIST
350g/12oz raw prawns [US shrimp], fresh or canned water chestnuts, pork fat, egg, spring onions [US scallions]

STAPLES
sesame oil, cornflour [US cornstarch], sugar, groundnut oil [US peanut oil]

PREPARATION TIME
15 minutes

COOKING TIME
10 minutes

SERVES 4, AS A FIRST COURSE

These crispy prawn balls are a savory snack often served in *dim sum* as a separate course. They are light with a wonderful fluffy texture. The secret is the use of egg white. The pork fat adds to the mouth-watering taste. These are very easy to make.

PRAWN MIXTURE
350g/12oz raw prawns, [US shrimp] peeled and deveined
110g/4oz peeled fresh or canned water chestnuts, finely chopped (page 92)
110g/4oz pork fat, finely chopped
1 tsp salt
½ tsp freshly ground white pepper
1 egg white
1 tsp sesame oil
2 tbsp spring onions, [US scallions] white part only, finely chopped
1 tbsp cornflour [US cornstarch]
2 tsp sugar

FOR FRYING
450ml/15fl oz/1⁵⁄₈ cups groundnut oil [US peanut oil]

FOR DIPPING
Seasoned Salt & Pepper (page 85)

Using a cleaver or sharp knife, chop the prawns coarsely and then mince them in a food processor to a fine paste. Put the paste into a bowl and mix in the rest of the ingredients for the prawn mixture. Alternatively, you could do this in a food processor. (This step can be done hours in advance, but you should then cover the paste tightly and keep it in the refrigerator until you need it.)

Using your hands, form the mixture into 3.5cm/1½in balls – about the size of a golf ball. Continue until you have used up all the paste. Heat the oil for frying in a deep-fat fryer or wok to a moderate heat (180° C/350°F). Deep-fry the prawn balls a few at a time, for about 3 minutes or until they are golden brown and puffed up.

117

Remove with a slotted spoon, and drain on paper towels. Serve with the Seasoned Salt & Pepper for dipping.

PRAWNS WITH HONEY-GLAZED WALNUTS

──────── SHOPPING LIST ────────

110g/4oz walnut halves, 450g/1lb raw prawns [US shrimp], egg, fresh ginger, garlic, spring onions [US scallions]

──────── STAPLES ────────

groundnut oil [US peanut oil], cornflour [US cornstarch], sugar, sesame oil, Shaoxing rice wine or dry sherry

──────── PREPARATION TIME ────────

2 hours or overnight for the walnuts + 40 minutes

──────── COOKING TIME ────────

15 minutes

SERVES 4

This exotic and unlikely combination is one of the best examples of how Chinese food practices evolve in Hong Kong. Classical dishes are given a refreshing new dimension. I have enjoyed this dish several times in Hong Kong, and I discovered a delicious version at the Hong Kong Flower Lounge in San Francisco. Here, the rich sweetness and crunchy texture of the walnuts works extremely well with the fresh, delicate taste and soft texture of the prawns. Although it takes a bit of time, it is well worth making for a special occasion or as the main course of a dinner party.

──────── WALNUTS ────────

110g/4oz/¼ cup shelled walnut halves
50g/2oz/⅛ cup sugar
240ml/8fl oz/1 cup groundnut oil [US peanut oil]

──────── PRAWNS ────────

450g/1lb raw prawns [US shrimp], peeled and deveined
1 egg white

2 tsp cornflour [US cornstarch]
1 tsp salt
1 tsp sesame oil
½ tsp freshly ground white pepper
350ml/12fl oz/1½ cups groundnut oil [US peanut oil] or water
1 tbsp finely chopped fresh ginger
2 tsp finely chopped garlic
1 tbsp Shaoxing rice wine or dry sherry
1 tsp salt
½ tsp freshly ground white pepper
2 tsp sesame oil

──────── GARNISH ────────

2 tbsp finely chopped spring onions [US scallions]

Bring a small pot of water to the boil. Add the walnuts and simmer for about 10 minutes to blanch them. Drain the nuts in a colander or sieve, then pat dry with paper towels and spread them on a baking tray. Sprinkle the sugar over the walnuts and roll them around in the sugar to coat them completely. Place the tray of sugared walnuts in a cool, drafty place. Let them dry for at least 2 hours, preferably overnight. (The recipe can be done ahead to this point.)

Heat a wok or large frying pan over high heat until it is hot. Add the oil and, when it is very hot and slightly smoking, fry the walnuts for about 2 minutes or until the sugar melts and the walnuts turn golden. (Watch the heat to prevent burning.) Remove the walnuts from the oil with a slotted spoon or strainer. Do not drain them on paper towels as the sugar would stick to the towels when it dries. Allow the walnuts to cool before using. (This step too can be done in advance: the honey walnuts can be kept in a sealed glass jar for about 2 weeks.)

Rinse the prawns and pat them dry with paper towels. Combine the prawns with the egg white, cornflour, salt, sesame oil, and pepper. Mix well and place in the refrigerator for 20 minutes.

Reserve 1½ tbsp of the groundnut oil. Heat a wok until it is very hot and then add the remaining oil. When the oil is very hot, remove the wok from the heat and immediately add the prawns, stirring vigorously to keep them from sticking. When the prawns turn white, about 2 minutes, drain them in a stainless steel colander.

If you choose to use water instead of oil, bring it to a boil in a saucepan. Remove the saucepan from the heat and immediately add the prawns, stirring vigorously to keep them from sticking. When the prawns turn white, about 2 minutes, quickly drain them in a stainless steel colander. Reheat the wok or a large frying pan over high heat until it is hot. Add the reserved oil. When it is very hot and slightly smoking, add the ginger and garlic and stir-fry for 10 seconds. Return the prawns to the wok, together with the rice wine or sherry, salt and pepper. Stir-fry the mixture for 1 minute. Now add the honey walnuts and stir gently for 1 minute to mix well. Stir in the sesame oil.

Turn onto a platter, garnish with spring onions, and serve at once.

PRAWNS IN HOT GARLIC SAUCE

──────── SHOPPING LIST ────────

450g/1lb raw prawns [US shrimp], egg, small onion, spring onions [US scallions], fresh red chillies, small fresh green chillies, fresh ginger, garlic

──────── STAPLES ────────

cornflour [US cornstarch], groundnut oil [US peanut oil], sesame oil, black beans, Shaoxing rice wine or dry sherry, light soy sauce, sugar, Chicken Stock

──────── PREPARATION TIME ────────

15 minutes

──────── COOKING TIME ────────

15 minutes

SERVES 4

This appetizing recipe was created by an unknown chef in a simple restaurant in Hong Kong, where fresh prawns are always available.

When I say 'fresh', I mean that they are usually swimming minutes before they go into the wok. Unlike prawn dishes served in Chinese restaurants in the West, the style of cooking in Hong Kong entails a minimum amount of sauce – to coat food, not to mask it. This modest dish is easy to make at home. Remember, get the freshest prawns possible.

──────── PRAWNS ────────

450g/1lb raw prawns [US shrimp], peeled and deveined
1 egg white
2 tsp cornflour [US cornstarch]
1 tsp salt
1 tsp sesame oil
½ tsp freshly ground white pepper
350ml/12fl oz/1½ cups groundnut oil [US peanut oil] or water

──────── HOT GARLIC SAUCE ────────

1½ tbsp finely chopped fresh ginger
3 tbsp coarsely chopped garlic
1 small onion
2 fresh red chillies, seeded and sliced
1 small fresh green chilli, seeded and sliced
3 spring onions [US scallions], sliced
1 tbsp coarsely chopped black beans
1 tbsp Shaoxing rice wine or dry sherry
2 tbsp light soy sauce
1½ tsp sugar
4 tbsp Chicken Stock (page 128)
2 tsp sesame oil

Rinse the prawns and pat them dry with paper towels. Combine the prawns with the egg white, cornflour, salt, sesame oil and pepper. Mix well and let them sit in the refrigerator for 20 minutes. Heat a wok until it is very hot and then add the groundnut oil. When the oil is very hot, remove the wok from the heat and immediately

119

add the prawns, stirring vigorously to keep them from sticking. When the prawns turn white, about 2 minutes, quickly drain them in a stainless steel colander set in a bowl. Discard all but 1½ tbsp of the oil.

If you choose to use water instead of oil, bring it to a boil in a saucepan. Remove the saucepan from the heat and immediately add the prawns, stirring vigorously to keep them from sticking. When the prawns turn white, about 2 minutes, quickly drain them in a stainless steel colander. Reheat the wok or a large frying pan over high heat until it is hot. Add the reserved 1½ tbsp of oil and, when it is very hot and slightly smoking, add the ginger and garlic. Stir-fry for 10 seconds. Then add the onion, chillies and spring onions and stir-fry for 1 minute. Add the black beans, rice wine or sherry, soy sauce, sugar and chicken stock. Continue to cook for 2 minutes. Return the prawns to the wok and stir-fry for 30 seconds, mixing well.

Stir in the sesame oil and mix well. Turn onto a platter and serve at once.

SCALLOPS AND PRAWNS IN HONEY SAUCE

——— SHOPPING LIST ———
225g/8oz scallops, including the corals [US sea scallops], 225g/8oz raw prawns [US shrimp], 450g/1lb red and green sweet peppers, garlic, fresh ginger, spring onions [US scallions], egg

——— STAPLES ———
cornflour [US cornstarch], sesame oil, groundnut oil [US peanut oil], black beans, Shaoxing rice wine or dry sherry, light soy sauce, honey

——— PREPARATION TIME ———
30 minutes

——— COOKING TIME ———
15 minutes
SERVES 4

This simple and delicious dish was inspired by the chef at the Hong Kong Flower Lounge in San Francisco. A native of Hong Kong, he manifests the innovative and exciting approach to traditional foods that is so typical of the new Hong Kong cuisine. In this recipe, red sweet peppers are combined with the rich seafood flavor of scallops and prawns in a gentle and subtle honey sauce that strikes just the right balance of flavors, colors, and textures. Essential to the dish, however, is that you use the best and freshest seafood.

225g/8oz scallops, including the corals [US sea scallops]
225g/8oz raw prawns [US shrimp], peeled and deveined
½ egg white
1 tsp cornflour [US cornstarch]
½ tsp salt
½ tsp sesame oil
¼ tsp freshly ground white pepper
240ml/8fl oz/1 cup groundnut oil [US peanut oil] or water
450g/1lb red and green sweet peppers, seeded and cut into 2.5cm/1in squares

——— HONEY SAUCE ———
1½ tbsp groundnut oil [US peanut oil]
1 tbsp finely chopped fresh ginger
1 tbsp finely chopped garlic
1 tbsp Shaoxing rice wine or dry sherry
1 tbsp coarsely chopped black beans
2 tbsp finely chopped spring onions [US scallions]
2 tsp light soy sauce
2 tsp honey
1 tsp salt
½ tsp freshly ground white pepper
2 tsp sesame oil

Remove any tough muscle bits from the scallops and discard. Rinse the prawns and pat them dry with paper towels. Combine the prawns with the egg white, cornflour, salt, sesame oil and pepper. Mix well and and let them sit in the refrigerator for 20 minutes.

Heat a wok until it is very hot and add the groundnut oil. When the oil is very hot, remove the wok from the heat and immediately add the prawns, stirring vigorously to keep them from sticking. When the prawns turn white, about 2 minutes, quickly drain them in a stainless steel colander.

If you choose to use water instead of oil, bring it to a boil in a saucepan. Remove the saucepan from the heat and immediately add the prawns, stirring vigorously to keep them from sticking. When the prawns turn white, about 2 minutes, quickly drain them in a stainless steel colander.

Reheat the wok or a large frying pan over high heat until it is hot. Add the 1¹/₂ tbsp oil for the sauce. When it is very hot and slightly smoking, add the ginger and garlic and stir-fry for 10 seconds. Add the sweet peppers and scallops and stir-fry for 3 minutes. Return the prawns to the wok, together with the rice wine or sherry. Stir-fry the mixture for 1 minute. Then add the rest of the honey sauce ingredients except for the sesame oil. Continue to stir-fry for 4 minutes until the scallops are firm. Now add the sesame oil and stir-fry for another minute. Serve at once.

SICHUAN-STYLE PRAWNS AND SCALLOPS

SHOPPING LIST

225g/8oz scallops, including the corals, 225g/8oz raw prawns [US shrimp], garlic, fresh ginger, spring onions [US scallions], egg

STAPLES

cornflour [US cornstarch], sesame oil, groundnut oil [US peanut oil], Shaoxing rice wine or dry sherry, light soy sauce, chilli bean paste, sugar

PREPARATION TIME
30 minutes

COOKING TIME
15 minutes

SERVES 4

Hong Kong chefs, always open to new ideas, have often drawn upon the spicy traditions of Sichuan to invigorate simple stir-fry dishes. In this recipe, scallops and prawns are combined in a zesty dish that one would not find in Sichuan itself. Being a landlocked province, seafood is not available there. Because we use fresh, delicately flavored seafood, the spices are muted, providing an accent rather than dominating the dish as would be the case in authentic Sichuan cooking. This is quick and easy to make and provides a satisfying main course with rice and vegetables.

225g/8oz scallops, including the corals [US sea scallops]
225g/8oz raw prawns [US shrimp], peeled and deveined
¹/₂ egg white
1 tsp cornflour [US cornstarch]
¹/₂ tsp salt
¹/₂ tsp sesame oil
¹/₄ tsp freshly ground white pepper
240ml/8fl oz/1 cup groundnut oil [US peanut oil] or water

SAUCE

1¹/₂ tbsp groundnut oil [US peanut oil]
1 tbsp finely chopped fresh ginger
1 tbsp finely chopped garlic
2 tbsp finely chopped spring onions [US scallions]
1 tbsp Shaoxing rice wine or dry sherry
2 tsp light soy sauce
1¹/₂ tbsp chilli bean paste
¹/₂ tsp freshly ground white pepper
1 tsp sugar
2 tsp sesame oil

Remove any tough muscle bits from the scallops and discard.

Rinse the prawns and pat them dry with paper towels. Combine the prawns with the egg white, cornflour, salt, sesame oil, and pepper. Mix well and and let them sit in the refrigerator for 20 minutes.

Heat a wok until it is very hot and then add the groundnut oil. When the oil is very hot, remove the wok from the heat and immediately add the prawns, stirring vigorously to keep them from sticking. When the prawns turn white, about 2 minutes, quickly drain them in a stainless steel colander.

If you choose to use water instead of oil, bring it to a boil in a saucepan. Remove the saucepan from the heat and immediately add the prawns, stirring vigorously to keep them from sticking. When the prawns turn white, about 2 minutes, quickly drain them in a stainless steel colander.

Reheat the wok or a large frying pan over high heat until it is hot. Add the oil for the sauce. When it is very hot and slightly smoking, add the ginger, garlic, and spring onions and stir-fry for 10 seconds. Add the scallops and stir-fry for 3 minutes. Then return the prawns to the wok, together with the rice wine or sherry. Stir-fry the mixture for 1 minute. Add the soy sauce, chilli bean paste, pepper, and sugar. Continue to stir-fry for 4 minutes or until the scallops are firm. Now add the sesame oil and stir-fry for another minute. Serve at once.

STIR-FRIED SCALLOPS WITH BROCCOLI

──────── SHOPPING LIST ────────

450g/1lb scallops, including the corals [US sea scallops], 450g/1lb broccoli, fresh ginger, garlic, spring onions [US scallions]

──────── STAPLES ────────

light soy sauce, Shaoxing rice wine or dry sherry, groundnut oil [US peanut oil], sugar, cornflour [US cornstarch], sesame oil, Chicken Stock

──────── PREPARATION TIME ────────
15 minutes

──────── COOKING TIME ────────
10 minutes

SERVES 4

Scallops are a favorite with the southern Chinese who are fortunate in having seafood so readily available to them. They like scallops both fresh and dried. Stir-frying works especially well with fresh scallops since it makes overcooking, which makes scallops tough, less likely. Just 5 minutes of stir-frying, as in this recipe, is quite sufficient to cook them thoroughly without robbing them of their sweet flavour. They are particularly tasty when paired with broccoli. This classical combination of a fresh green vegetable with a delicate seafood is typical of Cantonese cooking and exemplifies the basis of its highly respected reputation. It is simple but elegant at the same time.

450g/1lb scallops, including the corals [US sea scallops]
450g/1lb broccoli
1¹/₂ tbsp groundnut oil [US peanut oil]
1 tbsp finely chopped fresh ginger
1 tbsp finely chopped garlic
2 tbsp finely chopped spring onions [US scallions]
1 tbsp Shaoxing rice wine or dry sherry
2 tsp light soy sauce
1 tsp sugar
¹/₂ tsp salt
¹/₂ tsp freshly ground white pepper
4 tbsp Chicken Stock (page 128)
1 tsp cornflour [US cornstarch] blended with 2 tsp water

MARINADE

1 tbsp ginger juice (page 45)
1 tbsp Shaoxing rice wine or dry sherry
^{1}/$_2$ tsp salt
^{1}/$_4$ tsp freshly ground white pepper
2 tsp sesame oil

Remove any tough muscle bits from the scallops and discard. Combine the scallops with the marinade ingredients. Allow to marinate for 20 minutes.

Divide the broccoli heads into small florets. Peel the skin off the stems as it is often fibrous and stringy, and then cut them into thin slices at a slight diagonal. This will ensure that the stems cook evenly with the florets. Bring a pot of salted water to the boil, add the broccoli florets and stems, and cook for about 5 minutes. Drain them, plunge into cold water, and drain again.

Heat a wok or large frying pan over high heat. Add the groundnut oil and, when it is very hot and slightly smoking, add the ginger, garlic, and spring onions. Stir-fry for 10 seconds. Drain the scallops and reserve the marinade. Add the scallops to the wok and stir-fry them for 2 minutes. Then add the reserved marinade and the rest of the ingredients except the cornflour and sesame oil. Add the broccoli and continue to stir-fry for 4 minutes or until the scallops are firm and thoroughly coated with the sauce. Now add the cornflour mixture and sesame oil and stir-fry for another minute. Serve at once.

CRAB BEAN THREAD CASSEROLE

SHOPPING LIST

40g/1^1/$_2$oz package of bean thread noodles, 1.35kg/ 3lb live or freshly cooked crab in the shell, garlic, fresh ginger, spring onions [US scallions], fresh red chillies

STAPLES

groundnut oil [US peanut oil], light and dark soy sauces, Shaoxing rice wine or dry sherry, Chicken Stock, sesame oil

PREPARATION TIME

20 minutes

COOKING TIME

20 minutes

SERVES 4

This recipe can only be made with fresh crabs, preferably live, in the shell since the shell serves to protect the delicate crabmeat during the quick stir-frying process. It is then cooked at very high heat in a clay pot. This dish is very popular in Hong Kong, as the first, short blast of heat infuses flavor into the crabs without drying them out. If you are feeling extravagant, you can also make this with lobster. The bean thread noodles absorb all the precious juices and aromas of the other ingredients. Nothing is wasted in this dish. I love to eat it with plain steamed rice and a vegetable dish. It makes a satisfying meal.

40g/1^1/$_2$oz package of bean thread noodles
1.35kg/3lb live or freshly cooked crab in the shell
2 tbsp groundnut oil [US peanut oil]
4 tbsp coarsely chopped garlic
2 tbsp finely shredded fresh ginger
6 tbsp finely chopped spring onions [US scallions]
2 tbsp seeded and finely shredded fresh red chillies
2 tbsp light soy sauce
1 tbsp dark soy sauce
2 tbsp Shaoxing rice wine or dry sherry
175ml/6fl oz/^{3}/$_4$ cup Chicken Stock (page 128)
2 tsp sesame oil

Soak the bean thread noodles in a large bowl of warm water for 15 minutes. When they are soft, drain them. Cut them into more manageable lengths using scissors or a knife.

If the crab is alive, remove the claws. Remove the tail-flap, stomach sac, and feathery gills from the crab. Remove the main shell. Using a heavy knife or cleaver, cut the crab body into quarters. Lightly crack the legs with the cleaver.

Heat a wok or large frying pan over high heat until it is hot. Add the oil and, when it is very hot and slightly smoking, add the crab, garlic, ginger, spring onions and chillies. Stir-fry for 2 minutes. Then add the soy sauces, rice wine or sherry and chicken stock and cook for a further 2 minutes.

Quickly pour this mixture into a clay pot or a large casserole. Add the drained noodles. Cover and cook over high heat for 10 minutes. Add the sesame oil. Turn the mixture onto a large, warm serving platter and serve. It is perfectly good manners to eat the crab with your fingers, but I suggest that you have a large bowl of water decorated with lemon slices on the table so that your guests can rinse their fingers.

CLAMS IN BLACK BEAN SAUCE

—— SHOPPING LIST ——
1.35kg/3lb fresh clams, garlic, fresh ginger, shallots, spring onions [US scallions]

—— STAPLES ——
groundnut oil [US peanut oil], black beans, dark and light soy sauces, Shaoxing rice wine or dry sherry, chilli bean paste, sugar, Chicken Stock, sesame oil

—— PREPARATION TIME ——
30 minutes

—— COOKING TIME ——
10 minutes
SERVES 4

Shellfish of all types are enjoyed by all who have access to them, and Chinese who are lucky enough to live near the sea savor the briny freshness of clams whenever possible. The clams are steamed or used in soups, or dried and served as a condiment, or, as in this recipe, stir-fried in a flavorful, aromatic combination with black bean sauce. In this way, my mother would turn ordinary clams into a feast. Clams cook very

quickly, making them perfect for those in a hurry. Serve with rice or vegetables for a nutritious and satisfying light meal. Mussels make a perfect substitute if clams are unavailable.

1.35kg/3lb fresh clams, thoroughly scrubbed
1 1/2 tbsp groundnut oil [US peanut oil]
1 1/2 tbsp coarsely chopped garlic
1 tbsp finely chopped fresh ginger
3 tbsp finely chopped shallots
2 tbsp coarsely chopped black beans
1 tbsp light soy sauce
2 tbsp dark soy sauce
2 tbsp Shaoxing rice wine or dry sherry
2 tsp chilli bean paste
1 tsp sugar
120ml/4fl oz/1/2 cup Chicken Stock (page 128)
2 tsp sesame oil
3 tbsp chopped spring onions [US scallions]

Rinse the clams in a large bowl of cold water, changing the water at least twice. Drain well.

Heat a wok or large frying pan over high heat until it is hot. Add the oil and, when it is very hot and slightly smoking, add the garlic, ginger, shallots, and black beans. Stir-fry for 15 seconds. Then add the clams, soy sauces, Shaoxing rice wine or dry sherry, chilli bean paste, sugar, and chicken stock. Cover the wok and cook over high heat for 3 minutes. Remove the clams as their shells open; discard any that remain unopened after 5 minutes. Stir the sesame oil and spring onions into the sauce remaining. Pour this over the clams and serve at once.

SALT AND PEPPER SQUID

—— SHOPPING LIST ——
700g/1 1/2lb fresh or frozen squid, fresh red chillies, garlic, spring onions [US scallions]

—— STAPLES ——
groundnut oil [US peanut oil], Sichuan peppercorns, potato starch or cornflour [US cornstarch]

Squid is an often unappreciated seafood. However, when cooked properly and imaginatively, it is delectable as well as inexpensive. Here it is cooked in popular southern Chinese style that results in a tender and tasty treat. The secret to tender squid is a minimal cooking time – just enough for the squid to firm up slightly. Cooking it too long will make it tough, like chewing on rubber bands, and this avoidable result is what most people believe squid is. Unlike most seafood, frozen squid can be quite good and when properly cooked it is often impossible to tell from fresh. In this recipe, it is deep-fried first, then tossed with an aromatic seasoning.

700g/1 1/2lb fresh or frozen squid
potato starch or cornflour [US cornstarch], for dusting
2 tsp sea salt
2 tsp roasted and ground Sichuan peppercorns (page 85)
1 tsp freshly ground white pepper
2 tbsp coarsely chopped garlic
3 tbsp coarsely chopped fresh red chillies, unseeded
2 tbsp finely chopped spring onions [US scallions]
450ml/15fl oz/1 5/8 cups groundnut oil [US peanut oil]

The edible parts of the squid are the tentacles and the body. If it has not been cleaned by your fishmonger you can do it yourself by pulling the head and tentacles away from the body. Then pull off and discard the skin. Using a small, sharp knife, split the body in half. Remove the translucent bony section. Wash the halves thoroughly under cold running water and then pull off and discard the skin. Cut the tentacles from the head, cutting just above the eye. (You may also have to remove the polyp or beak from the base of the ring of tentacles.) If you are using frozen squid make sure it is properly thawed before cooking it.

Cut the squid meat into 4cm/1 1/2in strips. Rinse the strips and tentacles in cold water, drain well, and blot completely dry with paper towels. Dust the squid with the potato starch or cornflour. Shake off any excess powder.

In a small bowl, combine the salt, peppercorns and pepper and set aside. In another small bowl, combine the garlic and chillies. Place the spring onions in a third bowl.

Heat a wok or large frying pan over high heat until it is hot. Add the oil and, when it is very hot and slightly smoking, add the squid and fry for several minutes or until the pieces are crispy. Drain them well on paper towels.

Pour off the oil from the wok, leaving 1 1/2 tbsp. Reheat the wok and oil and, when it is hot, add the garlic and chilli mixture and stir-fry for 10 seconds. Then add the salt mixture and stir-fry for 10 seconds. Return the squid to the wok and stir-fry over high heat for about 2 minutes or until the spices have thoroughly coated the squid. Add the spring onions. Mix well, turn onto a serving platter, and serve at once.

POULTRY

CHICKEN STOCK MASTER RECIPE

Chicken stock is an all-purpose base for soups and sauces. Its chief ingredient is inexpensive; it is light and delicious; and it marries well with other foods, enhancing and sustaining them. Small wonder it is an almost universally present ingredient in Chinese cookery. Thus, from the Imperial kitchens to the most humble food stalls, good stock is the basic ingredient. The usual Chinese chicken stock is precisely that, the essence of chicken, with complements of ginger and spring onions often added. Combined with the condiments that give Chinese food its distinctive flavor, good stock captures the essential taste of China. Many of the most famous recipes in the repertory require such stock. There are two basic types: one is a clear stock made from chicken bones and meat; the other is a richer stock that uses ham and pork bones. The different recipes call for different stocks but both types make a solid base for soups and sauces.

During the Qing dynasty, the last Imperial dynasty (1644–1911), Chinese cuisine reached its peak of classical perfection. One of the most highly prized dishes featured in the Imperial banquets was a bowl of clear soup, a consommé of chicken stock, much appreciated for its subtle, light, flavorful elegance. This serves as a reminder that stock so prepared can also be used as a clear soup. I find that the richer stocks made with ham or pork bones are heavier and less to my taste. This simple recipe for stock reflects what I believe works best for any Chinese dish.

There are commercially prepared canned or cubed (dried) stocks but many of them are of inferior quality, being either too salty or containing additives and colorings that adversely affect your health as well as the natural taste of good foods. Stock does take time to prepare but it is easy to make your own – and when homemade, it is the best. Your first step on the path to success with Chinese cooking must be to prepare and maintain an ample supply of good chicken stock. I prefer to make large quantities of it at a time and freeze it. Once you have a supply of stock available you will be able to prepare any number of soups or sauces very quickly. Here are several important points to keep in mind when making stock:

● Good stock requires meat to give it richness and flavor. It is therefore necessary to use at least some chicken meat, if not a whole bird.
● The stock should never boil. If it does it will be undesirably cloudy and the fat will be incorporated into the liquid. Flavors and digestibility come with a clear stock.
● Use a tall, heavy pot so the liquid covers all the solids and evaporation is slow.
● Simmer slowly and skim the stock regularly. Be patient – you will reap the rewards each time you prepare a Chinese dish.
● Strain the finished stock well through several layers of muslin or cheesecloth or a fine mesh sieve or strainer.
● Let the stock cool completely. Refrigerate and remove any fat before freezing it.

The classic Chinese method to ensure a clear stock is to blanch the meat and bones before simmering. I find this unnecessary. My method of careful skimming achieves the same result with far less work. Remember to save all your uncooked chicken bones for stock. They can be frozen until you are ready to make it.

This recipe makes about 4 litres/7 pints/17½ cups (if you find the portions too large for your needs, cut the recipe in half).

2kg/4½lb uncooked chicken bones, such as backs, feet, wings, etc.
700g/1½lb chicken pieces, such as wings, thighs, drumsticks, etc.
4 litres/7 pints/17½ cups cold water

Previous page: Soy Sauce Chicken Wings; Stuffed Chicken Slices

3 slices fresh ginger
6 spring onions [US scallions]
6 garlic cloves, unpeeled
1 tsp salt

Put the chicken bones and chicken pieces into a very large pot. (The bones can be put in either frozen or thawed.) Cover them with the cold water and bring it to a simmer. Meanwhile cut the ginger into diagonal slices, 5 x 1cm/2 x ½ in. Remove the green tops of the spring onions. Lightly crush the garlic cloves without removing their outer skins.

Using a large, flat spoon, skim off the scum as it rises from the bones. Watch the heat as the stock should never boil. Keep skimming until the stock looks clear. This can take from 20 to 40 minutes. Do not stir or disturb the stock.

Now turn the heat down to a low simmer. Add the ginger, white part of the spring onions, garlic cloves, and salt. Simmer the stock on a very low heat for between 2 and 4 hours, skimming any fat off the top at least twice during this time. The stock should be rich and full-bodied which is why it needs to be simmered for such a long time. This way the stock (and any soup you make with it) will have plenty of flavor.

Strain the stock through several layers of dampened muslin or cheesecloth or through a very fine mesh sieve or strainer, and then let it cool completely. Remove any fat that has risen to the top. It is now ready to be used or transferred to containers and frozen for future use.

STEEPED CHICKEN, MASTER RECIPE

—————— SHOPPING LIST ——————
1.5–1.75kg/3½-4lb cornfed chicken, fresh ginger, spring onions [US scallions]

—————— STAPLES ——————

—————— FOR SOY SAUCE CHICKEN ——————
Chicken Stock, light and dark soy sauces, Shaoxing rice wine or dry sherry, rock or ordinary sugar, star anise, cinnamon bark or sticks, cumin seeds

—————— FOR DRUNKEN CHICKEN ——————
Chicken Stock, Shaoxing rice wine, rock or ordinary sugar, light soy sauce

—————— PREPARATION TIME ——————
10–20 minutes

—————— COOKING TIME ——————
20 minutes simmering + 1 hour steeping
SERVES 4–6

When Chinese chefs cook with boiling liquid, they never overcook the food, as is so often done in the West. Rather they employ a most wonderful technique called steeping. This is used for delicate foods, such as chicken or fish. It applies the gentlest possible heat so that the flesh of the chicken or fish remains extremely moist with a velvet texture which the Chinese describe as smooth. The liquid used may be water, a soy sauce mixture, or rice wine.

The food simmers in liquid for about 15 minutes, then the heat is turned off, the pot tightly covered, and the food left to steep in the heat remaining to finish cooking slowly. This method results in a texture quite different from that of foods cooked at a constant simmer or higher heat. It takes longer, but the results are worth the extra effort and care.

This is a good technique to use when you are preparing many dishes on a small hob. Once the food begins to steep, the pot can be removed from the hob. The result is a delicately textured chicken, succulent, moist, and full of flavor, which marries nicely with a number of different regional sauces.

129

1.5–1.75kg/3¹/₂-4lb cornfed chicken
1 tbsp salt
6 slices fresh ginger
6 whole spring onions [US scallions]
freshly ground black pepper, to taste

Rub the chicken evenly with the salt. Put the chicken in a pot large enough to hold it, cover with water, and bring to a boil. Add the ginger and spring onions. Reduce the heat and simmer for 20 minutes, skimming all the while. Then cover tightly, remove from the heat, and leave for 1 hour. Serve the chicken with the sauce of your choice.

To make Soy Sauce Chicken:

My friends are often surprised at their first taste of Soy Sauce Chicken. Instead of the saltiness they expect, given the name of the dish, they taste tender, succulent chicken bathed in a rich and subtle sauce. The technique of steeping used here ensures that the chicken is moist and tender, and allows the rich flavors of the sauce to permeate the meat gently. The chicken may be served hot but I think it is best cooled and served at room temperature, or refrigerated and served cold. It also makes a delicious picnic dish. The steeping liquid may be used as a sauce, and the rest may be frozen and re-used.

1.5–1.75kg/3¹/₂-4lb cornfed chicken

———————— STEEPING LIQUID ————————
900ml/1¹/₂ pints/3³/₄ cups Chicken Stock (page 128)
900ml/1¹/₂ pints//3³/₄ cups dark soy sauce
450ml/15fl oz/1⁵/₈ cups light soy sauce
300ml/10fl oz/1¹/₄ cups Shaoxing rice wine or
dry sherry
175g/6oz/1 cup rock sugar or ordinary sugar
5 whole star anise
5 pieces cinnamon bark or cinnamon sticks
3 tbsp cumin seeds

Combine all the ingredients in a very large pot and bring to a simmer. Add the chicken and simmer and steep as in the Master recipe.

To make Drunken Chicken:

This popular dish from Eastern China makes the best use of the rich yellow rice wine from the region. It is best to leave the chicken in the liquid for at least 2 days for good results. Because it can be prepared at least 2 days ahead, it makes an ideal dish for a party or a large gathering or special occasion.

1.5–1.75kg/3¹/₂-4lb cornfed chicken

———————— RICE WINE MIXTURE ————————
900ml/1¹/₂ pints/3³/₄ cups Chicken Stock (page 128)
1.35 litres/3 pints/6¹/₂ cups Shaoxing rice wine or
dry sherry
225g/8oz/1 cup rock sugar or ordinary sugar
3 tbsp light soy sauce
1 tbsp salt

Combine all the ingredients for the rice wine mixture in a large pot and bring to a simmer. Add the chicken and simmer as in the master recipe. Steep for 2 days. Remove the chicken and arrange it on a serving platter. Pour some of the wine mixture over the chicken to moisten it. The remaining wine can be kept in the refrigerator and used for cooking other dishes that call for rice wine.

Dipping Sauces for Steeped Chicken:

———————— JIANGXI NORTHERN-STYLE SAUCE ————————
2 tbsp finely chopped garlic
2 large fresh red chillies, thinly sliced with or
without seeds
6 tbsp finely chopped spring onions [US scallions]
2 tbsp finely chopped fresh coriander [US cilantro]
120ml/4fl oz dark soy sauce
1 tbsp chilli bean paste
1 tbsp Shaoxing rice wine or dry sherry
1 tbsp white rice vinegar
2 tsp sugar
1 tbsp groundnut oil [US peanut oil] or
vegetable oil
2 tsp sesame oil

Place all the ingredients except the oils in a stainless steel bowl and mix well. Heat a wok, then add the two oils. When very hot and smoking, pour the oil into the sauce ingredients and mix well. The sauce is now ready to serve.

— NORTHERN-STYLE GARLIC-VINEGAR SAUCE —
1 tbsp finely chopped garlic, 2 tbsp Chinese white rice vinegar, 2 tbsp light soy sauce, 2¹/₂ tbsp finely chopped spring onions [US scallions], white part only

Mix all the ingredients together.

—— CANTONESE-STYLE DIPPING SAUCE ——
4 tbsp finely chopped spring onions [US scallions], white part only, 1 tbsp finely chopped fresh ginger, 2 tsp salt, 3 tbsp groundnut oil [US peanut oil]

Combine the spring onions, ginger and salt in a small heatproof bowl. Heat the oil until it is smoking and pour it over the spring onion mixture. Allow to cool before serving.

—— OTHER TIPS ——
- Save the steeping liquid and use it to cook rice.
- Both the Soy Sauce steeping liquid and the Rice Wine mixture can be frozen and re-used.
- Steeped Chicken can be used for chicken salad.

STEAMED CHICKEN WITH SAUSAGE AND HAM

—— SHOPPING LIST ——
450g/1lb boneless, skinless chicken breasts, prosciutto (Parma ham), Chinese (wind-dried) sausages, spring onions [US scallions]

—— STAPLES ——
Shaoxing rice wine or dry sherry, light and dark soy sauces, sesame oil, sugar

—— PREPARATION TIME ——
10 minutes

—— COOKING TIME ——
8 minutes
SERVES 4

Steaming is the preferred Chinese technique for preparing chicken. The process preserves the delicate texture and subtle flavor of the food, a particularly important consideration in the preparation of both fish and chicken. This is a simpler version of my mother's recipe which calls for a whole chicken; here I use only chicken breasts, but the spirit and taste are the same. This is a quick, healthy way to prepare chicken.

Serve it with a fried rice dish and a stir-fried vegetable.

450g/1lb boneless, skinless chicken breasts
50g/2oz prosciutto (Parma ham)
50g/2oz Chinese (wind-dried) sausages

—— COATING MIXTURE ——
2 tbsp Shaoxing rice wine or dry sherry
1¹/₂ tbsp light soy sauce
2 tsp sesame oil
1 tsp dark soy sauce
1 tsp sugar
¹/₂ tsp salt
¹/₄ tsp freshly ground black pepper

—— GARNISH ——
chopped spring onions [US scallions]

Make slashes 4cm/1¹/₂in long in each chicken breast, without cutting all the way through. Cut the ham into slices and diagonally slice the sausage. Insert a piece of ham and a slice of sausage into the slashes in the chicken. Arrange the chicken on a heatproof plate. Pour the ingredients for the coating mixture over the chicken.

Set up a steamer or put a rack into a wok or deep pan and add about 5cm/2in of hot water. Bring the water to a simmer. Put the plate with the chicken into the steamer or onto the rack. Cover tightly and gently steam over medium heat for 8 minutes or until the chicken is cooked. Replenish the water in the steamer from time to time as needed.

Remove from the steamer, garnish, and serve at once.

PORTUGUESE CHICKEN
CHICKEN WITH CREAMY CURRY SAUCE

──────── SHOPPING LIST ────────

450g/1lb boneless, skinless chicken thighs, fresh ginger, garlic, Madras curry paste, canned coconut milk, carrots, potatoes

──────── STAPLES ────────

light and dark soy sauces, Shaoxing rice wine or dry sherry, sesame oil, cornflour [US cornstarch], groundnut oil [US peanut oil], Chicken Stock

──────── PREPARATION TIME ────────
1 hour

──────── COOKING TIME ────────
25 minutes
SERVES 4

This a popular dish in both Macao and Hong Kong. Its origins are clearly an amalgam of Southeast Asian styles and Portuguese predilections. It is a hearty as well as delicious dish that is easy to make. Moreover, it can be made in advance and reheats well. The coconut milk adds a rich and sweet flavor. This dish goes well with plain rice or makes a very satisfying one-dish meal.

450g/1lb boneless, skinless chicken thighs, cut into 2.5cm/1in pieces

──────── MARINADE ────────
1¹/₂ tbsp light soy sauce
2 tsp dark soy sauce
1¹/₂ tbsp Shaoxing rice wine or dry sherry
2 tsp salt
2 tsp sesame oil
2 tsp cornflour [US cornstarch]

──────── SAUCE ────────
1¹/₂ tbsp groundnut oil [US peanut oil] or vegetable oil
1 tbsp finely chopped fresh ginger

2 tsp finely chopped garlic
1 tbsp light soy sauce
1 tbsp dark soy sauce
1 tbsp Shaoxing rice wine or dry sherry
3 tbsp Madras curry paste
1 tbsp sugar
1 tsp salt
freshly ground black pepper, to taste
400ml/14fl oz/1³/₄ cups canned coconut milk
200ml/7fl oz/⁷/₈ cup Chicken Stock (page 128)
225g/8oz carrots, peeled and cut into 5cm/2in pieces
225g/8oz potatoes, peeled and cut into 5cm/2in pieces

──────── GARNISH ────────
chopped spring onions [US scallions]

Combine the chicken with the marinade ingredients in a glass bowl and mix well. Let it marinate for 1 hour. Drain well and reserve the marinade.

Heat a wok over high heat until it is hot, then add the oil. When the oil is hot and slightly smoking, add the ginger and garlic and stir-fry for 20 seconds. Then add the chicken and stir-fry for 3 minutes or until it is lightly browned. Transfer the contents of the wok to a large pot. Add the rest of the sauce ingredients and the reserved marinade and bring to a boil. Lower the heat and simmer for 20 minutes.

Garnish with spring onions and serve at once.

GENERAL TANG'S CHICKEN

──────── SHOPPING LIST ────────
450g/1lb boneless, skinless chicken thighs, garlic

──────── STAPLES ────────
light soy sauce, Shaoxing rice wine or dry sherry, sesame oil, cornflour [US cornstarch], plain flour [US all-purpose flour], baking powder, groundnut oil [US peanut oil], dried red chillies, white rice vinegar, Chicken Stock

PREPARATION TIME
25 minutes

COOKING TIME
20 minutes

SERVES 4

This dish is said to have been created for a certain General Tang who, besides being noted for his military skills, was also famous as a gourmand. Given the zestful nature of this recipe, I am almost inclined to believe that its name was invented by a modern marketing expert. Nevertheless, the influences of Hunan, a province in southern China well known for its fiery cuisine, are obvious in the hot and spicy flavors of this dish. It certainly has 'tang'. The chicken is coated with a light, airy batter and deep-fried to ensure a crispy texture. Then it is tossed with a clear, chilli-laden, piquant sauce with mounds of sliced garlic.

The sauce is at once spicy and sweet, which is typical of Hunan sauces and cooking. The dish goes well with plain rice and a vegetable.

450g/1lb boneless, skinless chicken thighs, cut into 2.5cm/1in pieces

MARINADE
1 tsp salt
1/2 tsp black pepper
1 tbsp light soy sauce
2 tsp Shaoxing rice wine or dry sherry
1 tsp sesame oil
2 tsp cornflour [US cornstarch]

BATTER
2 tbsp cornflour [US cornstarch]
50g/2oz/1/2 cup plain flour [US all-purpose flour]
1 tsp baking powder
150ml/5fl oz/5/8 cup water
1/2 tsp salt
1 tsp groundnut oil [US peanut oil] or vegetable oil
1 tsp sesame oil

SAUCE
1 1/2 tbsp groundnut oil [US peanut oil] or vegetable oil
5 dried red chillies, halved, unseeded
5 garlic cloves, finely sliced
1 tsp salt
3 tbsp sugar
300ml/10fl oz/1 1/4 cups Chicken Stock (page 128) or water
2 tsp white rice vinegar
1 tsp cornflour [US cornstarch] blended with 1 tsp water

FOR DEEP-FRYING
1.2 litres/2 pints/5 cups groundnut oil [US peanut oil] or vegetable oil

Combine the chicken with the marinade ingredients in a bowl and let it sit for 20 minutes.

Mix the batter ingredients together in a blender until smooth with *no* lumps. Put it through a sieve or strainer if necessary. Combine the batter with the chicken.

For the sauce, heat a saucepan over medium heat until it is hot, then add the oil. When the oil is hot and slightly smoking, add the chillies and garlic and stir for 30 seconds or until the garlic begins to brown. Then add the salt, sugar, stock, and rice vinegar and bring the mixture to a boil. Thicken this with the cornflour mixture. Turn the heat to low and simmer, uncovered, for 10 minutes.

Heat a wok over high heat until it is hot, then add the oil for deep-frying. When the oil is hot and slightly smoking, remove the chicken from the batter with tongs and deep-fry, in two or three batches, until golden and crispy. Drain well on paper towels and set on a warm platter. Immediately pour the sauce over the chicken and serve at once.

SWEET AND SOUR CHICKEN

SHOPPING LIST

450g/1lb boneless, skinless chicken breasts, 225g/ 8oz red or green sweet peppers, egg, spring onions [US scallions], canned lychees, tomato paste or ketchup, garlic

STAPLES

cornflour [US cornstarch], groundnut oil [US peanut oil], Chicken Stock, light and dark soy sauces, sesame oil, Chinese white rice vinegar, sugar

PREPARATION TIME

25 minutes

COOKING TIME

12 minutes

SERVES 2–4

This dish is often featured in the West where, in mediocre Chinese restaurants, it invariably appears as a sweet, gluey, reddish concoction. Properly prepared, however, it is the perfect balance of sweet and sour paired with moist, succulent chicken meat. This simple dish reflects the influence of southern and eastern Chinese cuisine.

450g/1lb boneless, skinless chicken breasts, cut into 2.5cm/1in cubes
1 egg white
^{1}/2 tsp salt
2 tsp cornflour [US cornstarch]
300ml/10fl oz/1^1/4 cups groundnut oil [US peanut oil] or water
225g/8oz red or green peppers, seeded and cut into 2.5cm/1in cubes
3 garlic cloves, finely sliced
5 spring onions [US scallions], cut into 5cm/2in sections
175g/6oz/1 cup drained canned lychees or fresh orange segments

SAUCE

150ml/5fl oz/^{5}/8 cup Chicken Stock (page 128)
1 tbsp light soy sauce
2 tsp dark soy sauce
2 tsp sesame oil
^{1}/2 tsp salt
^{1}/2 tsp freshly ground white pepper
2 tbsp Chinese white rice vinegar or cider vinegar
1^1/2 tbsp sugar
2 tbsp tomato paste or ketchup
2 tsp cornflour [US cornstarch] blended with 1 tbsp water

Combine the cubes of chicken with the egg white, salt, and cornflour in a small bowl. Refrigerate for about 20 minutes.

Heat a wok or frying pan over high heat until it is hot, then add all but 1 tbsp of the oil. When the oil is very hot, remove the wok from the heat and immediately add the chicken pieces, stirring vigorously to keep them from sticking. When the chicken pieces turn white, about 2 minutes, quickly drain them in a stainless steel colander set in a bowl. Discard the oil.

If you choose to use water instead of oil, bring it to a boil in a saucepan. Remove the saucepan from the heat and immediately add the chicken pieces, stirring vigorously to keep them from sticking. When the chicken pieces turn white, about 2 minutes, quickly drain the chicken in a stainless steel colander set in a bowl. Discard the water.

Wipe the wok or pan clean and reheat until it is very hot. Add the reserved 1 tbsp of oil. When it is very hot, add the peppers, garlic, spring onions, and lychees and stir-fry them for 2 minutes. Then add all the sauce ingredients except the cornflour mixture and cook for 2 minutes. Add the cornflour mixture and cook for 1 minute more. Add the drained chicken to the wok and stir-fry for another 2 minutes, coating the chicken thoroughly with the sauce. Serve at once.

SALT ROASTED CHICKEN

---------- SHOPPING LIST ----------

1.5–1.75kg/3¹/₂-4lb cornfed chicken, 2.5–3kg/5–6lb rock salt, fresh ginger, garlic, spring onions [US scallions], fresh coriander [US cilantro]

---------- STAPLES ----------

groundnut oil [US peanut oil], whole bean sauce, light soy sauce, Shaoxing rice wine or dry sherry, sugar, star anise, Sichuan peppercorns, Chicken Stock

---------- PREPARATION TIME ----------

2 hours (drying time) + 15 minutes

---------- COOKING TIME ----------

1¹/₂ hours

SERVES 4

This is a popular southern Chinese technique for cooking chicken. The result is not salty, but succulent and flavorful. The salt acts to seal in the juices of the chicken as it slowly cooks.

Filling the cavity with a piquant sauce makes the chicken even tastier. It makes a delicious treat whether served hot or cold.

1.5–1.75kg/3¹/₂-4lb cornfed chicken
2.5–3kg/5–6 lb rock salt

---------- SAUCE ----------

1 tbsp groundnut oil [US peanut oil]
3 slices fresh ginger
3 garlic cloves, lightly crushed
5 spring onions [US scallions], cut into 7.5cm/3in segments
1 tbsp whole bean sauce
2 tbsp light soy sauce
1¹/₂ tbsp Shaoxing rice wine or dry sherry
1 tbsp sugar
2 star anise
2 tsp whole Sichuan peppercorns, roasted (page 85)
150ml/5fl oz/ ⁵/₈ cup Chicken Stock (page 128)
10 sprigs whole fresh coriander [US cilantro]

Wipe the chicken dry inside and out with paper towels and let it sit, loosely wrapped, in the refrigerator for at least 2 hours.

For the sauce, heat a wok or large frying pan over high heat until it is hot. Add the oil and, when it is very hot and slightly smoking, add the ginger, garlic, and spring onions. Stir-fry for 2 minutes. Add the rest of the sauce ingredients. Turn down the heat and simmer for 5 minutes. Pour the sauce into a bowl and allow it to cool completely.

Preheat the oven to 180°C/350°F/gas mark 4. Put half of the salt in a large flameproof casserole (big enough to hold the chicken) and the other half in another pot. Heat both pots of salt for at least 30 minutes.

Put the cold sauce into the body cavity of the chicken. Secure it with a bamboo skewer tied with kitchen string. Lay the chicken in the casserole – and pour the hot salt from the second pot onto the chicken. The salt should cover the chicken completely. Cover the casserole tightly and transfer to the oven. Cook for 1¹/₂ hours.

When the chicken is cooked, carefully remove the hot salt by scraping it off. Let the chicken cool slightly. Drain the sauce from the chicken. Carve the bird and serve it with the sauce on the side.

SOY SAUCE CHICKEN WINGS

---------- SHOPPING LIST ----------

1.35–1.5kg/3–3¹/₂lb chicken wings, fresh ginger, spring onions [US scallions], fresh coriander [US cilantro]

---------- STAPLES ----------

Chicken Stock, light and dark soy sauces, Shaoxing rice wine or dry sherry, rock or ordinary sugar, star anise, cinnamon bark or stick, cumin seeds

15 minutes

——————— COOKING TIME ———————
45 minutes
SERVES 4

When used properly and in the right amount, soy sauce results in dishes that are not salty but rather are rich in flavor and aroma. Here the tender, succulent chicken wings are bathed in a rich and subtle sauce. Gentle simmering ensures the chicken wings remain moist and tender, and allows the rich flavors of the sauce to permeate the meat. The chicken wings may be served hot, but I think they are best cooled and then served at room temperature, or refrigerated and served cold. The wings also make a delicious picnic dish or a wonderful cold first course. The steeping liquid may be used as a sauce, and the rest may be frozen and re-used for making more Soy Sauce Chicken Wings.

1.35–1.5kg/3–3¹/₂lb chicken wings

——————— SAUCE ———————
2.25 litres/4 pints/10 cups Chicken Stock (page 128) or water
600ml/1 pint/2¹/₂ cups dark soy sauce
150ml/5fl oz/⁵/₈ cup light soy sauce
300ml/10fl oz/1¹/₄ cups Shaoxing rice wine or dry sherry, or 150ml/5fl oz/⁵/₈ cup dry sherry mixed with 150ml/5fl oz/⁵/₈ cup Chicken Stock (page 128)
175g/6oz/1 cup rock sugar or ordinary sugar
6 slices fresh ginger
6 spring onions [US scallions]
2 tbsp salt
1 tsp freshly ground black pepper
5 star anise
5 cinnamon bark or cinnamon sticks
3 tbsp cumin seeds

——————— GARNISH ———————
fresh coriander sprigs [US cilantro]

First make the sauce. Combine all the sauce ingredients in a very large pot and bring to a simmer. Add the chicken wings. If the sauce does not cover the chicken, add a little more stock. Bring it back to a simmer and simmer for about 15 minutes, covered. Uncover and skim from time to time. Cover the pot tightly and continue to simmer the wings gently for 30 minutes more.

After this time remove the chicken wings from the sauce with a slotted spoon and put them on a plate to cool. They can now be cut up into pieces and served or put into the refrigerator.

Remove any surface fat from the sauce. Spoon some of the sauce over the chicken wings. Garnish with fresh coriander sprigs before serving.

FRAGRANT CRISPY CHICKEN

——————— SHOPPING LIST ———————
700g/1¹/₂lb boneless, skinless chicken thighs, spring onions [US scallions], fresh ginger, honey

——————— STAPLES ———————
Shaoxing rice wine or dry sherry, light and dark soy sauces, five spice powder, Sichuan peppercorns, groundnut oil [US peanut oil], sesame oil, sugar

——————— PREPARATION TIME ———————
50 minutes

——————— COOKING TIME ———————
15 minutes
SERVES 4

This eastern Chinese flavored chicken is one of my favorites because it combines succulent meat with a simple but extremely tasty marinade.

The method is to deep-fry the chicken *twice*, once at a low temperature and then at a much higher temperature. The result is a crispy textured chicken that is very moist within.

700g/1¹/₂lb boneless, skinless chicken thighs

MARINADE

3 tbsp Shaoxing rice wine or dry sherry, 1 tbsp light soy sauce, 2 tsp dark soy sauce, 3 spring onions [US scallions], 2 slices fresh ginger, 1 tbsp honey, 1/2 tsp freshly ground black pepper, 1 tsp five spice powder, 1 tsp roasted and ground Sichuan peppercorns (page 85), 1 tsp salt

FOR FRYING

600ml/1 pint/2 1/2 cups groundnut oil [US peanut oil]

SAUCE

2 tbsp finely chopped spring onions [US scallions]
2 tsp sesame oil
2 tsp sugar

Place each chicken thigh between two pieces of cling film [US plastic wrap] and pound them lightly until they are evenly flat. Put them in a large mixing bowl.

Combine the rice wine, soy sauces, spring onions, and ginger in a blender and purée. Strain the liquid into the bowl with the chicken. Add the rest of the marinade ingredients and mix well. Let the chicken marinate for 45 minutes. Remove the chicken from the bowl and reserve the marinade. Heat a wok or large frying pan over high heat (200°C/400°F) until it is hot. Add the oil and, when it is very hot and slightly smoking, add the chicken. Fry for 5 minutes. Remove and drain the chicken. Reheat the oil in the wok until it is very hot (200°C/400°F). Fry the chicken again until it is crispy and golden brown. Remove the chicken and drain well on paper towels.

Drain off all the oil and discard it. Cut the chicken into slices and arrange on a platter.

Reheat the wok over medium heat. Add the reserved marinade and the sauce ingredients. Bring to a boil, and pour this over the chicken. Serve at once.

STUFFED CHICKEN SLICES

SHOPPING LIST

450g/1lb boneless, skinless chicken breasts, 110g/4oz raw prawns [US shrimp], fresh or canned water chestnuts, egg, spring onions [US scallions], Chinese dried black mushrooms

STAPLES

sesame oil, Shaoxing rice wine or dry sherry, cornflour [US cornstarch], groundnut oil [US peanut oil]

PREPARATION TIME

30 minutes

COOKING TIME

20 minutes

SERVES 4

Here is a Chinese recipe that gives an added dimension to chicken. The process seems complex but it is actually very easy to prepare. The dish can serve as a tasty first course or as an unusual main course.

450g/1lb boneless, skinless chicken breasts

STUFFING

15g/1/2oz Chinese dried black mushrooms (page 26)
110g/4oz fresh water chestnuts or 175g/6oz canned water chestnuts (page 92)
110g/4oz raw prawns [US shrimp], peeled and deveined
1 egg white
2 tsp salt
1/2 tsp freshly ground black pepper
2 tsp sesame oil
2 tsp Shaoxing rice wine or dry sherry
2 tsp cornflour [US cornstarch] + extra for dusting
3 tbsp finely chopped spring onions [US scallions]

FOR FRYING

450ml/15fl oz/1 5/8 cups groundnut oil [US peanut oil]

FOR DIPPING

Seasoned Salt & Pepper (page 85)

Hold each chicken breast flat on a chopping board. With a sharp cleaver or knife, carefully split the breast in half horizontally without cutting all the way through. Set aside.

Coarsely chop the prawns. Put the water chestnuts, prawns, and mushrooms into a bowl with the rest of the filling ingredients, and mix them together very well.

Dust the inside of each split chicken breast lightly with some cornflour. Spoon a small layer of stuffing between the two halves and reshape the breast to enclose the filling. Dust the outside of the chicken breasts with cornflour, shaking off any excess.

Heat a wok or large frying pan over high heat until it is hot. Add the oil and, when it is very hot and slightly smoking, turn the heat down to moderate. Add the chicken and fry gently for 5 minutes or until cooked. Drain the chicken on paper towels. When it is cool enough to handle, gently slice crosswise and serve at once with the Seasoned Salt and Pepper.

BEGGAR'S CHICKEN

──────── SHOPPING LIST ────────

1.35–1.5kg/3–3¹/₂lb cornfed chicken, boneless pork, Chinese dried black mushrooms, fresh water chestnuts, cloud ears or tree ears, spring onions [US scallions], fresh ginger, Sichuan preserved vegetable

──────── STAPLES ────────

sesame oil, light soy sauce, Shaoxing rice wine or dry sherry, groundnut oil [US peanut oil], sugar

──────── PREPARATION TIME ────────

40 minutes

──────── COOKING TIME ────────

1 hour 5 minutes

SERVES 4

Of several legends concerning the origin of this recipe, the most common is that a beggar, having stolen a chicken and believing he had eluded his pursuers, started to cook the chicken over a campfire by a river. When the chicken was half cooked, he suddenly heard his pursuers in the distance. In a panic, he buried the chicken in the mud by the riverbank and ran off. The pursuers arrived, but not finding him or the chicken, they soon departed. The beggar returned and retrieved the mud-encased chicken, finished cooking it, and cracked it open to discover an incredibly succulent meal. How else but by accident could one hit upon so unorthodox a cooking technique?

The original recipe is quite complicated and requires a boned chicken with stuffing, wrapped in lotus leaves and then encased in wet clay before it is baked – a project best left to professional restaurants. Here is a simplified version that is much easier to make while still producing a spectacular centerpiece for any meal.

1.35–1.5kg/3–3¹/₂lb cornfed chicken

──────── PORK MIXTURE ────────

110g/4oz minced [US ground] pork
4 tsp light soy sauce
2 tsp + 1 tbsp Shaoxing rice wine or dry sherry
1 tsp sesame oil
¹/₂ tsp salt
¹/₂ tsp freshly ground white pepper
50g/2oz Chinese dried black mushrooms (page 26)
25g/1oz cloud ears or tree ears (page 34)
1¹/₂ tbsp groundnut oil [US peanut oil]
3 tbsp finely chopped spring onions [US scallions]
1 tbsp finely chopped fresh ginger
50g/2oz peeled or canned fresh water chestnuts, coarsely chopped (page 92)
50g/2oz/¹/₂ cup Sichuan preserved vegetable, rinsed and coarsely chopped
2 tsp sugar

Thoroughly dry the chicken inside and out with paper towels.

Combine the pork in a small bowl with 2 tsp of the soy sauce, 2 tsp Shaoxing rice wine or dry sherry, the sesame oil, salt, and pepper.

Remove and discard the mushroom stems and coarsely chop the caps.

Remove and discard any hard bits from the cloud ears or tree ears and coarsely chop.

Heat a wok or large frying pan over high heat until it is hot. Add the oil and, when it is very hot and slightly smoking, add the spring onions and ginger. Stir-fry for 10 seconds. Then add the pork mixture and continue to stir-fry for 3 minutes. Add the mushrooms, tree ears, water chestnuts, Sichuan vegetable, remaining Shaoxing rice wine or dry sherry and soy sauce, and the sugar. Continue to stir-fry for 5 minutes. Turn into a bowl and allow the mixture to cool completely.

Preheat the oven to 230°C/450°F/gas mark 8.

When the pork mixture is thoroughly cool, put it into the cavity of the chicken and close with a skewer. Put the chicken in a baking dish.

Roast the chicken for 15 minutes or until it is brown. Then turn the temperature down to 180°C/350°F/gas mark 4 and continue to roast for 50 minutes more. Remove from the oven and let the chicken rest for at least 15 minutes before carving and serving.

BEAN SAUCE CHICKEN

─────── SHOPPING LIST ───────

450g/1lb skinless, boneless chicken breasts, 225g/8oz red sweet pepper, fresh or canned water chestnuts, shelled raw peanuts, egg

─────── STAPLES ───────

cornflour [US cornstarch], groundnut oil [US peanut oil], light soy sauce, whole bean sauce, hoisin sauce, Shaoxing rice wine or dry sherry, sesame oil

─────── PREPARATION TIME ───────

15 minutes

─────── COOKING TIME ───────

10 minutes

SERVES 4

This straightforward chicken dish, redolent of rich bean sauce flavor and enlivened by the textural crunch of nuts, is easy to make. You may substitute your own favorite ingredients. Simply follow the same procedure for the same delicious result.

450g/1lb skinless, boneless chicken breasts
1 egg white
1 tsp salt
2 tsp cornflour [US cornstarch]
175g/6oz peeled fresh or canned water chestnuts (page 92)
225g/8oz red sweet pepper, seeded
350ml/12fl oz/1¹/₂ cups groundnut oil [US peanut oil] or water
110g/4oz/¹/₄ cup shelled raw peanuts
1 tbsp light soy sauce
2 tsp Shaoxing rice wine or dry sherry
1¹/₄ tbsp whole bean sauce
2 tbsp hoisin sauce
2 tsp sesame oil

Cut the chicken into 1cm/¹/₂in cubes. Combine with the egg white, salt and cornflour in a bowl. Mix well and chill in the refrigerator for about 20 minutes.

Meanwhile, cut the water chestnuts and red pepper into rough dice about 1cm/¹/₂in square.

Reserve 1 tbsp groundnut oil. Heat a wok until it is very hot and then add the remaining oil. When the oil is very hot, remove the wok from the heat and immediately add the chicken cubes, stirring vigorously to keep them from sticking. When the chicken pieces turn white, about 2 minutes, quickly drain them in a stainless steel colander.

If you choose to use water instead of oil, bring it to a boil in a saucepan. Remove the saucepan from the heat and immediately add the chicken pieces, stirring vigorously to keep them from sticking. When the chicken pieces turn white, about 2 minutes, quickly drain them in a stainless steel colander.

Heat the wok until it is hot and add the reserved 1 tbsp of oil. When the oil is hot, add the peanuts and stir-fry for 1 minute or until they are lightly browned. Then add the vegetables and stir-fry for 1 minute. Add the soy sauce, rice wine or sherry, bean sauce, and hoisin sauce and continue to stir-fry for 2 minutes. Return the drained chicken to the wok, stir to mix well, and add the sesame oil. Give the mixture a few more stirs and then turn it onto a warm serving platter. Serve at once.

CRISPY AROMATIC CHICKEN

SHOPPING LIST

700g/1¹/₂lb boneless, skinless chicken thighs, garlic, fresh ginger, small onion

STAPLES

light and dark soy sauces, Shaoxing rice wine or dry sherry, five spice powder, cornflour [US cornstarch], groundnut oil [US peanut oil]

PREPARATION TIME

20 minutes + overnight marinating time in the refrigerator

COOKING TIME

30 minutes

SERVES 4

I first enjoyed this deliciously satisfying dish at a family dinner in Beijing a few years ago. Invited into the kitchen to observe the process, I was impressed by how easy it is to make. The essential point is to marinate the chicken for at least a few hours, and preferably overnight. This means that the chicken can be prepared well in advance of the meal. The marinade itself is a superb combination of classical Chinese flavorings. Serve the chicken with stir-fried vegetables and plain rice.

700g/1¹/₂lb boneless, skinless chicken thighs
2 tsp salt

MARINADE

2 tbsp finely chopped garlic
2 tbsp finely chopped fresh ginger
1¹/₂ tbsp light soy sauce
1¹/₂ tbsp dark soy sauce
1 small onion, finely chopped
2 tbsp Shaoxing rice wine or dry sherry
2 tsp five spice powder

FOR FRYING

cornflour [US cornstarch], for dusting
450ml/15 fl oz/1⁵/₈ cups groundnut oil [US peanut oil]

Rub the chicken thighs evenly with the salt and allow to sit in the refrigerator for 20 minutes. Mix the marinade ingredients and rub evenly on the chicken. Wrap in cling film [US plastic wrap] and marinate overnight in the refrigerator.

The next day, set up a steamer or put a rack into a wok or deep pan and add 5cm/2in of water. Bring the water to the boil over a high heat. Put the chicken onto a heatproof plate and then carefully lower it into the steamer or onto the rack. Turn the heat to low and cover the wok or pan tightly. Steam gently for 20 minutes.

Remove the cooked chicken and let it cool in a drafty room on a baking tray. The chicken should be slightly dried.

Dust the chicken pieces with cornflour. Heat a wok or deep frying pan until it is very hot, then add the oil. When the oil is hot and slightly smoking, deep-fry the chicken pieces in two or three batches until golden and crisp. Remove and drain the chicken on paper towels. When cool enough to handle, quickly cut the chicken into slices and arrange on a warm platter. Serve at once.

CANTONESE-STYLE BRAISED CHICKEN

——————— SHOPPING LIST ———————
1.35–1.5kg/3–3¹/₂lb cornfed chicken, small onion, garlic, fresh ginger, spring onions [US scallions]

——————— STAPLES ———————
lily buds, wood ears or cloud ears, Chinese dried black mushrooms, groundnut oil [US peanut oil], Shaoxing rice wine or dry sherry, oyster sauce, light and dark soy sauces, sugar, Chicken Stock, cornflour [US cornstarch]

——————— PREPARATION TIME ———————
30 minutes

——————— COOKING TIME ———————
45 minutes–1 hour
SERVES 4

My mother frequently served this easy-to-make dish because it is delicious when reheated. That meant she could prepare it a day in advance. Slow braising kept the chicken moist and the earthy flavors complement each other very well. Serve it with rice and another vegetable dish for a satisfying home-style meal.

1.35–1.5kg/3–3¹/₂lb cornfed chicken
1 tbsp salt
25g/1oz lily buds (page 51)
25g/1oz wood ears or cloud ears (page 34)
50g/2oz Chinese dried black mushrooms (page 26)
3 tbsp groundnut oil [US peanut oil]
1 small onion, finely chopped
3 garlic cloves, crushed

3 slices fresh ginger
6 spring onions, cut into 5cm/2in pieces
3 tbsp Shaoxing rice wine or dry sherry
3 tbsp light soy sauce
1¹/₂ tbsp dark soy sauce
2 tsp sugar
3 tbsp oyster sauce
240ml/8fl oz/1 cup Chicken Stock (page 128)
2 tsp cornflour [US cornstarch] blended with 1 tbsp water

Evenly rub salt inside and all over the outside of the chicken. Set aside.

Remove and discard the hard stem on each end of the lily buds and shred them in halves.

Remove any trace of sand from the wood ears or cloud ears. Remove any hard stems and, if you are using wood ears, finely shred them in thin strips. Leave cloud ears whole.

Remove and discard dried mushroom stems and finely shred the caps into thin strips.

Pat the chicken dry with paper towels. Heat a wok or large frying pan over high heat until it is hot. Add the oil and, when it is very hot and slightly smoking, add the onion, garlic, ginger and spring onions. Stir-fry for 1 minute. Then add the chicken, turn the heat down to medium, and slowly brown the chicken on all sides for 8 minutes. Remove the chicken. Add the lily buds, wood ears or cloud ears, and mushrooms and stir-fry for 3 minutes. Add the Shaoxing rice wine or dry sherry, soy sauces, sugar, oyster sauce, and chicken stock. Bring to a simmer.

Transfer half of the mixture from the wok to a large casserole. Place the chicken, breast side down, on top and add the remaining mixture from the wok. Bring to a boil, then turn the heat down to low, cover, and slowly braise for about 45 minutes to 1 hour.

When the chicken is done, remove it to a warm platter. When it is cool enough to handle, carve it into serving portions. Thicken the juices with the cornflour mixture, cook for 1 minute and pour over the chicken. Serve at once.

SMOKED CHICKEN

SHOPPING LIST
1.5–1.75kg/3¹/₂-4lb cornfed chicken, spring onions [US scallions], ginger, black tea leaves, long-grain white rice, brown sugar

STAPLES
Sichuan peppercorns, five spice powder, star anise, cinnamon bark or sticks

PREPARATION TIME
10 minutes + overnight marinating

COOKING TIME
1 hour steaming + 25 minutes smoking
SERVES 4

Among the many methods the Chinese have for preserving food as well as making it appetizing, perhaps the most appealing is smoking. We do not often practice this technique in our modern homes, but it is easier to do than you may think. The process is long, but the cooking itself is quite quick. The chicken is first marinated, then gently steamed, and finally lightly smoked. The result is a surprisingly succulent chicken with the savoriness one expects with smoked food. This dish can be served cold or warm. It makes a wonderful picnic item, as well as an unusual first course for any meal.

1.5–1.75kg/3¹/₂-4lb cornfed chicken
2 tbsp salt
2 tbsp roasted and ground Sichuan peppercorns (page 85)
2 tsp five spice powder
1 tsp freshly ground white pepper
6 slices fresh ginger
6 spring onions [US scallions]

SMOKING INGREDIENTS
50g/2oz/¹/₄ cup long-grain white rice
50g/2oz/¹/₄ cup brown sugar
50g/2oz/¹/₄ cup black tea leaves
3 star anise, broken into sections
2 cinnamon bark or cinnamon sticks, broken into sections

Rub the chicken evenly inside and out with the salt, Sichuan peppercorns, five spice powder, and white pepper. Wrap it well in cling film [US plastic wrap] and refrigerate overnight.

The next day, unwrap the chicken and place the spring onions and ginger inside the cavity.

Set up a steamer or put a rack into a wok or deep pan and add 5cm/2in of water. Bring the water to the boil over a high heat. Put the chicken on a heatproof plate and then carefully lower it into the steamer or onto the rack. Turn the heat to low and cover the wok or pan tightly. Steam gently for 1¹/₄ hours or until the chicken is cooked, replenishing the water as necessary. Allow the chicken to cool completely.

Line the inside of a wok with aluminum foil. Place the smoking ingredients on the bottom. Rub a rack with oil and place it over the smoking ingredients. Place the chicken on the rack. Now heat the wok over high heat until the smoking mixture begins to burn. Turn the heat down to moderate, cover, and let it smoke for 15 minutes. Remove from the heat and allow it to sit, covered, for another 10 minutes. Remove the chicken and discard the smoking ingredients with the aluminum foil. Carve or cut up the chicken and serve.

CANTONESE PRESSED DUCK

SHOPPING LIST
1.5–1.75kg/3¹/₂-4lb fresh or frozen duck, eggs

STAPLES

Chicken Stock, dark and light soy sauces, Shaoxing rice wine or dry sherry, rock or ordinary sugar, star anise, cinnamon bark or cinnamon sticks, cornflour [US cornstarch], groundnut oil [US peanut oil]

PREPARATION TIME

20 minutes

COOKING TIME

1 hour braising + 20 minutes steaming + 10 minutes deep-frying

SERVES 4

This Cantonese specialty is said to have originated in northern China and been brought south during the Ming Dynasty when the Manchus invaded China and the Emperor and his court fled south. Traditionally, the duck was boned and then literally flattened before being steamed and cured with various spices and finally deep-fried.

Much of the work here is in the preparation. The duck is braised, then boned, steamed and finally deep-fried. The result is an unusual and delicious duck, unlike any you have ever had. Fortunately, much of the preparation can be done ahead of time. It would make a superb main course for any dinner party as well as for a special family meal.

1.5–1.75kg/3¹/₂-4lb fresh or frozen duck

SAUCE

900ml/1¹/₂ pints/3³/₄ cups Chicken Stock (page 128) or water
900ml/1¹/₂ pints/3³/₄ cups dark soy sauce
350ml/12 fl oz/1¹/₂ cups light soy sauce
350ml/12 fl oz/1¹/₂ cups Shaoxing rice wine or dry sherry .
110g/4oz/¹/₂ cup rock or ordinary sugar
5 star anise
3 cinnamon barks or cinnamon sticks

FOR STEAMING

2 eggs, beaten
cornflour [US cornstarch], for dusting

FOR FRYING

900ml/1¹/₂ pints/3³/₄ cups groundnut oil [US peanut oil]

Cut the duck in half, lengthways. Dry the halves thoroughly with paper towels. Combine all the sauce ingredients together in a large pot and bring to a boil. Add the duck halves and turn the heat down to a simmer. Cover the pot and slowly braise the duck for 1 hour or until it is tender.

Skim off the large amount of surface fat that will be left when the duck is cooked. Remove the duck and allow to cool. Once the sauce has cooled, remove any lingering surface fat. Reserve the sauce.

When the duck is quite cool, carefully remove all the bones, keeping the meat and skin intact. Place the duck halves between two pieces of cling film [US plastic wrap] and press the meat and skin together. Unwrap and brush the duck halves with the beaten egg. Dust with cornflour.

Next, set up a steamer or put a rack into a wok or deep pan and add 5cm/2in of water. Bring the water to the boil over a high heat. Put the duck onto a heatproof plate and then carefully lower it into the steamer or onto the rack. Turn the heat to low and cover the wok or pan tightly. Steam gently for 20 minutes. Allow the duck to cool completely. (The dish can be completed to this stage a day in advance.)

When you are ready to serve the duck, heat a wok or large frying pan over high heat until it is hot. Add the oil and, when it is very hot and slightly smoking, add the duck halves. Deep-fry until they are crispy. Remove and drain well on paper towels. Heat some of the reserved sauce and serve with the duck.

143

MEAT

ORANGE-FLAVORED BEEF

SHOPPING LIST

450g/1lb lean beef fillet or sirloin steak, fresh ginger, garlic, fresh red chillies, Sichuan preserved vegetables

STAPLES

light and dark soy sauces, Shaoxing rice wine or dry sherry, sesame oil, sugar, cornflour [US cornstarch], groundnut oil [US peanut oil], dried citrus peel, Chicken Stock, chilli bean paste, Sichuan peppercorns

PREPARATION TIME

20 minutes

COOKING TIME

15 minutes

SERVES 4

Beef plays but a secondary role in Chinese cuisine. Often relegated to this status because of its tendency to be bland to the palate, beef can, however, be made quite sumptuous when it is enhanced by a distinctively flavored marinade, as in this Kweichow-inspired recipe. I personally prefer and recommend this zesty recipe in which tart citrus peel is stir-fried with the beef fillet or sirloin. This tasty and robust dish makes an elegant dinner when combined with rice, soup, and a vegetable dish.

450g/1lb lean beef fillet or sirloin steak

MARINADE

2 tsp light soy sauce
2 tsp dark soy sauce
1 tbsp Shaoxing rice wine or dry sherry
2 tsp finely chopped fresh ginger
2 tsp sesame oil
2 tsp salt
1 tsp sugar
2 tsp cornflour [US cornstarch]

FOR THE SAUCE

3 tbsp groundnut oil [US peanut oil] or vegetable oil for cooking
2 tbsp finely chopped garlic
2 tbsp finely chopped fresh ginger
1 small onion, coarsely chopped
3 tbsp rinsed and finely chopped Sichuan preserved vegetable
2 large fresh red chillies, seeded and finely shredded
2 tbsp dried citrus peel, soaked and coarsely chopped or fresh orange zest
2 tbsp Chicken Stock (page 128)
1^1/$_2$ tbsp Shaoxing rice wine or dry sherry
1 tbsp chilli bean paste
1 tbsp dark soy sauce
2 tsp roasted ground Sichuan peppercorns (page 85)
2 tsp sugar
2 tsp sesame oil
salt, to taste

GARNISH

chopped spring onions [US scallions]

Cut the beef into slices about 3cm/1^1/$_2$in long and 5mm/^{1}/$_4$in thick. Then stack the slices and finely shred the meat. Put the beef into a bowl. Add the marinade ingredients and mix well.

Heat a wok over high heat until it is hot, then add the oil. When the oil is very hot and begins to smoke, add the beef. Let the meat brown for 1 minute, then carefully stir-fry for another minute. Drain the beef in a colander, leaving 1 tbsp of oil in the wok.

Quickly reheat the wok and the oil. When it is hot, add the garlic and ginger and stir-fry for 20 seconds over medium heat. Then add the onion, preserved vegetable, fresh chillies, and citrus peel and stir-fry for another 20 seconds. Add the stock, rice wine, chilli bean paste, soy sauce, peppercorns, sugar, and sesame oil. Cook over high heat for 30 seconds. Return the meat to the wok, add salt to taste, and give the mixture several stirs to mix well. Turn onto a platter, garnish with spring onions, and serve at once.

BEEF AND TURNIP STEW

──────── SHOPPING LIST ────────

1kg/2¼lb beef brisket, 450g/1lb Chinese white radish, fresh ginger, spring onions [US scallions], garlic

──────── STAPLES ────────

Shaoxing rice wine or dry sherry, groundnut oil [US peanut oil], light and dark soy sauces, hoisin sauce, ground bean sauce, chilli bean paste, rock or ordinary sugar, star anise, Chicken Stock

──────── PREPARATION TIME ────────

25 minutes

──────── COOKING TIME ────────

2 hours

SERVES 4

Most beef in China tends to be quite tough – traditionally cattle are not butchered until they are too old to work; therefore, braising is the best way to cook beef, using a blend of Chinese spices which infuses it with complex flavors. Since it requires a long cooking time, a cheap cut such as brisket (preferably with a bit of fat and tendon) is perfect. Chinese white radish, known as mooli or daikon, is often paired with it. If unavailable, you can substitute carrots or turnips. Plain rice is a perfect accompaniment and the whole is wonderful as an autumn or winter dish. It reheats very well.

1kg/2½lb beef brisket (with some fat and tendon), cut into 4cm/1½in cubes
2 tbsp groundnut oil [US peanut oil] or vegetable oil
2 tbsp finely chopped fresh ginger
4 spring onions [US scallions], cut into 5cm/2in segments
4 garlic cloves, crushed slightly
450g/1lb Chinese white radish, peeled and cut into 5cm/2in segments

──────── BRAISING SAUCE ────────

3 tbsp Shaoxing rice wine or dry sherry
2 tbsp dark soy sauce
1 tbsp light soy sauce
3 tbsp hoisin sauce
2 tbsp ground yellow bean paste
2 tbsp chilli bean sauce
2 tbsp rock sugar or ordinary sugar
3 star anise
½ tsp freshly ground black pepper
salt, to taste
1.2 litres/2 pints/5 cups Chicken Stock (page 128)

──────── GARNISH ────────

chopped spring onions [US scallions]

Bring a large pot of salted water to a boil. Put in the meat and blanch for 10 minutes. Skim the surface constantly to remove all impurities. Drain the meat and discard the water.

Heat a wok until it is hot, then add the oil. When the oil is hot and slightly smoking, add the ginger, spring onions, and garlic and stir-fry for 1 minute. Then add the beef and continue to stir-fry for 10 minutes or until the meat is brown. Drain off any excess fat or oil.

Transfer the meat to a large flameproof casserole or pot. Add all the braising sauce ingredients and bring to the boil. Turn down the heat, cover the pot, and simmer for 1½ hours or until the meat is tender. Add the radish and continue to cook for 30 minutes more.

Skim off any surface fat, garnish with spring onions and serve immediately. Or, cool and reheat later.

SPICY STIR-FRIED HUNAN BEEF

──────── SHOPPING LIST ────────

450g/1lb lean beef fillet or sirloin steak, large fresh red chillies, large fresh green chillies, fresh ginger, garlic

— STAPLES —
*Chicken Stock, light soy sauce, Shaoxing rice wine,
sesame oil or dry sherry cornflour [US cornstarch],
groundnut oil [US peanut oil], black beans, sugar*

— PREPARATION TIME —
5 minutes

— COOKING TIME —
5 minutes
SERVES 4

As is usual when beef is served in Chinese cuisine, this dish utilizes strong, pungent, and aromatic ingredients to enhance the color and taste of the meat. This hearty dish is a wonderful treat at the height of the chilli season in China, when the chillies are in full bloom, abundant, and inexpensive. Before they are preserved by pickling, they are often simply stir-fried as in this recipe. This is delightful just with plain rice and an easy soup.

*450g/1lb lean beef fillet or sirloin steak
3 tbsp groundnut oil [US peanut oil] or vegetable oil
2 tbsp coarsely chopped black beans
2 tbsp finely chopped garlic
1 tbsp finely chopped fresh ginger
110g/4oz large, fresh red chillies, seeded and finely
shredded
110g/4oz large, fresh green chillies, seeded and
finely shredded
3 tbsp Chicken Stock (page 128)
1¹/₂ tbsp Shaoxing rice wine or dry sherry
1 tbsp light soy sauce
2 tsp sugar
2 tsp sesame oil*

— MARINADE —
*2 tsp light soy sauce
1 tbsp Shaoxing rice wine or dry sherry
2 tsp sesame oil
2 tsp salt
2 tsp cornflour [US cornstarch]*

Cut the beef into slices about 3cm/1¹/₄in long and 5mm/¹/₄in thick. Then stack the slices and finely shred the meat. Put it into a bowl. Add the marinade ingredients and mix well.

Heat a wok over high heat until it is hot, then add the oil. When the oil is very hot and begins to smoke, add the beef mixture. Let the meat brown for 1 minute, then carefully stir-fry for another minute. Drain the beef in a colander, leaving 1 tbsp of oil in the wok.

Quickly reheat the wok and the oil. When it is hot, add the black beans, garlic, and ginger and stir-fry for 20 seconds over medium heat. Add the chillies and stir-fry for another 20 seconds. Then add the stock, rice wine, soy sauce, sugar, and sesame oil. Cook over high heat for 30 seconds. Return the meat to the wok and give the mixture several stirs to mix well. Turn onto a platter and serve at once.

STIR-FRIED BEEF IN BLACK BEAN SAUCE

— SHOPPING LIST —
*450g/1lb lean beef steak, shallots, spring onions
[US scallions], fresh ginger, garlic*

— STAPLES —
*light soy sauce, sesame oil, Shaoxing rice wine or
dry sherry, cornflour [US cornstarch], groundnut
oil [US peanut oil], black beans, Chicken Stock,
oyster sauce*

— PREPARATION TIME —
25 minutes

— COOKING TIME —
10 minutes
SERVES 4

This popular recipe is a favorite in Chinese restaurants and understandably so. The fragrance of the black bean sauce mixed with garlic and ginger is a perfect savory combination.

450g/1lb lean beef steak

— MARINADE —

1 tbsp light soy sauce

2 tsp sesame oil

1 tbsp Shaoxing rice wine or dry sherry

2 tsp cornflour [US cornstarch]

— BLACK BEAN SAUCE —

3 tbsp groundnut oil [US peanut oil]

1 tbsp finely chopped fresh ginger

1¹/₂ tbsp finely chopped garlic

3 tbsp sliced shallots

6 spring onions [US scallions], cut into 5cm/2in
segments

2¹/₂ tbsp coarsely chopped black beans

¹/₄ tsp salt

¹/₄ tsp freshly ground black pepper

150ml/5floz/⁵/₈ cup Chicken Stock (page 128) or water

1 tbsp oyster sauce

— GARNISH —

2 tbsp finely chopped spring onions [US scallions]

Cut the beef into slices 5cm/2in long and 5mm/
¹/₄in thick. Put them in a bowl. Add the marinade ingredients, mix and leave for 20 minutes.

Heat a wok or large frying pan until very hot.
Add the oil and, when slightly smoking, add the
beef slices. Stir-fry for 5 minutes or until they
are lightly browned. Remove and drain them
well in a colander inside a bowl. Save 1 tbsp of
the drained oil and discard the rest.

Wipe the wok or pan clean and reheat it over a
high heat until it is hot. Add the reserved 1 tbsp
of oil. Then add the ginger, garlic, shallots, spring
onions, and black beans and stir-fry for 2 minutes. Add the salt, pepper, chicken stock, and
oyster sauce and bring the mixture to a boil.
Return the drained beef slices and toss them
thoroughly with the sauce. Turn the mixture onto
a serving platter, garnish it with the spring onions, and serve at once.

SICHUAN PEPPERCORN ONION BEEF

— SHOPPING LIST —

450g/1lb lean beef steak, onion, leeks

— STAPLES —

light soy sauce, sesame oil, Shaoxing rice wine or
dry sherry, cornflour [US cornstarch], groundnut
oil [US peanut oil], sugar, Sichuan peppercorns

— PREPARATION TIME —

25 minutes

— COOKING TIME —

10 minutes

SERVES 4

This highly aromatic and fragrant dish from
Sichuan illustrates the Chinese talent for taking
quite ordinary foods and turning them into
something extraordinary – a quick, easy, and
delicious main course, which is perfect served
with rice.

450g/1lb lean beef steak

3 leeks, white part only, finely shredded

4 tbsp groundnut oil [US peanut oil]

1 onion, finely sliced

1 tbsp Shaoxing rice wine or dry sherry

2 tsp salt

1 tsp sugar

2 tsp sesame oil

2 tsp roasted and ground Sichuan peppercorns
(page 85)

— MARINADE —

1 tbsp light soy sauce

2 tsp sesame oil

1 tbsp Shaoxing rice wine or dry sherry

2 tsp cornflour [US cornstarch]

Cut the beef into thin slices 5cm/2in long and
5mm/¹/₄in thick. Put them into a bowl. Add the
marinade ingredients and mix well.

Let the beef marinate for 20 minutes.

149

Heat a wok or large frying pan until it is very hot. Add the 3 tbsp oil and, when it is very hot and slightly smoking, add the beef slices. Stir-fry for 5 minutes or until they are lightly browned. Remove them and drain them well in a colander.

Wipe the wok or pan clean and reheat it over a high heat until it is hot. Add the remaining 1 tbsp oil, then add the leeks and onion and stir-fry for 2 minutes. Add the rice wine and continue to stir-fry for 5–8 minutes. Then add the drained beef slices, salt, sugar, sesame oil and Sichuan peppercorns and toss thoroughly to mix. Turn the mixture onto a serving platter and serve at once.

RED COOKED OXTAIL STEW

———— SHOPPING LIST ————
1.35kg/3lb oxtail, 450g/1lb carrots, garlic, fresh ginger, fermented bean curd or chilli-fermented bean curd

———— STAPLES ————
groundnut oil [US peanut oil], Shaoxing rice wine or dry sherry, hoisin sauce, dark soy sauce, five spice powder, whole bean sauce, star anise, cinnamon bark or stick, rock or ordinary sugar

———— PREPARATION TIME ————
20 minutes

———— COOKING TIME ————
2 hours
SERVES 4

Oxtail makes a tasty and lusty dish because it lends itself to long stewing. This extensive cooking process allows it both to impart and to absorb flavors slowly. Chinese aromatics and spices are a perfect foil for the rich, strong taste of oxtail. The beauty of this dish is that it can be made days in advance and is even better reheated.

3 tbsp groundnut oil [US peanut oil]
1.35kg/3lb oxtail, separated into sections
450g/1lb carrots

———— SAUCE ————
2 tbsp finely chopped garlic
3 fresh ginger slices
6 cubes fermented bean curd or chilli-fermented bean curd
3 tbsp Shaoxing rice wine or dry sherry
6 tbsp hoisin sauce
5 tbsp dark soy sauce
1 tbsp five spice powder
1 tbsp salt
1 tbsp whole bean sauce
2 tsp freshly ground black pepper
3 star anise
3 pieces cinnamon bark or cinnamon stick
50g/2oz/¼ cup rock sugar or ordinary sugar
2.8 litres/5 pints/12½ cups water

Heat a wok or large frying pan over high heat until it is hot. Add the oil and, when it is very hot and slightly smoking, add the oxtail. Turn the heat down and brown the meat. Remove the oxtail and set aside. Drain off all but 1 tbsp of the oil and fat from the wok. Discard the rest.

Reheat the wok and reserved oil and, when it is hot, add the garlic, ginger, and fermented bean curd. Stir-fry the mixture for 30 seconds. Then add the rest of the sauce ingredients and bring the mixture to a simmer.

Transfer the sauce to a large flameproof casserole. Add the oxtail and bring to a boil. Turn the heat to very low, cover, and let it cook for 2 hours or until the meat is very tender.

While the oxtail is cooking, peel the carrots and roll-cut them into 5cm/2in segments. When the meat is cooked, add the carrots and cook for an additional 30 minutes. Skim off all surface fat, put the stew onto a platter, and serve at once.

PEARL MEATBALLS

———— SHOPPING LIST ————

225g/8oz glutinous rice, 450g/1lb minced [US ground] fatty pork, fresh or canned water chestnuts, cooked ham, egg, fresh ginger, spring onions [US scallions], fresh coriander [US cilantro]

———— STAPLES ————

light soy sauce, Shaoxing rice wine or dry sherry, sugar, sesame oil, Sichuan peppercorns, cornflour [US cornstarch]

———— PREPARATION TIME ————

8 hours (for soaking rice) + 15 minutes

———— COOKING TIME ————

15 minutes

SERVES 4

Steaming is the best technique for bringing out delicate flavors.

Here tasty meatballs are rolled in glutinous rice and steamed until they glisten like pearls… hence the name of the dish. Glutinous rice must be soaked overnight and can withstand a long cooking time without falling apart. It also absorbs all the savory marinade and pork flavors. I find these meatballs, sometimes served in dim sum snack restaurants, a delectable alternative to traditional meat dishes. Use this dish as a first course for any meal or for parties.

225g/8oz/1 cup glutinous rice, soaked overnight

———— MEATBALLS ————

450g/1lb fatty minced [US ground] pork
175g/6oz peeled fresh or canned water chestnuts finely chopped (page 92)
50g/2oz cooked ham, finely diced
2 tbsp light soy sauce
1 tbsp Shaoxing rice wine or dry sherry
1 tbsp finely chopped fresh ginger
2 tbsp finely chopped spring onions [US scallions]
1 tsp salt

2 tsp sugar
1 egg, beaten
1 tbsp sesame oil
2 tsp roasted ground Sichuan peppercorns (page 85)
2 tsp cornflour [US cornstarch]

———— GARNISH ————

chopped fresh coriander [US cilantro]

Drain the rice and spread it out on a baking tray. Combine all the ingredients for the meatballs and mix them well.

Take about 2 tbsp of the meatball mixture and roll it between your palms into a ball about the size of a golf ball. Then roll this ball over the rice until the surface is evenly covered. Repeat until you have used up all the mixture. Put the pearl balls on a heatproof plate.

Set up a steamer or put a rack into a wok or deep pan and add about 5cm/2in of hot water. Bring the water to a simmer. Put the plate with the meatballs into the steamer or onto the rack. Cover tightly and gently steam over medium heat for 15 minutes. Check the water in the steamer and replenish it from time to time, as needed. You will have to steam the pearl balls in two batches.

Arrange the pearl balls on a platter, garnish with chopped coriander, and serve at once.

SAVORY DEEP-FRIED WONTON

———— SHOPPING LIST ————

225g/8oz wonton wrappers [US wonton skins], 350g/12oz raw prawns [US shrimp], 110g/4oz minced [US ground] pork, tomato paste or ketchup, spring onions [US scallions], egg

———— STAPLES ————

Shaoxing rice wine or dry sherry, sugar, sesame oil, Chinese white rice vinegar, cornflour [US cornstarch], groundnut oil [US peanut oil]

151

PREPARATION TIME

25 minutes

COOKING TIME

10 minutes

SERVES 4 (MAKES 30–35)

Prosaic wontons become savory treats when dipped in a sweet and sour sauce. They make a great snack or first course for any meal.

The sweet and sour sauce can be made a day in advance, refrigerated and then brought to room temperature before serving. The recipe can easily be doubled for those who want more sauce.

225g/8oz wonton wrappers [US wonton skins]

FILLING

*350g/12oz peeled raw prawns [US shrimp],
deveined and coarsely chopped
110g/4oz minced [US ground] pork
2 tsp salt
$^1/_2$ tsp freshly ground white pepper
4 tbsp finely chopped spring onions [US scallions]
2 tsp Shaoxing rice wine or dry sherry
1 tsp sugar
2 tsp sesame oil
1 egg white, lightly beaten*

SWEET AND SOUR SAUCE

*150ml/5fl oz/$^5/_8$ cup water
2 tbsp sugar
3 tbsp Chinese white rice vinegar
3 tbsp tomato paste or tomato ketchup
1 tsp salt
$^1/_2$ tsp freshly ground white pepper
1 tsp cornflour [US cornstarch] blended with
2 tsp water*

FOR DEEP-FRYING

*600ml/1 pint/2$^1/_2$ cups groundnut oil [US peanut
oil] or vegetable oil*

Put the prawns and pork in a large bowl, add the salt and pepper, and mix well, either by kneading with your hand or by stirring with a wooden spoon. Then add all the other filling ingredients and stir them well into the prawn and pork mixture. Cover the bowl tightly and chill for at least 20 minutes.

In a small saucepan, combine all the ingredients for the sweet and sour sauce, except the cornflour mixture. Bring to a boil. Stir in the cornflour mixture and cook for 1 minute. Allow to cool.

Put 1 tbsp of the filling in the center of each wonton wrapper. Dampen the edges with a little water and bring up the sides around and over the filling. Pinch the edges together at the top so that the wonton is sealed. It should look like a small, filled bag.

Heat a wok over high heat until it is hot, then add the oil. When the oil is hot and slightly smoking, add a handful of wontons and deep-fry for 3 minutes, or until golden and crispy. Drain on paper towels. Continue to fry the wontons until you have finished all of them. Serve them immediately, with the sweet and sour sauce.

STEWED PORK SPARERIBS

SHOPPING LIST

*450g/1lb meaty pork spareribs, garlic, fresh ginger,
spring onions [US scallions]*

STAPLES

*groundnut oil [US peanut oil], five spice powder,
rock or ordinary sugar, dark soy sauce, Chinese
black vinegar, Shaoxing rice wine or dry sherry,
Chicken Stock*

PREPARATION TIME

15 minutes

COOKING TIME

40 minutes

SERVES 4

Having a fire burning all day and all night to ward off the cold, the cooks of northern China made a virtue of necessity and concocted many dishes that can simmer at the back of the fireplace. Here is one of my favorites that utilizes spareribs. The meat is blanched first to rid it of excess fat; then the spareribs are stir-fried briefly to give them color, and finally braised to make them succulent and tender. The sauce is unusual and piquant. It is a dish that goes very well with rice and is easy to reheat.

450g/1lb meaty spareribs
2 tbsp groundnut oil [US peanut oil] or vegetable oil
8 garlic cloves, crushed
8 slices fresh ginger, finely chopped
4 spring onions [US scallions], cut into 7.5cm/3in segments
2 tsp five spice powder
3 tbsp rock sugar or ordinary sugar
2 tbsp dark soy sauce
150ml/5fl oz/ ⁵/₈ cup Chinese black vinegar
150ml/5fl oz/ ⁵/₈ cup Shaoxing rice wine or dry sherry
150ml/5fl oz/ ⁵/₈ cup Chicken Stock (page 128)

Cut the spareribs into 5cm/2in pieces. Blanch them in salted boiling water for 10 minutes. Drain well and discard the water.

Heat a wok over high heat until it is hot, then add the oil. When the oil is hot and slightly smoking, add the garlic, ginger and spring onions and stir-fry for 1 minute. Then add the spareribs and stir-fry for 4 minutes or until they are lightly browned. Add the rest of the ingredients and bring the mixture to a boil.

Transfer the contents to a flameproof casserole. Cover and simmer for 40 minutes or until the meat on the ribs is very tender. Serve the dish immediately.

SHREDDED PORK IN BEAN PASTE

SHOPPING LIST
450g/1lb lean, minced [US ground] pork, garlic, spring onions [US scallions]

STAPLES
light and dark soy sauces, Shaoxing rice wine or dry sherry, sugar, sesame oil, cornflour [US cornstarch], groundnut oil [US peanut oil], hoisin sauce, ground bean sauce

PREPARATION TIME
10 minutes

COOKING TIME
5 minutes

SERVES 4

This dish shows off the renowned Peking – inspired rich sauce, which is here paired with the most popular Chinese meat – pork. It is a savory dish that goes well with plain rice and your favorite vegetable dish. It is quick and easy to make.

450g/1lb lean, minced [US ground] pork

MARINADE
2 tsp dark soy sauce
2 tsp light soy sauce
2 tsp Shaoxing rice wine or dry sherry
¹/₂ tsp sugar
¹/₄ tsp salt
1 tsp sesame oil
2 tsp cornflour [US cornstarch]

SAUCE
1¹/₂ tbsp groundnut oil [US peanut oil] or vegetable oil
2 tbsp finely chopped garlic
2 tbsp ground bean sauce
1 tbsp Shaoxing rice wine or dry sherry
1 tbsp hoisin sauce
4 spring onions [US scallions], shredded

Combine the pork and marinade ingredients.

153

Heat a wok until it is hot, then add the oil. When the oil is hot and slightly smoking, add the pork mixture and stir-fry for 1 minute. Add the garlic, bean sauce, and rice wine and stir-fry for another minute. Then add the hoisin sauce and spring onions and continue to stir-fry for another minute, mixing well. Turn onto a platter and serve at once.

STEAMED PORK WITH FRAGRANT RICE CRUMBS

———————— SHOPPING LIST ————————
450g/1lb pork fillet [US pork tenderloin] or boneless pork chops, ginger, spring onions [US scallions], long-grain white rice

———————— STAPLES ————————
dark soy sauce, Shaoxing rice wine or dry sherry, chilli bean paste, sesame oil, Sichuan peppercorns, five spice powder

———————— PREPARATION TIME ————————
35 minutes

———————— COOKING TIME ————————
20 minutes
SERVES 4

This is an unusual but delicious method for flavoring pork. Similar to breadcrumbs in European cookery, rice crumbs are used in China to add texture to foods. The rice is stir-fried to 'roast' it, coarsely crushed, and used to coat marinated pork which is then gently steamed. The result is a fragrant and tasty pork dish with unique qualities. It is easy to make.

450g/1lb pork fillet [US pork tenderloin] or tender, boneless pork chops

———————— MARINADE ————————
1 tbsp dark soy sauce
1 tbsp Shaoxing rice wine or dry sherry
2 tsp finely chopped fresh ginger
2 tsp chilli bean paste

1 tbsp finely chopped spring onions [US scallions]
2 tsp sesame oil
1 tsp salt
1 tsp roasted and crushed Sichuan peppercorns (page 85)

———————— RICE CRUMBS ————————
110g/4oz/¹/₂ cup long-grain white rice
1 tsp Sichuan peppercorns
¹/₂ tsp five spice powder
¹/₄ tsp freshly ground black pepper

Cut the pork into slices about 5cm/2in long, 2.5cm/1in wide and 5mm/¹/₄in thick. Combine with the marinade ingredients and let sit at room temperature for 30 minutes.

Meanwhile, prepare the rice crumbs. Heat a wok or large frying pan over high heat until it is hot. Add the rice, peppercorns, five spice powder and pepper. Turn the heat to moderate and continue to stir-fry until the rice is lightly browned. Allow the mixture to cool thoroughly. Then coarsely grind the rice mixture in a blender or food processor, making sure not to overprocess the rice to a powder. The mixture should be slightly coarse.

Coat the marinated pork slices in the rice crumbs. Next set up a steamer or put a rack into a wok or deep pan and add 5cm/2in of water. Bring the water to the boil over a high heat. Put the pork onto a heatproof plate, one layer thick, and carefully lower it into the steamer or set on the rack. Turn the heat to low and cover tightly. Steam gently for 15 minutes. (You will have to cook the pork in two batches.) When it is done, remove the plate from the steamer and serve at once.

SHREDDED STRANGE-FLAVOR PORK

———— SHOPPING LIST ————

450g/1lb boneless, lean pork, egg, garlic, fresh ginger, spring onions [US scallions]

———— STAPLES ————

cornflour [US cornstarch], groundnut oil [US peanut oil], dark soy sauce, Chinese black vinegar, chilli bean paste, sesame oil, Shaoxing rice wine or dry sherry, Sichuan peppercorns

———— PREPARATION TIME ————

25 minutes

———— COOKING TIME ————

5 minutes

SERVES 4

This is the pork counterpart to a fragrant Sichuan dish popularly known as 'Strange-Taste Chicken' because it incorporates so many flavors, being hot, spicy, sour, sweet, and salty all at the same time. The combination of flavors is often used with fish as well. Delicious as a hot dish, it complements plain rice very well. The bonus is that it is also very easy to make.

450g/1lb boneless, lean pork, from the loin or chops
1 egg white, ¹/₂ tsp salt
2 tsp cornflour [US cornstarch]
300ml/10fl oz/1 cup groundnut oil [US peanut oil] or water

———— SAUCE ————

1 tbsp groundnut oil [US peanut oil]
1 tbsp finely chopped garlic
1 tbsp finely chopped fresh ginger
1¹/₂ tbsp finely chopped spring onions [US scallions]
2 tsp dark soy sauce
2 tsp Chinese black rice vinegar or cider vinegar
2 tsp chilli bean paste
2 tsp sesame oil
2 tsp sugar
1 tbsp Shaoxing rice wine or dry sherry
1 tsp roasted and ground Sichuan peppercorns
(page 85)

Cut the pork into thin shreds about 7.5cm/3in long and 5mm/¹/₄in wide. Combine them with the egg white, salt, and cornflour in a small bowl. Refrigerate for about 20 minutes.

Heat a wok until it is very hot and then add the oil. When the oil is very hot, remove the wok from the heat, and immediately add the pork, stirring vigorously to keep the shreds from sticking. When the pork shreds turn white, about 1 minute, quickly drain them in a stainless steel colander set in a bowl. Discard the oil.

Wipe the wok clean. Heat it until it is hot, then add the 1 tbsp of oil for the sauce. Immediately add the garlic, ginger, and spring onions and stir-fry for 30 seconds or until they are slightly brown. Add the remaining sauce ingredients and bring to the boil. Return the cooked pork to the wok and stir-fry the mixture for 2 minutes more, coating the meat thoroughly with the sauce. Serve at once.

CRISPY FRIED PORK CHOPS

———— SHOPPING LIST ————

225g/8oz lean, boneless pork chops, lemon, egg, dry breadcrumbs

———— STAPLES ————

Shaoxing rice wine or dry sherry, light soy sauce, five spice powder, sugar, groundnut oil [US peanut oil], cornflour [US cornstarch]

———— PREPARATION TIME ————

35 minutes

———— COOKING TIME ————

5 minutes

SERVES 4

This is an unusual dish that has recently become popular in Hong Kong and Taiwan. It bears some resemblance to a similar dish in Japanese cookery. Whatever its origins, the Chinese like to serve it sliced and dipped in a Sichuan peppercorn and salt mixture. Like many such dishes, it is quick to make and therefore popular among busy Hong Kong families.

225g/8oz thick, lean, boneless pork chops

MARINADE
---

1 tbsp Shaoxing rice wine or dry sherry
1 tsp light soy sauce
¹/₂ tsp five spice powder
¹/₂ tsp salt
¹/₄ tsp freshly ground black pepper
2 tsp sugar

FOR COATING

Cornflour [US cornstarch], for dusting
1 egg, beaten
dry breadcrumbs

FOR DEEP-FRYING

600ml/1 pint/2¹/₂ cups groundnut oil [US peanut oil]

GARNISH
---

1 lemon, cut into wedges
Seasoned Salt & Pepper (page 85)

Put the pork chops between two sheets of cling film [US plastic wrap] and pound them with a mallet until the pieces of pork are about 5mm/¹/₄in thick. Put the pork in a bowl and add the marinade ingredients. Mix well, then let sit for about 30 minutes.

Dip the pieces of pork in the cornflour, shaking off any excess. Then dip them in the egg and finally roll them in the breadcrumbs.

Heat a wok or large frying-pan over high heat until it is hot. Add the oil and, when it is very hot and slightly smoking, deep-fry the pork pieces for about 1¹/₂ minutes or until they are golden brown. Drain them well on paper towels. Slice the pork and arrange it on a platter. Serve immediately with lemon wedges and the Seasoned Salt & Pepper.

COLD PORK WITH GARLIC SAUCE

SHOPPING LIST

450g/1lb boneless piece of pork leg or shoulder [US fresh ham or pork butt], fresh ginger, spring onions [US scallions], garlic

---
STAPLES

Shaoxing rice wine or dry sherry, dark soy sauce, Chinese white rice vinegar, sugar, chilli oil

---
PREPARATION TIME
---

5 minutes

COOKING TIME
---

45 minutes

SERVES 4

In the hot, humid region of Sichuan, this cold dish is a stimulating first course for any meal. It is beautifully spicy and is easy to make.

450g/1lb boneless piece of pork leg or shoulder [US fresh ham or pork butt]
2 tbsp Shaoxing rice wine or dry sherry
3 slices fresh ginger
3 spring onions [US scallions]

SAUCE
---

3 tbsp finely chopped garlic
3 tbsp dark soy sauce
2 tbsp Chinese white rice vinegar
2 tbsp sugar
1 tbsp chilli oil (page 23)

GARNISH
---

3 tbsp finely chopped spring onions [US scallions]

Bring a large pot of water to the boil, add the pork, rice wine or sherry, ginger, and spring onions. Let the liquid come back to the boil, then turn the heat to very low, cover, and cook for 45 minutes.

Combine the sauce ingredients. Mix well and set aside.

Remove the pork from the liquid, and allow it to cool completely.

Then cut it into very thin slices and arrange them on a platter. Pour the sauce onto the pork, garnish with the spring onions, and serve.

MU SHU PORK WITH CHINESE PANCAKES

───────── SHOPPING LIST ─────────

450g/1lb boneless lean pork, eggs, spring onions [US scallions], dried lily buds, tree ears

───────── STAPLES ─────────

cornflour [US cornstarch], groundnut oil [US peanut oil], sugar, Shaoxing rice wine or dry sherry, light soy sauce, sesame oil, hoisin sauce, plain flour [US all-purpose flour]

───────── PREPARATION TIME ─────────

25 minutes

───────── COOKING TIME ─────────

15 minutes

SERVES 4

This popular northern Chinese dish has become fashionable in the West. It is not difficult to see why. The shredded ingredients have a delightful textural quality and the combination of flavors, enhanced by hoisin sauce (in Beijing a salty bean paste would be used), enclosed by Chinese pancakes, makes for a delicious dish that works beautifully.

450g/1lb boneless, lean pork, from the loin or chops
1 egg white
1/2 tsp salt
2 tsp cornflour [US cornstarch]
25g/1oz dried lily buds, soaked (page 51)
50g/2oz tree ears, soaked (page 34)
300ml/10fl oz groundnut oil [US peanut oil]
or water
4 eggs, beaten
6 spring onions [US scallions], finely shredded

1 tsp sugar
1 tsp salt
1 tsp freshly ground black pepper
1 tbsp Shaoxing rice wine or dry sherry
1 1/2 tbsp light soy sauce
2 tsp sesame oil

───────── FOR DIPPING ─────────

hoisin sauce

Cut the pork into thin strips about 7.5cm/3in long. Combine them with the egg white, salt, and cornflour in a small bowl. Refrigerate for about 20 minutes.

Set aside 1 1/2 tbsp oil for later use. Heat a wok until it is very hot and then add the remaining oil. When the oil is very hot, remove the wok from the heat and immediately add the pork, stirring vigorously to keep the strips from sticking to the side. When the strips turn white, about 1 minute, quickly drain them in a stainless steel colander set in a bowl. Save 2 tbsp of oil and discard the rest.

Wipe the wok clean. Heat it until it is hot, then add the 2 tbsp of oil. Immediately add the eggs and gently stir-fry by lifting them up and around until they are scrambled. Remove them immediately and drain on paper towels.

Wipe the wok clean and reheat. When it is very hot, add the reserved 1 1/2 tbsp of oil. Then add the lily buds, tree ears, and spring onions and stir-fry for 1 minute. Add the rest of the ingredients and stir-fry for 2 minutes more. Return the cooked pork and egg to the wok or pan and stir-fry the mixture for another 2 minutes, mixing thoroughly. Serve at once with Chinese pancakes and hoisin sauce.

───────── CHINESE PANCAKES ─────────

These pancakes are the classic accompaniment to Peking Duck and reflect the northern Chinese use of wheat instead of rice. The pancakes

157

are easy to make once you get the knack, which comes with practice. The unusual method of rolling 'double' pancakes is designed to ensure thinner, moister pancakes with less risk of over-cooking them. Since they can be frozen, it is possible to make them weeks ahead. They can also be used with other dishes, such as the Mu Shu Pork recipe above.

275g/10oz/2 cups plain flour [US all-purpose flour]
225ml/8fl oz/1 cup very hot water
2 tbsp sesame oil

Put the flour into a large bowl. Stir the hot water gradually into the flour, mixing all the while with chopsticks or a fork until the water is fully incorporated. Add more water if the mixture seems dry. Turn the mixture onto a board and knead it with your hands until it is a smooth dough. This should take about 8 minutes. Put the dough back into the bowl, cover it with a clean, damp towel, and let it rest for about 30 minutes.

After the resting period take the dough out of the bowl and knead it again for about 5 minutes, dusting with a little flour if it is sticky. Once the dough is smooth, form it into a roll about 45cm/18in long and about 2.5cm/1in in diameter. Take a knife and cut the roll into equal segments. There should be about 18. Roll each segment into a ball.

Take two of the dough balls. Dip one side of one ball into the sesame oil and place the oiled side on top of the other ball. Take a rolling pin, and roll the two simultaneously into a round about 15cm/6in in diameter. It is important to roll double pancakes in this way because the resulting dough will remain moist inside and you will be able to roll them thinner but avoid the risk of overcooking them later.

Heat a frying pan or wok over a very low flame. Put the double pancake into the wok or pan and cook it until it has dried on one side. Flip it over and cook the other side. Remove from the pan, peel the 2 pancakes apart and set them aside. Repeat this process until all the dough balls have been cooked. (There should be about 18 pancakes in all.)

Steam the pancakes to reheat them. Or, alternatively, wrap them tightly in a double sheet of foil, put them into a pan containing 2.5cm/1in of boiling water, cover, and simmer over a very low heat until they are hot. Don't be tempted to reheat them in the oven as this will dry them out too much. If you want to freeze the cooked pancakes, wrap them tightly in cling film [US plastic wrap] first. When using pancakes that have been frozen, let them thaw in the refrigerator first before reheating them.

CHIU CHOW STYLE SWEET AND SOUR PORK

—————— **SHOPPING LIST** ——————
450g/1lb fatty, minced [US ground] pork, 225g/8oz caul fat, fresh or canned water chestnuts, egg, green and red sweet peppers, carrots, spring onions [US scallions], canned lychees

—————— **STAPLES** ——————
light and dark soy sauces, Shaoxing rice wine or dry sherry, sugar, cornflour [US cornstarch], groundnut oil [US peanut oil], sesame oil, Chicken Stock, Chinese white rice vinegar

—————— **PREPARATION TIME** ——————
30 minutes

—————— **COOKING TIME** ——————
20 minutes
SERVES 4

This is a delicious and unusual version of sweet and sour pork, based on a recipe that originated in a region of southern China. It is unlike most sweet and sour pork dishes offered in restaurants, where the dish has become a cliché bereft of its true character. The minced pork is combined with crispy sweet water chestnuts, seasoned and covered in caul fat. This is then lightly dusted with cornflour and deep-fried. The result is a tender morsel of pork with a light, balanced sweet and sour taste. It is not difficult to make and your guests will surely be surprised at how good this classic dish can really be. Serve it with plain rice and a stir-fried vegetable dish.

450g/1lb fatty, minced [US ground] pork
1 egg white
4 tbsp cold water
175g/6oz peeled fresh or *canned water chestnuts,*
coarsely chopped (page 92)
2 tbsp light soy sauce
1 tbsp dark soy sauce
2 tbsp Shaoxing rice wine or *dry sherry*
1¹/₂ tbsp sugar
2 tsp salt
¹/₂ tsp freshly ground black pepper
225g/8oz caul fat, for wrapping
110g/4oz green sweet pepper (about 1)
110g/4oz red sweet pepper (about 1)
110g/4oz carrots
50g/2oz spring onions [US scallions] (about 4)
cornflour [US cornstarch], for dusting
450ml/15fl oz/1⁵/₈ cup groundnut oil [US peanut oil]
75g/3oz/¹/₃ cup drained canned lychees or *fresh*
orange segments

────────── **SAUCE** ──────────
150ml/5fl oz/⁵/₈ cup Chicken Stock (page 128)
1 tbsp light soy sauce
2 tsp dark soy sauce
2 tsp sesame oil
¹/₂ tsp salt
1 tsp freshly ground white pepper
1¹/₂ tbsp Chinese white rice vinegar
1 tbsp sugar
2 tbsp tomato paste or *ketchup*

Mix the pork with the egg white and cold water by hand. The mixture should be light and fluffy. Do not use a blender as it would make the mixture too dense. Then add the water chestnuts, soy sauces, Shaoxing rice wine or dry sherry, sugar, salt, and pepper and mix for another 30 seconds. Divide the pork into small balls, about the size of golf balls. Cut the caul fat into 7.5cm/3in squares. Wrap caul fat around each pork ball.

Cut the green and red peppers into 2.5cm/1in squares. Peel and thinly slice the carrots on a diagonal. Cut the spring onions into 2.5cm/1in pieces. (The uniform size of meat and vegetables adds to the visual appeal of the dish.) Bring a pot of water to the boil and blanch the carrots and peppers for about 4 minutes or until just tender; drain and set aside.

Dust the pork balls with cornflour, shaking off any excess. Heat the oil in a deep-fat fryer or large wok until it is slightly smoking. Turn the heat to moderate and deep-fry the pork balls until they are cripsy. Drain them thoroughly on paper towels.

Combine the sauce ingredients in a large saucepan. Bring to the boil. Add the carrots, peppers, and spring onions, and stir well. Cook for 2 minutes. Turn the heat down so that the mixture is simmering. Add the lychees or oranges and pork balls.

Mix well, then turn the mixture onto a deep platter and serve at once.

EGGS

HOME-STYLE OMELETTE

— SHOPPING LIST —

175g/6oz minced [US ground] pork, large eggs, spring onions [US scallions], Sichuan preserved vegetable

— STAPLES —

sesame oil, groundnut oil [US peanut oil], Shaoxing rice wine or dry sherry, light soy sauce, sugar

— PREPARATION TIME —

10 minutes

— COOKING TIME —

10 minutes

SERVES 2–4

The Chinese cook can take common everyday ingredients and imaginatively turn them into a tasty, exotic treat. This home-style omelette is a good example of a quick, easy and appetizing dish that can serve as a main course or as part of a meal. Like many Chinese dishes, meat is used sparely, almost as a condiment.

Serve it with plain rice and a vegetable dish.

6 size 1 or 2 [US extra large] eggs, beaten
6 tbsp finely chopped spring onions [US scallions]
175g/6oz minced [US ground] pork
50g/2oz/³/₄ cup Sichuan preserved vegetable, thoroughly rinsed and finely chopped
¹/₄ tsp freshly ground white pepper
1 tsp sesame oil
3 tbsp groundnut oil [US peanut oil]
2 tsp Shaoxing rice wine or dry sherry
2 tsp light soy sauce
1 tsp sugar

In a large bowl, combine the eggs with half of the spring onions, pork, and preserved vegetable, together with the pepper and sesame oil.

Heat a wok or large frying pan over high heat until it is hot. Add the groundnut oil and, when it is very hot and slightly smoking, add the egg mixture. Fry until the omelette is brown. Carefully turn it over and fry the other side. Remove it from the wok and drain well on paper towels. Pour off most of the oil, leaving 1 tbsp in the wok. Reheat the wok until it is hot. Add the remaining spring onions, pork, and preserved vegetable, the Shaoxing rice wine or dry sherry, soy sauce, and sugar. Stir-fry for 2 minutes. Pour this over the omelette and serve at once.

MEAT-FILLED OMELETTE

— SHOPPING LIST —

225g/8oz minced [US ground] pork, eggs, fresh ginger, spring onions [US scallions], garlic, cloud ears, lily buds

— STAPLES —

flour, sesame oil, sugar, Shaoxing rice wine or dry sherry, light and dark soy sauces, Sichuan peppercorn, groundnut oil [US peanut oil], cornflour [US cornstarch], Chicken Stock

— PREPARATION TIME —

30 minutes

— COOKING TIME —

20 minutes

SERVES 4

This hearty dish is representative of the type of Chinese home cooking I love. It is full of rich flavors and aromas that typify the country cuisine of Sichuan. Not all Sichuan food is hot and spicy; as this recipe demonstrates, some of the dishes are quite mild, yet full of rich seasoning. The omelette (which is actually an egg wrapping) absorbs the juice from the filling as well as the sauce. Serve this with rice and vegetables for robust winter fare.

OMELETTE WRAPPERS

3 eggs, beaten

3 tbsp flour

1 tbsp sesame oil

a pinch of salt

groundnut oil [US peanut oil], for greasing

FOR THE FILLING

225g/8oz minced [US ground] pork

1 tbsp finely chopped fresh ginger

3 tbsp finely chopped spring onions [US scallions]

1 tbsp light soy sauce

2 tbsp Shaoxing rice wine or dry sherry

2 tsp sesame oil

1 egg white, beaten

2 tsp cornflour [US cornstarch]

1 tsp roasted and ground Sichuan peppercorns (page 85)

$1/2$ tsp salt

$1/2$ tsp freshly ground black pepper

beaten egg, for sealing

SAUCE

$1^1/2$ tbsp groundnut oil [US peanut oil]

3 tbsp finely shredded spring onions [US scallions]

4 garlic cloves, thinly sliced

12g/$^1/2$oz cloud ears, soaked and rinsed (page 34)

25g/1oz lily buds, soaked and ends removed (page 51)

2 tbsp Shaoxing rice wine or dry sherry

1 tbsp light soy sauce

1 tbsp dark soy sauce

2 tsp sugar

1 tsp roasted and ground Sichuan peppercorns (page 85)

1 tsp salt

300ml/10fl oz/$1^1/4$ cups Chicken Stock (page 128)

2 tsp sesame oil

Mix the eggs, flour, sesame oil and salt in a blender to make a smooth batter with *no* lumps. Put the batter through a fine sieve or strainer. Heat a wok over medium heat until it is hot, then use a paper towel to grease the surface of the wok with oil. Put 2 tbsp of the egg batter in the wok and tilt the wok in all directions to coat the bottom (approximately 13cm/5in in diameter). When the batter has set, carefully peel it off and lay it on a plate. Repeat the process until you have used all the batter. Makes 8 wrappers.

Combine the filling ingredients in a bowl and mix well. Put about 2 tbsp of filling in the center of each omelette wrapper. Moisten the edges with the beaten egg and fold in half, pressing to seal. It should be like a half-moon-shaped dumpling. Repeat the process until you have used up all the omelette wrappers and filling. Left-over filling can be used in the sauce.

Heat a wok over high heat until it is hot, then add the oil. When the oil is hot and slightly smoking, add the spring onions and garlic. Stir-fry for 20 seconds, then add the cloud ears and lily buds and stir-fry for 1 minute. Add the rest of the sauce ingredients except the sesame oil. Bring to a boil. Put the dumplings in the sauce. Turn the heat to very low, cover, and simmer for 15 minutes. When the dumplings are cooked, add the sesame oil. Turn the dish onto a platter and serve at once.

STEAMED EGG CUSTARD WITH CLAMS

SHOPPING LIST

450g/1lb fresh clams, eggs, fresh ginger, spring onions [US scallions]

STAPLES

Chicken Stock, Shaoxing rice wine or dry sherry, groundnut oil [US peanut oil]

PREPARATION TIME

20 minutes

COOKING TIME

10 minutes

SERVES 4

There are many different varieties of clams harvested off the coast of eastern China. A favorite way to prepare them is to steam them open and then shuck them at the table and dip them in vinegar and sugar. In this Shanghai-inspired dish, cooked clam is mixed with beaten egg and then steamed. The result is a savoury velvet- or satin-textured custard. Only the freshest clams should be used because the taste of the clams must not overwhelm the delicate custard.

450g/1lb fresh clams, thoroughly scrubbed
150ml/5fl oz/⁵⁄₈ cup boiling water

CUSTARD

3 eggs
300ml/10fl oz/1cup Chicken Stock (page 128)
1 tbsp finely chopped fresh ginger
1¹⁄₂ tbsp Shaoxing rice wine or dry sherry
¹⁄₂ tsp freshly ground white pepper
1 tsp salt

GARNISH

3 tbsp spring onions [US scallions], white part only, finely chopped
1 tbsp groundnut oil [US peanut oil]

Cook the clams in the boiling water in a large pot. Remove them as soon as they begin to open. Finish opening them by hand and remove them from their shells. Reserve any clam juices. Mix the custard ingredients in a bowl and add the reserved clam liquid. Pour this mixture into a heatproof, shallow bowl and arrange the cooked clams attractively around the edge.

Next set up a steamer or put a rack into a wok or deep pan and add 5cm/2in of water. Bring the water to the boil over a high heat. Carefully lower the bowl with the clams and custard into the steamer or onto the rack. Turn the heat to low and cover the wok or pan tightly. Steam gently for 10 minutes or until the custard has set. Remove the custard and sprinkle with the spring onions. Quickly, heat the oil in a small pan until it begins to smoke. Pour this over the custard and serve at once.

STEAMED EGG CUSTARD WITH MEAT SAUCE

SHOPPING LIST

350g/12oz minced [US ground] pork, Chinese dried black mushrooms, eggs, spring onions [US scallions]

STAPLES

groundnut oil [US peanut oil], Shaoxing rice wine or dry sherry, sesame oil, dark soy sauce, five spice powder, sugar, Chicken Stock

PREPARATION TIME

20 minutes

COOKING TIME

15 minutes

SERVES 4

This is a delectable dish with an ambrosial aroma and a satisfying and unusual silky texture. The contrast between the hearty meat sauce and the smooth custard makes this dish a great favorite of many cooks. The eggs, assisted by the chicken stock, stand up well against the robust sauce. It is easy to make and goes well with plain rice.

MEAT SAUCE

40g/1¹⁄₂oz Chinese dried black mushrooms (page 26)
1¹⁄₂ tbsp groundnut oil [US peanut oil]
350g/12oz minced [US ground] pork, chopped
3 tbsp finely chopped spring onions [US scallions]
1¹⁄₂ tbsp Shaoxing rice wine or dry sherry
2 tsp sesame oil
2 tbsp dark soy sauce
1 tsp five spice powder
1 tsp salt
1 tsp sugar
¹⁄₂ tsp freshly ground white pepper

CUSTARD

4 eggs
450ml/15fl oz/1⁵⁄₈ cup Chicken Stock (page 128)
1 tsp salt

3 tbsp finely chopped spring onions [US scallions], green part only

Remove and discard the mushroom stems and finely chop the caps. Heat a wok or large frying pan over high heat until it is hot. Add the oil and, when it is very hot and slightly smoking, add the pork and stir-fry for 2 minutes. Drain the pork and return to the wok. Add the spring onions, rice wine or sherry, sesame oil, soy sauce, five spice powder, salt, sugar, pepper, and mushrooms and continue to stir-fry for 3 minutes. Remove from the heat and set aside.

Mix the custard ingredients in a bowl. Rub a heatproof, shallow bowl with groundnut oil or vegetable oil. Pour the custard mixture into the heatproof bowl.

Next, set up a steamer or put a rack into a wok or deep pan and add 5cm/2in of water. Bring the water to the boil over a high heat. Carefully lower the bowl into the steamer or onto the rack. Turn the heat to low and cover the wok or pan tightly. Steam gently for 10–12 minutes or until the custard has set.

Add the stir-fried meat mixture and spread it over the top of the custard. Cover and steam for another 4 minutes. Remove the custard, sprinkle with the spring onions, and serve at once.

EGGS WITH STIR-FRIED VEGETABLES

110g/4oz minced [US ground] pork, bamboo shoots, green beans, Chinese dried black mushrooms, spring onions [US scallions], eggs

light soy sauce, groundnut oil [US peanut oil], salt, white pepper, Shaoxing rice wine or dry sherry, sesame oil

10 minutes

10 minutes

SERVES 4

This easy-to-make home-style dish utilizes only a few prosaic ingredients but transforms them into a wholesome and delicious meal. It illustrates the versatility and imagination of Chinese cooking. This recipe can easily be altered to accommodate bits of left-over vegetables and meats you may have in your refrigerator.

25g/1oz Chinese dried black mushrooms, (page 26)
2 tbsp groundnut oil [US peanut oil]
110g/4oz minced [US ground] pork
110g/4oz bamboo shoots, shredded
110g/4oz green beans, finely sliced at a slight diagonal
4 spring onions [US scallions], finely shredded
1 tsp salt
1/2 tsp freshly ground white pepper
1 tbsp light soy sauce
1 tbsp Shaoxing rice wine or dry sherry
2 tsp sesame oil
6 eggs, beaten

Remove and discard the mushroom stems and finely shred the caps into thin strips.

Heat a wok or large frying pan over high heat until it is hot. Add the oil and, when it is very hot and slightly smoking, add the pork. Stir-fry for 2 minutes. Then add the mushrooms, bamboo shoots, green beans, and spring onions and stir-fry for 3 minutes more. Add the salt, pepper, soy sauce, rice wine or sherry, and sesame oil. Stir-fry for 1 minute. Now add the beaten eggs and stir-fry gently until the eggs are cooked and slightly browned. Remove the mixture to a platter and serve at once.

PRAWNS STIR-FRIED WITH EGGS

———— SHOPPING LIST ————

225g/8oz raw prawns [US shrimp], 110g/4oz green beans, 25g/1oz Chinese dried black mushrooms, spring onions [US scallions], eggs

———— STAPLES ————

light soy sauce, groundnut oil [US peanut oil], salt, white pepper, Shaoxing rice wine or dry sherry, sesame oil

———— PREPARATION TIME ————

15 minutes

———— COOKING TIME ————

10 minutes

SERVES 4

This simple dish is typical of the home-style dishes that one finds on the tables of many Chinese homes. The small amount of seafood makes it quite economical. This recipe can easily be altered to accommodate bits of left-over vegetables and meats you may have in your refrigerator.

225g/8oz raw prawns [US shrimp], peeled and deveined
25g/1oz Chinese dried black mushrooms (page 26)
2 tbsp groundnut oil [US peanut oil]
4 spring onions [US scallions], finely shredded
1 tbsp light soy sauce
1 tsp salt
1/2 tsp freshly ground white pepper
1 tbsp Shaoxing rice wine or dry sherry
2 tsp sesame oil
6 eggs, beaten

Remove and discard the mushroom stems and finely shred the caps into thin strips.

Heat a wok or large frying pan over high heat until it is hot. Add the oil and, when it is very hot and slightly smoking, add the prawns and stir-fry for 2 minutes. With a slotted spoon, re-move the prawns and set aside. Then add the mushrooms and spring onions and stir-fry for 3 minutes. Add the soy sauce, salt, pepper, rice wine and sesame oil. Stir-fry for 1 minute. Now add the beaten eggs and stir-fry gently until the eggs are cooked and slightly firm. Return the prawns and mix well. Remove the mixture to a platter and serve at once.

SHANGHAI-STYLE EGG WITH CRAB MEAT

———— SHOPPING LIST ————

225g/8oz fresh crabmeat, 110g/4oz bamboo shoots, 25g/1oz Chinese dried black mushrooms, eggs

———— STAPLES ————

light soy sauce, groundnut oil [US peanut oil], salt, white pepper, Shaoxing rice wine or dry sherry

———— PREPARATION TIME ————

10 minutes

———— COOKING TIME ————

10 minutes

SERVES 4

I first had this modest egg dish in a Shanghai home and was surprised by its deliciousness. It was made with the famous Shanghai hairy crabs, which are usually filled with rich, savory crab roe. The secret is the freshness of sweet crabmeat, so only the best will do.

225g/8oz fresh crabmeat
1 tbsp Shaoxing rice wine or dry sherry
6 eggs, beaten
1 tsp salt
1/2 tsp freshly ground white pepper
25g/1oz Chinese dried black mushrooms (page 26)
110g/4oz bamboo shoots
2 tbsp groundnut oil [peanut oil]
1 tbsp light soy sauce

Put the crabmeat in a medium-size bowl and sprinkle it with the Shaoxing rice wine or dry sherry. Then add the eggs, salt and pepper and mix well.

Remove and discard the mushroom stems and finely shred the caps into thin strips. Finely shred the bamboo shoots.

Heat a wok or large frying pan over high heat until it is hot. Add the oil and, when it is very hot and slightly smoking, add the mushrooms and bamboo shoots and stir-fry for 2 minutes. Then add the soy sauce and continue to stir-fry for 30 seconds. Now add the crab mixture and stir-fry gently until the eggs are cooked and slightly browned. Remove the mixture to a platter and serve at once.

STIR-FRIED EGGS WITH PRESERVED VEGETABLES

———————— SHOPPING LIST ————————
50g/2oz Sichuan or Tianjian preserved vegetable, spring onions [US scallions], eggs

———————— STAPLES ————————
light soy sauce, groundnut oil [US peanut oil], white pepper

———————— PREPARATION TIME ————————
10 minutes

———————— COOKING TIME ————————
10 minutes
SERVES 4

Whenever my mother was in a great hurry, she would whip up this easy semi-vegetarian dish, which uses preserved vegetables. These add a savory dimension to this surprisingly simple but delicious egg dish. Although my mother used Chinese chives, here I have substituted spring onions, which work equally well.

110g/4oz Sichuan or Tianjian preserved vegetable
4 spring onions [US scallions], finely chopped
1 tbsp light soy sauce
1/2 tsp freshly ground white pepper
6 eggs, beaten
2 tbsp groundnut oil [peanut oil]

Rinse the preserved vegetables in several changes of cold water. Pat them dry with paper towels and finely chop them.

In a medium-size bowl, combine the preserved vegetables with the spring onions, soy sauce, pepper and beaten eggs and mix well.

Heat a wok or large frying pan over high heat until it is hot. Add the oil and, when it is very hot and slightly smoking, add the egg mixture. Turn the heat to low and cook until slightly browned and crispy on the base, then turn over and cook until the other side is brown. Remove to a platter and serve at once.

VEGETABLES

VEGETARIAN DELIGHT

—————— SHOPPING LIST ——————

eggs, Chinese dried black mushrooms, cloud ears, bean thread noodles, pressed seasoned bean curd, cucumber, small onion, fresh ginger, garlic

—————— STAPLES ——————

sesame oil, groundnut oil [US peanut oil], light soy sauce, whole bean sauce, Shaoxing rice wine or dry sherry, hoisin sauce

—————— PREPARATION TIME ——————

30 minutes

—————— COOKING TIME ——————

15 minutes

SERVES 4

Daoists and Buddhists introduced vegetarianism into China many hundreds of years ago. The style never became very popular, for two main reasons in my opinion. First, the Chinese diet was, and remains, heavily weighted in favor of grains and vegetables – animal sources of nutrition are quite tertiary in importance. Second, there were, and are today, powerful demographic and ecological forces which demand that all edible sources of nutrition be utilized. Meat, poultry, and fish were, therefore, well integrated into, but without in any way dominating, Chinese cuisine.

Nonetheless, vegetable dishes were, and remain, highly regarded for their taste, color and nutrition, as this recipe demonstrates. It uses a classic array of popular vegetables, made even more nutritious by the addition of fresh eggs. It is a common feature of Sunday family dinners, perhaps because it requires a fair amount of preparation. The result is well worth the effort, and not only for vegetarians.

6 eggs, beaten
1 tsp salt
4 tsp sesame oil

25g/1oz Chinese dried black mushrooms (page 26)
12g/¹/₂oz cloud ears (page 34)
50g/2oz bean thread noodles
110g/4oz pressed seasoned bean curd
225g/8oz cucumber
3 tbsp groundnut oil [US peanut oil]
1 small onion, sliced
2 tbsp finely chopped fresh ginger
2 tbsp finely chopped garlic
3 tbsp light soy sauce
2 tbsp whole bean sauce
3 tbsp Shaoxing rice wine or dry sherry
1 tbsp hoisin sauce

In a small bowl, combine the egg, salt, and 2 tsp sesame oil and set aside.

Remove and discard the mushroom stems and finely shred the caps into thin strips. Remove and discard any hard stems from the cloud ears. Set aside. Soak the bean thread noodles in warm water for 15 minutes. Drain well and set aside. Cut the pressed bean curd into thin strips. Peel and seed the cucumbers and cut them into thin strips.

Heat a wok or large frying pan over high heat until it is hot. Add 1¹/₂ tbsp of the oil and, when it is very hot and slightly smoking, turn the heat down to moderate. Add the egg mixture and stir-fry for a few minutes or until the egg has barely scrambled. Remove the egg from the wok and drain on paper towels.

Wipe the wok clean and reheat it. When it is hot, add the remaining 1¹/₂ tbsp of oil. When it is very hot and slightly smoking, quickly add the onion, ginger and garlic and stir-fry for 2 minutes. Then add the mushrooms, cloud ears, pressed bean curd, bean thread noodles, and cucumbers and stir-fry for 2 more minutes. Add the soy sauce, bean sauce, Shaoxing rice wine or dry sherry, hoisin sauce, and remaining sesame oil and continue to stir-fry for 3 min-

Previous page: *Stir-Fried Silk Squash with Garlic; Crispy Seaweed* utes. Finally, add the cooked eggs and stir-fry for 1 minute. Turn onto a serving platter and serve at once.

VEGETARIAN DUMPLINGS

———————— SHOPPING LIST ————————

225g/8oz wonton wrappers [US wonton skins], 225g/8oz Chinese white cabbage (pak choi or bok choy), 225g/8oz Peking cabbage (Chinese leaves or Napa cabbage), fresh or frozen peas, Sichuan preserved vegetable, garlic, spring onions [US scallions]

———————— STAPLES ————————

groundnut oil [US peanut oil], Shaoxing rice wine or dry sherry, dark soy sauce, sugar, sesame oil, Chicken Stock, chilli oil, white rice vinegar

———————— PREPARATION TIME ————————

1 hour

———————— COOKING TIME ————————

5 minutes

SERVES 4–6 (MAKES 35–40 DUMPLINGS)

Dumplings in any form are universally popular in China. In northern China, they are a specialty in restaurants and a staple in home kitchens. To this day, making them is a family affair and social occasion, with Sunday mornings, before the big lunch, devoted to their preparation. Dumplings in general may be shallow-fried, boiled, poached or steamed. One very popular way to make them is simply to poach them in hot water or broth and then dip them in a mixture which you concoct yourself.

In China, dumplings are made with finely chopped pork or vegetarian-style as in this recipe. Both versions are very satisfying. The Chinese preserved vegetable adds a very tasty flavor to the dumplings. Make your own dipping sauce with chilli oil, dark soy sauce and Chinese white rice vinegar or cider vinegar. In this version, I have used wonton wrappers which are simple to use, light, and easily available.

225g/8oz wonton wrappers [US wonton skins]
1.2 litres/2 pints/5 cups Chicken Stock (page 128) or water

———————— FILLING ————————

1 tbsp groundnut oil [US peanut oil] or vegetable oil
2 tbsp finely chopped garlic
225g/8oz Chinese white cabbage (pak choi or bok choy) finely chopped
225g/8oz Peking cabbage (Chinese leaves or Napa cabbage), finely chopped
110g/4oz/¼ cup fresh or frozen peas, thawed
25g/1oz Sichuan preserved vegetable, thoroughly rinsed and finely chopped
2 tbsp Shaoxing rice wine or dry sherry
1 tbsp dark soy sauce
2 tsp sugar
1 tsp sesame oil
1 tsp salt
½ tsp freshly ground black pepper
2 tbsp finely chopped spring onions [US scallions]

———————— GARNISH ————————

small bowl of chilli oil (page 23)
small bowl of white rice vinegar
small bowl of dark soy sauce
spring onions [US scallions], chopped

For the filling, heat a wok over high heat until it is hot, then add the oil. When the oil is hot and slightly smoking, add the garlic and stir-fry for 20 seconds. Then add both kinds of cabbage, peas, and the preserved vegetables and continue to stir-fry for 1 minute. Add the rice wine, dark soy sauce, sugar, sesame oil, salt, and pepper. Continue to cook for 3 minutes, and then add the spring onions. Cook for 3 minutes more or until most of the liquid has evaporated. Put the mixture in a bowl and allow it to cool completely. Put about 1 tbsp of filling in the center of each wonton wrapper and then fold it in half. Moisten the edges with water and pinch together with

171

KEN HOM'S CHINESE KITCHEN

your fingers. Pleat around the edge, pinching to seal well. Transfer the finished dumplings to a floured tray and keep covered with a damp cloth until you have filled all the dumplings in this way.

Bring the stock or water to a simmer in a large pot. Add the dumplings and poach for 1 minute or until they float to the top. Continue to simmer them for 2 minutes. Using a slotted spoon, transfer to a platter. Arrange three small bowls, each containing white rice vinegar, chilli oil, and dark soy sauce, at each place setting. The idea is to let each person concoct their own dipping sauce by mixing these three things exactly to their taste. Garnish the dumplings with spring onions and serve immediately.

AUBERGINE WITH SESAME SAUCE

──────── SHOPPING LIST ────────
700g/1¹/2lb Chinese aubergine [US Chinese eggplant] or regular variety, garlic, fresh coriander [US cilantro]

──────── STAPLES ────────
sesame paste, Sichuan peppercorns, sesame and chilli oils, sugar, chilli bean paste

──────── PREPARATION TIME ────────
15 minutes

──────── COOKING TIME ────────
35–50 minutes
SERVES 4

This simple aubergine dish is easy to make and is delicious as a first course or when served as part of a meal. I found it often in the street markets of Beijing and Chengdu. Try to obtain the smaller, more delicately flavored Chinese aubergines, if you can. I deviate from the traditional Chinese method of steaming the aubergines and instead prefer roasting. The roasting is, in fact, a steaming process which leaves the aubergines sweet, tender, and moist, and increases their receptivity to the classic sesame sauce. As a tasty

first course it is served cold, and it may be made hours in advance; the sauce, however, should not be mixed with the cooked aubergines until you are ready to serve the dish.

700g/1¹/2lb Chinese aubergine [US Chinese eggplant] or regular variety

──────── SESAME SAUCE ────────
2 tbsp sesame paste
¹/2 tsp roasted and ground Sichuan peppercorns (page 85)
2 tbsp sesame oil
2 tsp chilli oil (page 23)
2 tsp sugar
1 tbsp finely chopped garlic
1¹/2 tsp salt
2 tsp chilli bean paste
2 tbsp finely chopped fresh coriander [US cilantro]

Pre-heat the oven to 200°C/400°F/gas mark 6. Put the aubergines in a roasting pan and bake for about 35 minutes if the Chinese variety or 50 minutes if the larger, regular variety. They should be charred outside and tender inside. Allow to cool completely and then peel them. Set them aside until you are ready to use them.

When you are ready to serve the dish, mix all the sauce ingredients together with the cooked aubergines and mash. Mix well. Serve at once, at room temperature.

BEIJING PAN-FRIED BEAN CURD

──────── SHOPPING LIST ────────
450g/1lb firm bean curd, egg, garlic, fresh ginger, spring onions [US scallions]

──────── STAPLES ────────
Shaoxing rice wine or dry sherry, cornflour [US cornstarch], whole bean sauce, chilli bean paste, sugar, Chicken Stock, sesame oil

──────── PREPARATION TIME ────────
5 minutes

172

15 minutes

SERVES 4

This is a delightful dish from Peking. The bean curd is coated with a batter, pan-fried slowly, and then braised over low heat until all the savory liquid is absorbed as into a sponge. Bean curd's versatility makes it adaptable to any seasoning. If you are a pure vegetarian, simply use wine or water instead of stock.

This goes well with noodles or rice and can be served as a vegetable accompaniment to any number of meat or fish dishes.

450g/1lb firm bean curd
cornflour [US cornstarch], for dusting
1 egg, beaten
300ml/10fl oz/1 cup groundnut oil [US peanut oil]
or vegetable oil
2 tbsp coarsely chopped garlic
2 tbsp finely chopped fresh ginger
3 tbsp spring onions [US scallions], white part only,
finely chopped
3 tbsp Shaoxing rice wine or dry sherry
2 tbsp whole bean sauce
1 tbsp chilli bean paste
2 tsp sugar
1 tsp salt
300ml/10fl oz/1¼ cups Chicken Stock (page 128)
or water
2 tsp sesame oil

Gently cut the bean curd into 5 x 2.5 x 1cm/2 x 1 x ½in pieces. Drain on paper towels for 10 minutes.

Dust the bean curd pieces with cornflour, then dip into the beaten egg to coat well.

Heat a wok until it is hot, then add the oil. When the oil is hot and slightly smoking add the bean curd and pan-fry for 4–5 minutes until golden.

Turn the pieces over and pan-fry the other side. Drain well on paper towels. Discard all the oil except for 1½ tbsp.

Reheat the wok and reserved oil over high heat until the oil is hot and slightly smoking. Add the garlic and ginger and stir-fry for 1 minute. Add the spring onions and stir-fry for another 30 seconds.

Return the bean curd to the wok, then add all the remaining ingredients and cook over low heat for 5 minutes or until the bean curd has absorbed all of the liquid. Transfer to a serving platter and serve at once.

BRAISED STUFFED BEAN CURD

SHOPPING LIST

450g/1lb firm bean curd, 110g/4oz raw prawns [US shrimp], fatty minced [US ground] pork, egg, spring onions [US scallions], fresh ginger, fresh coriander [US cilantro]

STAPLES

cornflour [US cornstarch], light and dark soy sauces, sesame oil, Shaoxing rice wine or dry sherry, sugar, oyster sauce, groundnut oil [US peanut oil], Chicken Stock

PREPARATION TIME

30 minutes

COOKING TIME

15 minutes

SERVES 4

Stuffed bean curd is one of the most delicious ways to enjoy this nutritious but bland food. The stuffing ingredients transform the plainness of the bean curd into a flavorful treat. The process is not as difficult as it appears. Each square of beancurd is cut into quarters, carefully hollowed out and then stuffed with the savory paste. The squares are pan-fried and then slowly braised, making them succulent and full of flavor.

450g/1lb firm bean curd
cornflour [US cornstarch], for dusting

─────── FILLING ───────

110g/4oz raw prawns [US shrimp], peeled
and deveined
90g/3oz fatty, minced [US ground] pork
1 egg white
1 tsp cornflour [US cornstarch]
1 tsp salt
1/4 tsp freshly ground white pepper
1 tbsp light soy sauce
1 tsp dark soy sauce
1 tsp sesame oil
2 tsp Shaoxing rice wine or dry sherry
1 tsp sugar
1 tsp finely chopped fresh ginger
1 tbsp finely chopped spring onions [US scallions]

─────── FOR FRYING ───────

3 tbsp groundnut oil [US peanut oil]

─────── SAUCE ───────

300ml/10fl oz/1¼ cups Chicken Stock (page 128)
3 tbsp oyster sauce
1/2 tsp salt
1/4 tsp freshly ground white pepper
2 tsp cornflour [US cornstarch] blended with
1 tbsp water
2 tbsp finely chopped fresh coriander [US cilantro]

Cut each bean curd square into quarters. With a paring knife, hollow out the squares, leaving a 5mm/¼in wall all the way around. Drain the bean curd on paper towels. Reserve the hollowed out bean curd; mash it with a fork and set aside. Next prepare the filling. Coarsely chop the prawns. Put the prawns into a bowl with the rest of the filling ingredients and the reserved mashed bean curd. Mix together very well.

Dust the inside of the bean curd squares lightly with cornflour and gently fill them with the prawn mixture.

Heat a wok or large frying pan over high heat until it is hot. Add the oil and, when it is very hot and slightly smoking, add the stuffed bean curd, filling side down. Turn the heat to medium and gently pan-fry, turning the bean curd squares until they are lightly browned on each side. Pour off any excess oil. Add any remaining filling and all the sauce ingredients except the cornflour mixture and coriander. Bring to a simmer, then cover and cook for 5 minutes. Add the cornflour mixture and cook for 2 minutes more. Add the coriander and cook for a final minute. Serve at once.

BEAN CURD CASSEROLE

─────── SHOPPING LIST ───────
450g/1lb fresh bean curd, Chinese dried black mushrooms, dried shrimp, fresh ginger, garlic, spring onions [US scallions]

─────── STAPLES ───────
groundnut oil [US peanut oil], Shaoxing rice wine or dry sherry, oyster sauce, dark and light soy sauces, sugar, Chicken Stock, sesame oil

─────── PREPARATION TIME ───────
20 minutes

─────── COOKING TIME ───────
20 minutes
SERVES 4

Once bean curd is fried, its texture changes from slippery and soft to tender and spongy with a light crispiness. Braised with Chinese black mushrooms and dried shrimp, fried bean curd readily takes on an appetizing and savory flavor. This is the type of semi-vegetarian dish which so many Chinese are fond of. It is easy to make and very nutritious. It also reheats well, making it suitable for preparation in advance.

450g/1lb fresh bean curd
50g/2oz Chinese dried black mushrooms (page 26)
25g/1oz dried shrimp

240ml/8 fl oz/1 cup groundnut oil [US peanut oil]
1 tbsp finely chopped fresh ginger
6 garlic cloves, lightly crushed
3 tbsp finely shredded spring onions [US scallions]

—————— SAUCE ——————

1¹/₂ tbsp Shaoxing rice wine or dry sherry
3 tbsp oyster sauce
1 tbsp dark soy sauce
1 tbsp light soy sauce
2 tsp sugar
¹/₂ tsp freshly ground black pepper
240ml/8fl oz/1 cup Chicken Stock (page 128)
2 tsp sesame oil

Drain and rinse the bean curd in cold water. Blot it dry with paper towels and cut into 1cm/¹/₂in cubes. Let them drain further on paper towels.

Remove and discard the mushroom stems and cut the caps into quarters.

Rinse the dried shrimp and soak in cold water for 5 minutes. Drain well and set aside.

Heat a wok or large frying pan over high heat until it is hot. Add the oil and, when it is very hot and slightly smoking, add the bean curd cubes. Fry until they are lightly brown on all sides. Remove with a slotted spoon and drain on paper towels.

Pour off most of the oil, leaving about 1¹/₂ tbsp in the wok. Reheat the oil, then add the ginger, garlic, and spring onions and stir-fry them for about 2 minutes. Add the mushrooms, dried shrimp, fried bean curd, and all the sauce ingredients except the sesame oil. Bring the mixture to the boil. Turn the heat down to a simmer, cover, and cook for 10 minutes. Add the sesame oil, give the mixture a few stirs, and turn onto a warm serving platter. Serve at once.

BEAN CURD-CHICKEN-SALT FISH CASSEROLE

—————— SHOPPING LIST ——————

450g/1lb fresh bean curd, 175g/6oz boneless, skinless chicken thighs, dried or preserved salted fish, garlic, fresh ginger, spring onions [US scallions]

—————— STAPLES ——————

groundnut oil [US peanut oil], Shaoxing rice wine or dry sherry, oyster sauce, dark and light soy sauces, sugar, Chicken Stock, sesame oil

—————— PREPARATION TIME ——————

20 minutes

—————— COOKING TIME ——————

20 minutes

SERVES 4

This is one of my favorite home-cooked dishes. It always transports me back to my mother's kitchen.

As prosaic and homely as it is, it has, nonetheless, come to be in high demand in restaurants throughout Hong Kong. I believe its popularity has much to do with nostalgia. Because so many wives are now working outside the home, and there is consequently much more dining out, people long for the 'home cooking' of their childhood. Few things are more satisfying than the enjoyment of this equivalent of, as it were, 'mom's apple pie'.

The bean curd in this casserole takes on the flavors of the various seasonings and blends in nicely with the equally congenial chicken. The recipe and technique are quite typically Chinese; the meal itself is both delicious and very nutritious. It goes well with plain rice.

450g/1lb fresh bean curd
240ml/8fl oz/1 cup groundnut oil [US peanut oil]
2 tbsp thinly sliced garlic

175

3 tbsp finely shredded fresh ginger
175g/6oz boneless, skinless chicken thighs,
coarsely chopped
3 tbsp finely chopped spring onions [US scallions]
3 tbsp salted fish, soaked and finely chopped

─────────── SAUCE ───────────
1¹/₂ tbsp Shaoxing rice wine or dry sherry
1¹/₂ tbsp oyster sauce
2 tsp dark soy sauce
2 tsp light soy sauce
2 tsp sugar
¹/₂ tsp freshly ground black pepper
120ml/4fl oz/¹/₂ cup Chicken Stock (page 128) or
water
2 tsp sesame oil

─────────── GARNISH ───────────
chopped spring onions [US scallions]

Drain the bean curd and rinse in cold water. Blot it dry with paper towels and cut into 1cm/¹/₂in cubes.

Heat a wok or large frying pan over high heat until it is hot. Add the oil and, when it is very hot and slightly smoking, add the bean curd cubes. Shallow-fry until they are lightly brown on all sides. Remove with a slotted spoon and drain on paper towels.

Pour off most of the oil, leaving about 1¹/₂ tbsp in the wok. Reheat the oil, then add the garlic, ginger, chicken, and spring onions and stir-fry them for about 1 minute. Add the salted fish and continue to stir-fry for 1 minute. Then add all the sauce ingredients except for the sesame oil. Bring the mixture to the boil. Pour it into a clay pot or casserole and add the bean curd. Cover and cook over moderate heat for 10 minutes. Remove from the heat and add the sesame oil. Give the mixture a few stirs and serve directly from the clay pot or casserole or, alternatively, turn onto a warm serving platter. Garnish with chopped spring onions and serve at once.

STIR-FRIED BEAN SPROUTS

─────────── SHOPPING LIST ───────────
450g/1lb fresh bean sprouts, spring onions [US scallions], garlic

─────────── STAPLES ───────────
groundnut oil [US peanut oil], light soy sauce, Chinese white rice vinegar, sesame oil

─────────── PREPARATION TIME ───────────
10 minutes

─────────── COOKING TIME ───────────
5 minutes
SERVES 4

Mung beans provide most of the bean sprouts consumed in China. The soybean is also sprouted but its sprouts are not as tender as those of the mung bean. Because mung beans are grown everywhere in China except the coldest and driest areas, their sprouts are a common item in the daily diet. In the West, sprouts were not cultivated until very recently, but they have been a staple in Asian cuisine for centuries. They are a nutritious food with many vitamins and minerals, but their popularity derives mainly from their sweet, nutty-flavored crunchiness and their congeniality with other foods. This last feature is why they are so commonly used in stir-fries. Use fresh, not canned, sprouts for the authentic taste experience. Do not overcook them to the point of losing their textural bite. Always choose the best and freshest sprouts. Serve this vegetable dish instead of a salad or as an accompaniment to meat dishes.

450g/1lb fresh bean sprouts
1 tbsp groundnut oil [US peanut oil]
3 spring onions [US scallions], finely shredded
2 tbsp thinly sliced garlic
1 tsp salt
2 tsp light soy sauce
1 tsp Chinese white rice vinegar
1 tsp sesame oil

Pick over the bean sprouts, removing any yellow or dark, soft sprouts. Rinse them several times and drain them well in a colander.

Heat a wok or large frying pan over high heat until it is hot. Add the oil and, when it is very hot and slightly smoking, quickly add the spring onions, garlic and salt and stir-fry for 10 seconds. Then add the bean sprouts and stir-fry for 2 minutes. Add the light soy sauce and stir to mix well. Add the vinegar and give the mixture several good stirs. Finally, add the sesame oil, give the mixture another good stir, put it onto a platter, and serve at once.

CHINESE BROCCOLI WITH OYSTER SAUCE

SHOPPING LIST
450g/1lb Chinese broccoli

STAPLES
oyster sauce, sesame oil, groundnut oil [US peanut oil]

PREPARATION TIME
8 minutes

COOKING TIME
5 minutes
SERVES 4

The robust character of this nutritious vegetable makes a delectable dish when combined with the distinct flavor of oyster sauce. It takes only minutes to prepare and will make a tasty treat with any meal.

450g/1lb Chinese broccoli
3 tbsp oyster sauce
1 tsp sesame oil
2 tsp groundnut oil [US peanut oil]

Trim any hard stems and yellow leaves from the broccoli.

Blanch the broccoli in a large pot of boiling salted water for 5 minutes. Drain well. Cut the broccoli in thirds and arrange on a large platter.

In a small bowl, combine the oyster sauce, and sesame and groundnut oils. Pour this over the broccoli and serve at once.

STIR-FRIED CELERY

SHOPPING LIST
450g/1lb celery, garlic, spring onions [US scallions]

STAPLES
groundnut oil [US peanut oil], Shaoxing rice wine or dry sherry, chilli bean paste, dark soy sauce, sugar, Sichuan peppercorns

PREPARATION TIME
10 minutes

COOKING TIME
10 minutes
SERVES 2–4

Chinese celery is virtually identical to European celery but differs in size. It is less compact and the stalks are thinner. Apparently they are the same species and represent divergent development over 1,500 years. Both have an aromatic flavor and crispy, externally stringy texture. The Chinese celery probably evolved from a wild Asian celery. In China it has a long history of use as a flavoring herb and vegetable, and today, it is one of the most widely grown vegetables.

450g/1lb celery
2 tbsp groundnut oil [US peanut oil]
2 tsp finely chopped garlic
2 tbsp finely chopped spring onions [US scallions]
1 tbsp Shaoxing rice wine or dry sherry
2 tsp chilli bean paste
1 tsp dark soy sauce
2 tsp sugar
1/2 tsp salt
3 tbsp water

177

*2 tsp roasted and ground Sichuan peppercorns
(page 85)*

Trim the base of the celery and all the top leaves. Separate the stalks. With a small, sharp knife, string a few of the tough stalks. Chop the stalks into 2.5cm/1in sections.

Heat a wok or large frying pan over high heat until it is hot. Add the oil and, when it is very hot and slightly smoking, add the garlic and spring onions. Stir-fry for 10 seconds. Then add the celery and continue to stir-fry for 1 minute. Add the rice wine, chilli bean paste, soy sauce, sugar, and salt and continue to stir-fry another minute. Add the water and cook over high heat for 3–4 minutes until the celery is just tender. Sprinkle the mixture with the peppercorns, mix well, pour onto a platter, and serve at once.

HOT AND SOUR CUCUMBER SALAD

—— SHOPPING LIST ——
450g/1lb cucumber, garlic

—— STAPLES ——
groundnut oil [US peanut oil], chilli oil, Chinese white rice vinegar

—— PREPARATION TIME ——
10 minutes

—— COOKING TIME ——
5 minutes
SERVES 4

Cucumbers are an inexpensive and popular vegetable in China. In summertime in northern China they are served cold as a first course. They are especially tasty and refreshing when combined with a spicy and sour flavor. Easy to prepare, they are perfect as a salad or for summer eating.

*450g/1lb cucumber
1 tsp salt
1 tbsp groundnut oil [US peanut oil]
3 garlic cloves, thinly sliced
1 tsp chilli oil (page 23)
2 tbsp Chinese white rice vinegar
1 tsp salt*

Peel the cucumber, halve it, and remove the seeds with a teaspoon. Then cut it into 2.5cm/1in cubes. Sprinkle the cubes with the salt and put in a colander to drain for 20 minutes. Rinse the cucumber cubes in cold running water and blot them dry with paper towels.

Heat a wok or large frying pan over high heat until it is hot. Add the oil and, when it is very hot and slightly smoking, turn the heat low and add the garlic slices. Stir-fry for 1 minute or until they are brown. Remove them from the wok and drain on paper towels.

In a large bowl, combine the chilli oil, vinegar, and salt. Add the cucumber cubes and garlic and toss well. Allow to sit for 5 minutes. Drain well before serving.

PICKLED CUCUMBER SALAD

—— SHOPPING LIST ——
350g/12oz pickling cucumber, fresh red chillies

—— STAPLES ——
sugar, Chinese white rice vinegar, sesame oil

—— PREPARATION TIME ——
10 minutes

—— REFRIGERATION TIME ——
overnight
SERVES 4

In private homes in Taiwan or in Beijing, I have often been served a modest dish of pickled cucumber which it is said helps to stimulate the appetite. It certainly works for me. The dish should be made the night before it is to be served. It is simple to prepare and makes a nice opener for summer meals. Try it also as an accompaniment to meat or vegetarian dishes.

350g/12oz pickling cucumber
1¹/₂ tbsp salt
3 tbsp sugar
2 tbsp Chinese white rice vinegar
3 tbsp sesame oil

———————— GARNISH ————————
2 fresh red chillies, seeded and thinly sliced

Trim the ends of the cucumber and thinly slice it.

In a large bowl, toss the cucumber with the salt and sugar. Cover tightly and refrigerate overnight.

Just before serving, squeeze out all the excess liquid. Then toss the cucumber with the vinegar and sesame oil. Garnish with the sliced red chillies and serve.

LOTUS ROOT SALAD

———————— SHOPPING LIST ————————
225g/8oz fresh lotus root, fresh ginger, spring onions [US scallions]

———————— STAPLES ————————
Chinese white rice vinegar, sugar

———————— PREPARATION TIME ————————
10 minutes

———————— REFRIGERATION TIME ————————
overnight
SERVES 4

This is a delectable, unusual, and exotic dish I learned of from my friend Lillian Rodyn, who traces her roots to Beijing. Lotus root has been aptly described as 'sweet and crisp, totally without any pulpy residue'. Cold dishes are uncom-

mon in Chinese cuisine, but they are very popular in the region of Beijing. Here, lotus root is thinly sliced and simply tossed with a tasty dressing that is itself quickly made. It is an ideal first course for any meal and may also serve as a side dish.

225g/8oz fresh lotus root
3 tbsp finely chopped fresh ginger
6 spring onions [US scallions], finely chopped
3 tbsp Chinese white rice vinegar
2 tsp salt
2 tsp sugar

Peel the lotus root and thinly slice it. In a large bowl, toss the lotus root gently with the remaining ingredients. Serve at once.

STUFFED CHINESE MUSHROOMS

———————— SHOPPING LIST ————————
225g/8oz raw prawns [US shrimp], peeled, 175g/ 6oz pork fat, large Chinese dried black mushrooms, fresh or canned water chestnuts, egg, spring onions [US scallions], fresh coriander [US cilantro], prosciutto (Parma ham)

———————— STAPLES ————————
cornflour [US cornstarch], sesame oil, Shaoxing rice wine or dry sherry, sugar, Chicken Stock, oyster sauce

———————— PREPARATION TIME ————————
35 minutes

———————— COOKING TIME ————————
10 minutes
SERVES

The Chinese are masters in making mushrooms even tastier by stuffing them with a savory paste of prawns. This is particularly true when they use Chinese mushrooms. The secret to the stuffing is the use of pork fat which adds richness to the paste, while the water chestnuts add texture. This is a rich but not heavy treat.

179

18 large Chinese dried black mushrooms (page 26)
3 tbsp cornflour [US cornstarch]

——— FILLING ———

110g/4oz peeled fresh or 150g/5oz canned water
chestnuts (page 92)
225g/8oz raw prawns [US shrimp], peeled
175g/6oz finely chopped pork fat
1 egg white
2 tsp cornflour [US cornstarch]
2 tsp salt
1 tsp freshly ground white pepper
2 tsp sesame oil
1 tbsp Shaoxing rice wine or dry sherry
1 tsp sugar
3 tbsp finely chopped spring onions [US scallions]

——— GARNISH ———

18 leaves fresh coriander [US cilantro]
25g/1oz prosciutto (Parma ham), finely chopped

——— SAUCE ———

150ml/5fl oz/⁵⁄₈ cup Chicken Stock (page 128)
¹⁄₄ tsp salt
¹⁄₄ tsp freshly ground white pepper
2 tsp sesame oil
1 tsp cornflour [US cornstarch] blended with
2 tsp water
1 tbsp oyster sauce

Dust the inside of each mushroom lightly with cornflour and set aside. Coarsely chop the prawns. Put the water chestnuts and prawns into a bowl with the rest of the filling ingredients and mix together very well.

Spoon a small layer of filling onto each mushroom cap. Use the spoon to smooth the filling. Place one coriander leaf on top of each cap and sprinkle with ham. Arrange the stuffed mushrooms on a heatproof plate.

Set up a steamer or put a rack into a wok or deep pan and add 5cm/2in of water. Bring the water to the boil over a high heat. Carefully lower the plate into the steamer or onto the rack. Turn the heat to low and cover tightly. Steam gently for 8 minutes. (You may have to do this in two batches.)

When the mushrooms are nearly done, heat a wok or large frying pan over high heat until it is hot. Put all the sauce ingredient, except the cornflour mixture in the wok and bring to a boil. Cook for 1 minute, then add the cornflour mixture. When the sauce has come to the boil again, pour it over the mushrooms and serve the dish immediately.

MUSHROOM BEAN CURD CASSEROLE

——— SHOPPING LIST ———

450g/1lb bean curd, Chinese dried black mushrooms, fresh ginger, spring onions [US scallions]

——— STAPLES ———

groundnut oil [US peanut oil], Shaoxing rice wine or dry sherry, sugar, light and dark soy sauces, sesame oil

——— PREPARATION TIME ———

15 minutes

——— COOKING TIME ———

18 minutes

SERVES 4

This is a simple vegetarian dish that builds upon the nutrition of subtle, fragile bean curd. Chinese dried black mushrooms, with their rich, smoky flavor, give the name and wonderful taste to this bean curd dish. The bean curd in this recipe is not deep-fried, but gently pan-fried so the center stays soft and custard-like. A special attraction is that this recipe is easy to reheat and even improves the second day.

450g/1lb bean curd
50g/2oz Chinese dried black mushrooms (page 26)
450ml/15fl oz/1⁵⁄₈ cups boiling water
2 tbsp groundnut oil [US peanut oil]

1 tbsp finely chopped fresh ginger
3 tbsp finely chopped spring onions [US scallions]
2 tbsp Shaoxing rice wine or dry sherry
2 tsp sugar
1 tbsp light soy sauce
2 tbsp dark soy sauce
1 tsp salt
1 tbsp sesame oil

Cut the bean curd into 5cm/2in cubes and drain well on paper towels.

Soak the mushrooms in the boiling water for 1 hour. (Place an empty plate on top of the mushrooms; this will keep them immersed in the liquid.) Then drain them and squeeze out the excess liquid. Reserve the mushroom soaking water. Remove and discard the stems and finely shred the caps into thin strips.

Heat a wok or large frying pan over high heat until it is hot. Add the oil and, when it is very hot and slightly smoking, add the bean curd, ginger, and spring onions. Turn down the heat and slowly pan-fry for 2 minutes. Then add the rice wine or sherry, sugar, soy sauces, salt, shredded mushrooms, and reserved mushroom liquid. Turn the heat down to a simmer and cover. Cook for 15 minutes. Add the sesame oil and serve at once.

PEANUTS WITH FIVE SPICE

──────── SHOPPING LIST ────────
225g/8oz shelled raw peanuts, garlic, fresh ginger

──────── STAPLES ────────
groundnut oil [US peanut oil], sugar, five spice powder, Sichuan peppercorns, hot chilli powder

──────── PREPARATION TIME ────────
10 minutes

──────── COOKING TIME ────────
5 minutes

SERVES 4

This is a fragrant and savory way to raise nuts to new heights. Serve them as a snack with drinks or as an easy addition to any meal. Although this recipe can be made ahead of time, it is best eaten within a day or two of preparation.

225g/8oz/1 cup shelled raw peanuts
300ml/10fl oz/1¹/₄ cups groundnut oil [US peanut oil] or vegetable oil
2 tbsp finely chopped garlic
1 tbsp finely chopped fresh ginger
1 tbsp sugar
2 tsp five spice powder
2 tsp salt
1 tsp roasted ground Sichuan peppercorns (page 85)
1 tsp chilli powder

Remove any loose skins from the peanuts.

Heat a wok over high heat until it is hot, then add the oil. When the oil is hot and slightly smoking, fry the peanuts for 2 minutes or until they are lightly brown. Remove and drain well on a baking sheet lined with paper towels.

Drain most of the oil from the wok (this oil can be saved for future use), leaving just 1¹/₂ tbsp. Reheat the wok and oil and, when it is hot and smoking slightly, add the garlic and ginger. Stir-fry for 1 minute. Then add the rest of the ingredients and return the peanuts to the wok. Continue to stir-fry for 2 minutes, stirring to mix well. Turn onto a baking sheet and allow to cool before serving.

FRIED STUFFED PEPPERS

──────── SHOPPING LIST ────────
700–900g/1¹/₂-2lb red, yellow or green sweet peppers or a mixture of the three colors, 225g/8oz minced [US ground] pork, fresh or canned water chestnuts, winter bamboo shoots, Chinese dried black mushrooms, egg, spring onions [US scallions]

181

cornflour [US cornstarch], groundnut oil [US peanut oil], sesame oil, Shaoxing rice wine or dry sherry

PREPARATION TIME

20 minutes

COOKING TIME

15 minutes

SERVES 4

Red or green sweet peppers are especially delicious when they are stuffed. Prepared as such, these snacks are featured on many *dim sum* menus in southern China. Easy to make, they also reheat well. The quick pan-frying before serving gives the peppers a crusty, brownish top. They make an attractive dish for a light lunch or supper.

700–900g/1¹/₂-2lb red, yellow, or green peppers or a mixture of the three

STUFFING

175g/6oz peeled fresh or canned water chestnuts (page 92)
50g/2oz winter bamboo shoots
50g/2oz Chinese dried black mushrooms (page 26)
225g/8oz minced [US ground] pork
1 egg white
2 tsp cornflour [US cornstarch]
2 tsp salt
1 tsp freshly ground black pepper
2 tsp sesame oil
1¹/₂ tbsp Shaoxing rice wine or dry sherry
1 tsp sugar
3 tbsp finely chopped spring onions [US scallions]

FOR FRYING

cornflour [US cornstarch], for dusting
350ml/12fl oz groundnut oil [US peanut oil]

Halve the peppers and remove the seeds and pulp. Next, prepare the stuffing. Coarsely chop the water chestnuts. Finely chop the bamboo

shoots. Remove and discard the mushroom stems and finely chop the caps.

Put the water chestnuts, bamboo shoots, mushrooms, and pork into a bowl with the rest of the stuffing ingredients, and mix together very well. Dust the pepper halves lightly with cornflour and fill them with the stuffing.

Heat a wok or large frying pan over high heat until it is hot. Add the oil and, when it is very hot and slightly smoking, add the peppers, stuffing side down. Fry until they are lightly browned, turning occasionally. Drain them well on paper towels and serve immediately.

STIR-FRIED SILK SQUASH WITH GARLIC

SHOPPING LIST

700g/1¹/₂lb silk squash, garlic, spring onions [US scallions]

STAPLES

groundnut oil [US peanut oil], oyster sauce, Chicken Stock, sesame oil

PREPARATION TIME

10 minutes

COOKING TIME

10 minutes

SERVES 4

This is an especially savory way to enjoy this unusual vegetable, which is sometimes called 'Chinese okra' even though it is not at all related to okra. When cooked it has a soft, pleasant texture and readily absorbs the garlic and oyster sauce flavors. Serve it as a simple vegetable dish with either a meat or poultry dish and rice for a complete meal.

700g/1¹/₂lb silk squash
1¹/₂ tbsp groundnut oil [US peanut oil]
3 garlic cloves, finely sliced

1 tsp salt
2 tbsp finely chopped spring onions [US scallions]
2 tbsp oyster sauce
2 tbsp Chicken Stock (page 128) or water
2 tsp sesame oil

Peel the squash and roll-cut it into 5cm/2in segments.

Heat a wok or large frying pan over high heat until it is hot. Add the oil and, when it is very hot and slightly smoking, add the garlic and salt. Stir-fry for 15 seconds. Then quickly add the squash and spring onions. Stir-fry for 3–4 minutes. Add the oyster sauce and chicken stock or water and continue to stir-fry for a few more minutes until the squash is cooked and soft. Drizzle with the sesame oil, turn onto a platter, and serve at once.

CRISPY 'SEAWEED'

SHOPPING LIST

1.1kg/2¹/₂lb Chinese white cabbage (pak choi or bok choy), pine nuts

STAPLES

groundnut oil [US peanut oil], sugar

PREPARATION TIME
20 minutes

COOKING TIME
5 minutes
SERVES 4

This is one of the most popular dishes among frequent Chinese restaurant diners in the U.K. I am not sure who was the first to bring this unique north-eastern Chinese dish to Britain; suffice it to say, however, that not 'seaweed' but cabbage is being used. A special type of seaweed, which is indeed used in China, is unfortunately not yet available in the West. The adaptability of Chinese cuisine is once again demonstrated in this dish: if the original ingredients are not available, then technique and ingenuity will overcome the deficiency. This dish is delicious and easy to make, and, speaking of adaptability, the recipe can also be tried with spinach leaves.

1.1kg/2¹/₂lb Chinese white cabbage (pak choi or bok choy)
900ml/1¹/₂ pints/3³/₄ cups groundnut oil [US peanut oil] or vegetable oil
1 tsp salt
2 tsp sugar
50g/2oz/¹/₄ cup pine nuts, lightly roasted

Preheat the oven to 130°C/250°F/gas mark ¹/₂. Separate the stalks from the stem of the cabbage and cut the green leaves from the white stalks. Save the stalks: you can stir-fry them with garlic (see recipe page 182) or use them for soup. Wash the green leaves in several changes of cold water. Drain them thoroughly in a colander and spin them dry in a salad spinner. Roll the leaves tightly and finely shred them. Lay them out on a baking sheet and put them in the oven for 20 minutes to dry. Remove from the oven and allow to cool. (This can be done the day before.) Heat a wok over high heat until it is hot, then add the oil. When the oil is hot and slightly smoking, deep-fry the cabbage in two or three batches. When it turns deep green, in about 30 seconds, remove it immediately and drain well on paper towels. Allow to cool.

Toss the crispy greens in salt and sugar. Top with the pine nuts and serve.

SPICY SPINACH SALAD

SHOPPING LIST
700g/1¹/₂lb fresh spinach, fresh ginger, spring onions [US scallions]

STAPLES
light soy sauce, sugar, sesame oil, Chinese white rice vinegar, chilli oil

183

——— PREPARATION TIME ———

5 minutes

——— COOKING TIME ———

5 minutes

SERVES 4

Summer in Sichuan province, with its hot, humid weather that goes on and on, always reminds me of my childhood summers in Chicago. Those who could, ran for relief to the lakes and rivers or at least sought out some shade. As in Chicago, so in Sichuan. In such weather, people eat light meals, especially salads such as this one. It is a delicious alternative to a lettuce salad and, being light and lively, makes a perfect accompaniment to grilled foods during the hot summer months.

700g/1¹/₂lb fresh spinach
2 tsp finely chopped fresh ginger
3 tbsp spring onions [US scallions], white part only, finely chopped
2 tbsp light soy sauce
2 tsp sugar
2 tsp sesame oil
1 tbsp white rice vinegar
1 tsp chilli oil (page 23)

Wash the spinach thoroughly. Remove all the stems, leaving just the leaves. In a small bowl, combine the ginger, spring onions, soy sauce, sugar, sesame oil, vinegar, and chilli oil. Mix well and set aside.

Blanch the spinach in a large pot of boiling salted water for just 2 minutes so that it has barely wilted. Remove and drain immediately. Add the sauce mixture to the spinach and toss well to coat the leaves thoroughly.

Transfer the spinach to a plate and pour off any excess liquid. Serve warm or cold.

STIR-FRIED SPINACH WITH SHRIMP PASTE

——— SHOPPING LIST ———

700g/1¹/₂lb fresh spinach, garlic, fresh ginger

——— STAPLES ———

shrimp paste, Shaoxing rice wine or dry sherry, sugar, groundnut oil [US peanut oil]

——— PREPARATION TIME ———

15 minutes

——— COOKING TIME ———

10 minutes

SERVES 4

When shrimp paste is used with other seasonings it does not have a 'fishy' taste, but becomes very aromatic. Paired with fresh spinach, the result is a most delectable and exotic vegetable dish. Since shrimp paste has an assertive punch, it must be used judiciously. However, a small amount can transform an ordinary stir-fry into a special treat. This dish is quick and easy, as well as being a different way to enjoy spinach.

700g/1¹/₂lb fresh spinach
2 tsp shrimp paste
1 tbsp Shaoxing rice wine or dry sherry
1 tsp sugar
1 tbsp groundnut oil [US peanut oil]
5 garlic cloves, lightly crushed
1 tbsp finely shredded fresh ginger

Wash the spinach thoroughly. Remove all the stems, leaving just the leaves. In a small bowl, combine the shrimp paste, Shaoxing rice wine or dry sherry and sugar. Mix well and set aside. Heat a wok or large frying-pan over high heat until it is hot. Add the oil and, when it is very hot and slightly smoking, add the garlic and ginger. Stir-fry for 1 minute or until the garlic is lightly browned. Then add the shrimp paste mixture and spinach. Stir-fry for about 2 minutes to coat the spinach leaves thoroughly with the oil, garlic, ginger, and shrimp paste mixture. When the spinach has wilted to about one-third of its original size, continue to stir-fry for another 4 minutes. Transfer the spinach to a plate and pour off any excess liquid. Serve hot or cold.

MIXED GREEN VEGETABLES

——— SHOPPING LIST ———
450g/1lb Peking cabbage (Chinese leaves or Napa cabbage), 350g/12oz Chinese white cabbage (pak choi or bok choy), 275g/10oz Shanghai pak choi, garlic

——— STAPLES ———
Chicken Stock, cornflour [US cornstarch], groundnut oil [US peanut oil]

——— PREPARATION TIME ———
10 minutes

——— COOKING TIME ———
5 minutes
SERVES 4

Vegetarian dishes are common throughout China. Historic religious influences and rituals played a part, but the availability of so many different green vegetables had a practical influence. Vegetables lend themselves to various modes of preparation and preservation, while retaining their essential nutrients and distinct characteristics. Peking cabbage, for example, was enjoyed pickled as well as fresh. Chinese white cabbage, now widely available in the West, is another popular vegetable of which this recipe uses two varieties. Here the vegetables are first stir-fried, then slowly braised in chicken stock (you can use water), and finally the stock is reduced and thickened with a little cornflour. A simple recipe but a delicious way to experience Chinese vegetables.

1¹/₂ tbsp groundnut oil [US peanut oil] or vegetable oil
6 garlic cloves, crushed
1¹/₂ tsp salt
¹/₂ tsp freshly ground white pepper
450g/1lb Peking cabbage (Chinese leaves or Napa cabbage), cut into 5cm/2in pieces widthways
200ml/7fl oz/⁷/₈ cup Chicken Stock (page 128) or water
350g/12oz Chinese White cabbage (pak choi or bok choy), cut into 5cm/2in pieces widthways
275g/10oz Shanghai pak choi, split in half
1 tsp cornflour [US cornstarch] blended with 2 tsp water

Heat a wok over high heat until it is hot, then add the oil. When the oil is hot and slightly smoking, add the garlic, salt and pepper. Stir-fry for 20 seconds. Add the Peking cabbage and stock and continue to stir-fry for 2 minutes. Add the Chinese white cabbage and Shanghai pak choi and stir-fry for another 2 minutes. Then turn the heat down, cover, and simmer for 8 minutes.

When the vegetables are cooked, remove them to a platter. Turn the heat to high and add the cornflour mixture to thicken the sauce. Cook for 30 seconds. Pour this sauce over the vegetables and serve at once.

RICE AND NOODLES

BRAISED NOODLES WITH BEAN SPROUTS AND HAM

SHOPPING LIST

450g/1lb dried or fresh wheat or egg noodles, 450g/1lb fresh bean sprouts, prosciutto (Parma ham), lean smoked bacon or cooked ham, garlic, spring onions [US scallions], fresh coriander [US cilantro]

STAPLES

Chicken Stock, dark and light soy sauces, Shaoxing rice wine or dry sherry, whole bean sauce, sugar, sesame oil

PREPARATION TIME

15 minutes

COOKING TIME

10 minutes

SERVES 4

Typical of many Chinese noodle dishes made at home or found in countless food stalls throughout China, this quick, savory plate is easy to make. And it is, if not the ultimate, then certainly the optimal fast food.

450g/1lb dried or fresh wheat or egg noodles
sesame oil
450g/1lb fresh bean sprouts
50g/2oz shredded prosciutto (Parma ham), lean smoked bacon or cooked ham

SAUCE

350ml/12fl oz/1¹/₂ cups Chicken Stock (page 128)
2 tbsp dark soy sauce
1 tbsp light soy sauce
2 tbsp Shaoxing rice wine or dry sherry
2 tbsp whole bean sauce
1¹/₂ tbsp finely chopped garlic
3 tbsp finely chopped spring onions [US scallions]
1 tsp sugar
1 tsp salt
¹/₂ tsp freshly ground white pepper
2 tsp sesame oil

GARNISH

3 tbsp finely chopped fresh coriander [US cilantro]
2 tbsp finely chopped spring onions [US scallions], green part only

If you are using fresh noodles, cook them for 3–5 minutes in a large pot of boiling water. If you are using dried noodles, cook them in boiling water for 4–5 minutes. Then immerse them in cold water, drain them thoroughly, and toss them with some sesame oil.

Put them aside until you are ready to use them. Now prepare the bean sprouts. I prefer to remove both ends of the bean sprouts as I think this gives them a cleaner look and taste. Cut the ham or bacon into 5cm/2in shreds.

Heat a wok or large pot. Add all the sauce ingredients, except the sesame oil, and bring to a simmer. Add the cooked noodles and stir to mix them well with the sauce. Then turn the heat to high and add the bean sprouts, sesame oil, and ham or bacon. Continue to stir-fry for 3 minutes or until the noodles are thoroughly heated. Toss them with fresh coriander and spring onions and mix well. Turn them onto a warm serving platter and serve at once.

STIR-FRIED RICE NOODLES WITH PRAWNS

SHOPPING LIST

225g/8oz rice noodles, rice vermicelli or rice sticks, 225g/8oz raw prawns [US shrimp], fresh red or green chillies, fresh or canned water chestnuts, garlic, fresh ginger, spring onions [US scallions]

STAPLES

groundnut oil [US peanut oil], light soy sauce, Shaoxing rice wine or dry sherry, Chicken Stock

PREPARATION TIME

20 minutes

COOKING TIME
10 minutes
SERVES 4

Rice noodles are a perfect alternative to egg noodles, as they need little cooking and combine well with other foods. Instead of blanching the noodles before stir-frying, all that is required is a bit of soaking. They make a perfect quick and easy dish that is right for these busy times. Here I have combined them with prawns, which also cook quickly and make a prosaic dish something very special.

225g/8oz rice noodles, rice vermicelli or rice sticks
110g/4oz fresh red or green chillies
225g/8oz peeled fresh or canned water chestnuts
(page 92)
2 tbsp groundnut oil [US peanut oil]
1 tbsp finely chopped garlic
2 tsp finely chopped fresh ginger
3 tbsp finely shredded spring onions [US scallions]
225g/8oz peeled raw prawns [US shrimp]
1 tsp salt
1/2 tsp freshly ground white pepper
2 tbsp light soy sauce
1 1/2 tbsp Shaoxing rice wine or dry sherry
120ml/4fl oz/1/4 cup Chicken Stock (page 128)

Soak the rice noodles in a bowl of warm water for 25 minutes. Then drain them in a colander or sieve. Set them aside until you are ready to use them.

Seed and finely shred the chillies. Finely shred the water chestnuts.

Heat a wok or large frying pan over high heat until it is hot. Add the oil and, when it is very hot and slightly smoking, add the garlic, ginger, and spring onions. Stir-fry for 15 seconds. Then add the prawns, shredded chillies, and shredded water chestnuts and stir-fry for about 1 minute. Put in the rest of the ingredients and

the drained noodles. Stir-fry the mixture for about 3 minutes or until it is well mixed and all the stock has been absorbed. Serve at once.

BEAN SAUCE NOODLES

SHOPPING LIST
225g/8oz fresh or dried egg or wheat noodles,
350g/12oz minced [US ground] boneless pork,
garlic, spring onions [US scallions], fresh ginger

STAPLES
groundnut oil [US peanut oil], ground bean sauce,
chilli bean paste, Shaoxing rice wine or dry sherry,
dark and light soy sauces, sugar, Chicken Stock,
sesame oil

PREPARATION TIME
10 minutes

COOKING TIME
10 minutes
SERVES 4

This northern Chinese dish can be found in small noodle restaurants as well as street food stalls everywhere in China. It is perhaps best described as the equivalent of Western pasta with meat sauce. Use the readily available dried Chinese egg noodles, or fresh egg noodles which are available in Chinese shops. With added vegetables, it makes a very satisfying light meal or snack.

2.25 litres/5 pints/12 1/2 cups water
2 tsp salt
225g/8oz fresh or dried egg or wheat noodles

SAUCE
1 1/2 tbsp groundnut oil [US peanut oil] or
vegetable oil
2 tbsp finely chopped garlic
2 tbsp spring onions [US scallions], white part only,
finely chopped
2 tsp finely chopped fresh ginger
350g/12oz boneless pork, minced [US ground]
2 tsp ground bean sauce

1 tbsp chilli bean sauce
1 tbsp dark soy sauce
1 tbsp light soy sauce
1 tbsp Shaoxing rice wine or dry sherry
150ml/5fl oz/ ⁵/₈ cup Chicken Stock (page 128)
2 tsp sugar
freshly ground black pepper, to taste
2 tsp sesame oil

───────── GARNISH ─────────

chopped spring onions [US scallions]

Bring the water to a boil in a large pot with the salt. Add the noodles. If you are using fresh noodles, boil them for 1¹/₂ minutes; if using dried noodles, boil them for 3 minutes. Separate the noodles, using chopsticks, while they are boiling. Drain in a colander and rinse under cold running water until they are cold, to stop them overcooking. Let the noodles drain in the colander, turning them several times so that all the water can drain off them. If you are not using them immediately, toss them with a little sesame oil before setting aside.

Heat a wok until it is hot, then add the oil. When the oil is hot and slightly smoking, add the garlic, spring onions, and ginger and stir-fry for 30 seconds. Then add the pork and stir well to break up all the pieces. Continue to stir-fry for 2 minutes or until it loses its pink color. Add the bean sauce, chilli bean paste, soy sauces, rice wine, chicken stock, sugar and pepper and continue to cook for 30 seconds. Mix well.

Return the noodles to the wok and cook over high heat for 2 minutes, mixing well. Stir in the sesame oil and mix again. Turn onto a platter and garnish with the spring onions. Serve at once.

LILLIAN'S SPRING ONION AND GINGER NOODLES

───────── SHOPPING LIST ─────────

350g/12oz dried or fresh thin egg or wheat noodles, ginger, spring onions [US scallions]

───────── STAPLES ─────────

groundnut oil [US peanut oil], sesame oil, oyster sauce

───────── PREPARATION TIME ─────────

10 minutes

───────── COOKING TIME ─────────

5 minutes

SERVES 4

Lillian is an excellent Chinese home-cook who grew up in Beijing. She has lived in the US for a number of years with her American husband, Phil. They often cook for groups of Chinese friends, students and artists from China. Being from the north of China, she prefers to serve noodles instead of rice with her extravagant dinners. Her northern Chinese origins notwithstanding, she occasionally serves this quick Cantonese version of simple-to-make noodles which are indeed an attractive and delicious alternative to rice.

350g/12oz dried or fresh thin egg noodles
1¹/₂ tbsp groundnut oil [US peanut oil]
2 tsp sesame oil
3 tbsp finely chopped fresh ginger
8 whole spring onions [US scallions],
finely chopped
1 tsp salt
¹/₂ tsp freshly ground white pepper
3 tbsp oyster sauce

Cook the noodles, allowing 3 minutes for fresh noodles and 5 minutes for dried in a pot of boiling water. Then rinse in cold water, drain thoroughly and toss them with a little sesame oil. Put them aside until you are ready to use them.

Heat a wok or large frying pan over high heat until it is hot. Add the two oils and, when very hot and slightly smoking, add the ginger. Stir-fry for 10 seconds. Add the spring onions and stir-fry for 30 seconds more. Remove from the heat and add the mixture to the noodles. Season with the salt and pepper and finally add the oyster sauce.

Turn the noodles onto a warm serving platter and serve at once.

HOT AND SOUR NOODLES

──────── SHOPPING LIST ────────
450g/1lb dried or fresh wheat or egg noodles, Sichuan preserved vegetable, spring onions [US scallions]

──────── STAPLES ────────
sesame oil, dark and light soy sauces, chilli oil, Chinese black rice vinegar, sugar

──────── PREPARATION TIME ────────
15 minutes

──────── COOKING TIME ────────
10 minutes
SERVES 4

The Chinese savor the sparkling contrast of hot and sour. This recipe is inspired by a dish from a simple Taipei noodle stall. I observed that this particular combination was quite popular, and, after sampling it, I understood why. It serves as a quick hot meal that is very tasty and quite satisfying. In Taipei, the noodles are cooked to order and the simple seasoning is mixed in at the last moment. It makes a marvelous vegetarian lunch dish.

450g/1lb dried or fresh wheat or egg noodles
1 tbsp sesame oil

──────── SAUCE ────────
1 tbsp dark soy sauce
2 tbsp light soy sauce
1 tbsp chilli oil (page 23)
1 tbsp sesame oil
1$^1/_2$ tbsp Chinese black rice vinegar or cider vinegar
2 tbsp rinsed and finely chopped Sichuan preserved vegetable
6 tbsp finely chopped spring onions [US scallions]
2 tsp sugar

If you are using fresh noodles, cook them for 3–5 minutes in a large pot of boiling water. If you are using dried noodles, cook them in boiling water for 4–5 minutes. Drain the noodles, toss them in the sesame oil, and then put them aside until you are ready to use them.

In a small bowl, combine all the sauce ingredients and set aside.

Before serving, plunge the noodles into boiling water for 20 seconds, and then drain them well in a colander or sieve. Quickly tip the noodles into a large bowl and pour the sauce over the top. Mix everything together and serve at once.

BRAISED NOODLES WITH CRAB MEAT

──────── SHOPPING LIST ────────
225g/8oz dried wheat noodles, 350g/12oz fresh white crab meat, Chinese dried black mushrooms, fresh ginger, Chinese yellow or green chives

──────── STAPLES ────────
groundnut oil [US peanut oil], light and dark soy sauces, Shaoxing rice wine or dry sherry, oyster sauce, sesame oil, sugar, Chicken Stock

──────── PREPARATION TIME ────────
20 minutes

──────── COOKING TIME ────────
15 minutes
SERVES 4

One of the most appealing aspects of walking through the streets of Hong Kong, Taipei, or Beijing, is to see the countless noodle stalls ladling out delicious, inexpensive noodle dishes that can be quickly eaten. These dishes have to be easy to make as many of the clients are in a great hurry, but it is 'fast food' that is nutritious as well as satisfying. The versatility of noodle dishes is such that, once everything is prepared, it literally takes seconds to put together a tasty one-dish meal.

225g/8oz dried wheat noodles
50g/2oz dried Chinese black mushrooms (page 26)
1¹/₂ tbsp groundnut oil [US peanut oil]
1 tbsp finely shredded fresh ginger
110g/4oz Chinese yellow or green chives, cut into
5cm/2in pieces
350g/12oz fresh white crab meat

—————————— SAUCE ——————————
1 tbsp light soy sauce
1 tbsp Shaoxing rice wine or dry sherry
2 tbsp oyster sauce
2 tsp dark soy sauce
1 tsp sesame oil
1 tsp sugar
240ml/8fl oz/1 cup Chicken Stock (page 128)

In a large pot of boiling water, blanch the noodles for 5 minutes or until they are soft. Drain well and set aside.

Remove and discard the mushroom stems and finely shred the caps into thin strips.

Heat a wok or large frying pan over high heat until it is hot. Add the oil and, when it is very hot and slightly smoking, add the shredded ginger and chives. Stir-fry them for 30 seconds. Then add the mushrooms and all of the sauce ingredients. Cook over high heat for 1 minute. Add the noodles and cook in the sauce for about 2 minutes or until the sauce is absorbed into the noodles. Add the crab meat and mix well. Ladle the noodles into a large bowl or individual bowls and serve at once.

CHINESE CHICKEN NOODLE SOUP

—————————— SHOPPING LIST ——————————
225g/8oz fresh or dried wheat noodles, 175g/6oz boneless, skinless chicken breasts, 175g/6oz Peking cabbage (Chinese leaves or Napa cabbage),Chinese dried black mushrooms, spring onions [US scallions]

—————————— STAPLES ——————————
Chicken Stock, Shaoxing rice wine or dry sherry, light soy sauce, sugar, sesame oil

—————————— PREPARATION TIME ——————————
20 minutes

—————————— COOKING TIME ——————————
10 minutes
SERVES 4

This is probably China's most popular soup – in fact, it may be the world's most popular soup! It is found in every region of China, every food stall and restaurant. It is light, tasty and easy to make. There are as many variations on its basic theme as there are cooks. This particular recipe carefully follows that of a delightful family restaurant I encountered in Yunnan province.

175g/6oz fresh or dried wheat noodles
25g/1oz Chinese dried black mushrooms (page 26)
175g/6oz boneless, skinless chicken breasts
175g/6oz Peking cabbage (Chinese leaves or
Napa cabbage)
900ml/1¹/₂ pints/3³/₄ cups Chicken Stock (page 128)
1 tbsp Shaoxing rice wine or dry sherry
2 tbsp light soy sauce
2 tsp sugar
1 tsp salt
¹/₄ tsp freshly ground black pepper

2 tsp sesame oil

3 tbsp finely chopped spring onions [US scallions]

Bring a large pot of salted water to boil. Add the noodles. If you are using fresh noodles, boil them for 3–5 minutes; if you are using dried noodles, boil them for 4–5 minutes. Separate the noodles while they are boiling, using chopsticks. Once the noodles are done, drain them in a colander and rinse under cold running water until they are cold, to prevent them from overcooking. Let the noodles drain in the colander, turning them several times so that all the water can drain off them. If you are not using them immediately, toss them with a little sesame oil before setting aside.

Remove and discard the mushroom stems and finely shred the caps into thin strips.

Finely shred the chicken and blanch it for 15 seconds in a pot of boiling salted water. Remove and drain well.

Shred the cabbage leaves.

Bring the chicken stock to a simmer in a wok or large pan. Add rice wine or sherry, soy sauce, sugar, salt, and pepper. Then add the cabbage leaves and mushrooms and simmer for 5 minutes. Now add the noodles and chicken and continue to simmer for 2 minutes. Add the sesame oil and spring onions and serve immediately.

EGG FRIED RICE

110g/4oz shelled fresh or frozen peas, 110g/4oz fresh bean sprouts, eggs, spring onions [US scallions], cold cooked rice

sesame oil, groundnut oil [US peanut oil]

10 minutes

5 minutes

SERVES 4

Egg fried rice is a quick and easy way to put together a dish without any complications. It is equally delicious served by itself or with the leftovers of other food. Here are a few important points to remember when making authentic Chinese fried rice.

● The cooked rice should be thoroughly cool, preferably cold. Once cooled, much of the moisture in the rice evaporates, allowing the oil to coat the dry grains and keep them from sticking. Store the cooked rice in the refrigerator until you are ready to use it.

● Never put any soy sauce into fried rice. This not only colors the rice unnaturally but makes it too salty. Any moisture will make the rice gummy. Fried rice should be quite dry.

● Always be sure the oil is hot enough to avoid saturating the rice. Saturated rice is greasy and heavy. The finished fried rice should have a wonderful smoky flavor.

If you follow these simple guidelines, you will be rewarded with perfect fried rice as it should be. Fried rice goes with almost any dish, but in China it is usually served at the end of a banquet in the unlikely event you are still hungry.

110g/4oz/¹/₂ cup shelled or frozen peas

4 eggs, beaten

2 tsp sesame oil

2 tbsp groundnut oil [US peanut oil]

steamed rice (see next recipe)

2 tsp salt

¹/₂ tsp spring onions

freshly ground black pepper
3 tbsp finely chopped spring onions [US scallions],
white part only
110g/4oz fresh bean sprouts

Blanch fresh peas in a saucepan of boiling water for about 5 minutes; simply thaw frozen peas. Drain them in a colander.

Combine the eggs and sesame oil in a small bowl and set aside.

Heat a wok or large frying pan over high heat until it is hot. Add the groundnut oil and, when it is very hot and slightly smoking, turn the heat to moderate and add the eggs. Stir-fry the eggs for 2 minutes, then add the cooked rice and stir-fry it for 3 minutes, mixing well. Then add the peas, salt and pepper. Continue to stir-fry the mixture for 5 minutes over a high heat. Add the spring onions and bean sprouts and continue to stir-fry for 2 minutes. Turn the mixture onto a plate and serve at once.

--- STEAMED RICE ---

enough long-grain rice to fill a glass measuring jug
to 400ml/14fl oz/1½ cups level
900ml/1½ pints/3¾ cups water

Put the rice into a large bowl and wash it in several changes of water until the water becomes clear. Drain the rice and put it into a heavy pot with the measured water. Bring to the boil. Boil until most of the surface liquid has evaporated. This should take about 5–10 minutes. The surface of the rice should have small indentations like a pitted crater.

At this point, cover the pot with a very tight-fitting lid, turn the heat as low as possible and let the rice cook undisturbed for 15 minutes. There is no need to 'fluff' the rice; just let it rest for 5 minutes before serving it.

SHANGHAI VEGETABLE RICE

--- SHOPPING LIST ---

350g/12oz Shanghai pale choi or Chinese white cabbage (pak choi or bok choy), long-grain white rice, Chinese dried black mushrooms, spring onions [US scallions], garlic

--- STAPLES ---

groundnut oil [US peanut oil], sesame oil

--- PREPARATION TIME ---

10 minutes

--- COOKING TIME ---

35 minutes

SERVES 4

This is a popular native Shanghai dish that combines so-called Shanghai pak choi with rice. This variety of cabbage is harvested young, when it is tender and its flavor is most intense. It is most congenial with the blander tastes of rice and mushrooms. Chefs variously cook the vegetables and rice together, or they partially cook the rice and then combine it with the vegetables. I prefer this second technique as it produces a tastier dish.

1½ cups cooked long-grain white rice (measured to about the 400ml/14fl oz mark in a measuring jug)
50g/2oz Chinese black dried mushrooms (page 26)
600ml/1 pint/2½ cups water
350g/12oz Shanghai pak choi or Chinese white cabbage (pak choi or bok choy)
1½ tbsp groundnut oil [US peanut oil]
3 tbsp finely chopped spring onions [US scallions]
2 tbsp finely chopped garlic
2 tsp salt
½ tsp freshly ground black pepper
2 tsp sesame oil

Put the rice into a large bowl and wash it in several changes of water until the water becomes clear.

Remove and discard the mushroom stems and coarsely chop the caps.

Wash and coarsely chop the pak choi.

Heat a wok or large frying pan over high heat until it is hot. Add the oil and, when it is very hot and slightly smoking, add the spring onions and garlic. Stir-fry for 10 seconds. Then add the mushrooms, pak choi, salt, pepper and sesame oil and continue to stir-fry for 2 minutes or until the pak choi has slightly wilted. Remove from the heat and set aside. Add to cooked rice and heat together for 5 minutes. Serve at once.

AROMATIC CHICKEN FRIED RICE

———— SHOPPING LIST ————
225g/8oz boneless, skinless chicken thighs, fresh or frozen peas, shallots, fresh ginger, garlic, spring onions [US scallions], eggs

———— STAPLES ————
groundnut oil [US peanut oil], sesame oil, chilli bean paste, shrimp paste, cooked long-grain white rice (page 194)

———— PREPARATION TIME ————
15 minutes

———— COOKING TIME ————
15 minutes

SERVES 4

The best chicken fried rice I have ever had was from a street food stall in Bangkok. Instead of tough, overcooked chicken, with the fried rice as an afterthought, the dish was cooked fresh from scratch. The cooking time literally took minutes and the result was delicious. I have created a similar version that comes very close to the original. It is quick and easy and makes a meal in itself. The rice to be fried is cooked beforehand.

110g/4oz/¼ cup shelled fresh or frozen peas
1½ tbsp groundnut oil [US peanut oil]
3 tbsp finely chopped shallots
2 tbsp finely chopped garlic
1 tbsp finely chopped fresh ginger
3 tbsp finely chopped spring onions [US scallions], white part only
225g/8oz boneless, skinless chicken thighs, coarsely chopped
2½ tsp salt
½ tsp freshly ground black pepper
4 eggs, beaten
2 tsp sesame oil cooked and cooled long-grain white rice (page 194)
1 tbsp chilli bean paste
2 tsp shrimp paste
3 tbsp finely chopped spring onions [US scallions], green part only

Blanch the peas in a saucepan of boiling water for about 5 minutes if they are fresh; if they are frozen, simply thaw them. Drain them well in a colander.

Heat a wok or large frying pan over high heat until it is hot. Add 1½ tbsp of oil and, when it is very hot and slightly smoking, add the shallots, garlic, ginger, and white parts of spring onions. Stir-fry for 1 minute. Then add the chicken, 2 tsp salt, and the pepper and continue to stir-fry for 3 minutes. Remove from the heat and put the contents in a bowl. Wipe the wok clean.

Combine the eggs, sesame oil, and remaining ½ tsp salt in a small bowl and set aside.

Reheat the wok or pan over high heat until it is hot. Add the remaining 1½ tbsp of oil and, when it is very hot and slightly smoking, turn the heat to moderate and add the egg mixture. Stir-fry the eggs for 2 minutes, then add the cooked rice and stir-fry for 3 minutes, mixing well. Add the peas, the cooked chicken mixture, chilli bean paste, and shrimp paste. Continue to stir-fry for

195

5 minutes over a high heat. Then add the green parts of spring onions and stir-fry for 2 minutes. Turn the mixture onto a plate and serve at once.

SAVORY GLUTINOUS RICE CASEROLE

—————— SHOPPING LIST ——————

350g/12oz glutinous rice, 450g/1lb minced [US ground] pork, Chinese dried black mushrooms, Chinese pork sausages, Smithfield ham or prosciutto (Parma ham), fresh or canned water chestnuts, spring onions [US scallions], fresh ginger

—————— STAPLES ——————

light soy sauce, Shaoxing rice wine or dry sherry, sesame oil, groundnut oil [US peanut oil], Chicken Stock

—————— PREPARATION TIME ——————

overnight soaking + 25 minutes

—————— COOKING TIME ——————

25 minutes

SERVES 4

My mother used to make this wonderful family dish on special occasions and for Chinese festivals. Sometimes it was served as a separate dish; sometimes it was stuffed inside a chicken or duck. In any case, I always appreciated it as a special treat. The casserole is rich, a bit like Italian risotto, as the rice absorbs all the flavors of the rest of the ingredients. Glutinous rice stands up well under long cooking, and this makes it ideal for this type of casserole. Another advantage is that it reheats well – you might even prefer it one day later.

350g/12oz/³/₄ cup glutinous rice
450g/1lb minced [US ground] pork
2 tbsp light soy sauce
3¹/₂ tbsp Shaoxing rice wine or dry sherry
1 tsp salt
1 tsp freshly ground black pepper

2 tsp sesame oil
50g/2oz Chinese dried black mushrooms (page 26)
1¹/₂ tbsp groundnut oil [US peanut oil]
4 tbsp finely chopped spring onions [US scallions]
2 tsp finely chopped fresh ginger
110g/4oz Chinese pork sausages, chopped
110g/4oz Smithfield ham or prosciutto (Parma ham), chopped
110g/4oz peeled fresh or canned water chestnuts, coarsely chopped
450ml/15fl oz/1⁵/₈ cups Chicken Stock (page 128)

Place the rice in a large bowl and cover it completely with water. Let it soak overnight. The next day, give the rice a good rinse and drain it well.

Combine the pork with 1 tbsp soy sauce, 1¹/₂ tbsp rice wine or sherry, the salt, ¹/₂ tsp pepper, and the sesame oil.

Remove and discard the mushroom stems and chop the caps.

Heat a wok or large frying-pan over high heat until it is hot. Add the groundnut oil and, when it is very hot and slightly smoking, add the pork mixture. Stir-fry for 2 minutes. Then add the spring onions and ginger and continue to stir-fry another minute. Now add the sausages, ham, water chestnuts, rice, and chicken stock. Bring the mixture to a simmer. Add the remaining rice wine or sherry, soy sauce, and pepper. Turn the heat to low, cover, and cook for 20 minutes or until the rice has absorbed all the liquid. Give the mixture a good stir, turn it onto a platter or bowl, and serve at once.

INDEX

angles luffa *see* silk squash
aubergine 10
    with sesame sauce 172

bamboo shoots 12
    eggs with stir-fried vegetables 165
    fried stuffed peppers 181–2
bean curd 13–14
    Beijing pan-fried 172–3
    braised stuffed 173–4
    casserole 174–5
    and chicken-salt fish casserole 175–6
    mushroom bean curd casserole 180–1
bean paste *see* bean sauce
bean sauce 15
    bean sauce noodles 189–90
    chicken 139–40
    shredded pork in bean paste 153–4
bean sprouts:
    braised noodles and ham with 188
    egg fried rice 193–4
    stir-fried 176–7
bean thread noodles 58–9
    braised catfish casserole 115–16
    crab bean thread casserole 123–4
    vegetarian delight 170–1
beans *see* black beans; broad beans; Chinese
        long beans
beef:
    beef soup with fresh coriander 103
    beef and turnip stew 147
    orange-flavored 146–7
    Sichuan peppercorn onion beef 149–50
    spicy stir-fried Hunan beef 147–8
    stir-fried, in black bean sauce 148–9
bird's nest 16
bitter melon 17
black beans 18
    clams in black bean sauce 124
    stir-fried beef in black bean sauce 148–9
black rice vinegar 74
bok choy *see* Chinese white cabbage
broad beans, stir-fried prawns with 116–7
broccoli:
    stir-fried scallops with 122–3
    see also Chinese broccoli
brown bean sauce *see* bean sauce
brown sugar slabs 91

cabbage *see* Chinese flowering; Chinese
        mustard; Chinese white; Peking; red in snow
        cabbage
canola oil 62
Cantonese-style dipping sauce 131
caul fat 19
    Chiu Chow style sweet and sour pork 158–9
celery, stir-fried 177–8
cellophane noodles 58–9
chee hou sauce 48
chicken:
    aromatic chicken fried rice 195–6
    and bean curd-salt fish casserole 175–6
    bean sauce 139–40
    beggar's 138–9
    braised, Cantonese-style 141–2
    Chinese chicken noodle soup 192–3
    crispy aromatic 140–1
    dipping sauces 130–1
    drunken 129, 130
    fragrant, crispy 136–7
    General Tang's 132–3
    oxtail-chicken soup 100
    Portuguese 132
    salt roasted 135
    Sichuan vegetable soup 102
    smoked 142
    Soy Sauce 129, 130, 135–6
    steamed, with sausage and ham 131–2
    steeped 129–31
    stuffed slices 137–8
    sweet and sour 134
    wonton soup 101–2
chicken stock 128–9
chilli bean paste (sauce) 20
chilli dipping sauce 23
chilli oil 23
chilli paste with garlic 20
chilli-fermented bean curd 14, 150
chillies, dried red 21
chillies, fresh 22
    spicy stir-fried Hunan beef 147–8
Chinese broccoli 24
    with oyster sauce 177
Chinese chives 25
    braised noodles with crab meat 191–2
Chinese dried black mushrooms 26
    bean curd casserole 174–5
    beggar's chicken 138–9
    Chinese cabbage soup 99–100
    Chinese chicken noodle soup 192–3
    double steamed mushroom soup 100–1
    fried stuffed peppers 181–2
    mushroom bean curd casserole 180–1

prawns stir-fried with eggs 166
Shanghai-style egg with crab meat 166–7
Shanghai vegetable rice 194–5
stuffed chicken slices 137–8
stuffed Chinese mushrooms 179–80
vegetarian delight 170–1
Chinese flowering cabbage 27
Chinese leaves *see* Peking cabbage
Chinese long beans 28
Chinese mustard cabbage 29, 68
Chinese okra *see* silk squash
Chinese parsley *see* coriander
Chinese white cabbage 30
crispy 'seaweed' 183
mixed green vegetables 185
Shanghai vegetable rice 194–5
vegetarian dumplings 171
Chinese white radish 31
beef and turnip stew 147
chives *see* Chinese chives
cilantro *see* coriander
cinnamon bark 32, 142–3
citrus peel 33
orange-flavored beef 146–7
clams:
in black bean sauce 124
with steamed egg custard 163–4
cloud ears 34
beggar's chicken 138–9
Cantonese-style braised chicken 141–2
meat-filled omelette 162–3
vegetarian delight 170–1
coconut milk 35
coriander 36
beef soup with fresh coriander 103
stuffed Chinese mushrooms 179–80
corn oil 61
cornflour 40
cornstarch 40
cottonseed oil 62
crab:
bean thread casserole 123–4
braised noodles with 191–2
Shanghai-style egg with 166–7
cucumbers:
hot and sour cucumber salad 178
pickled cucumber salad 178–9
stuffed cucumber soup 98
curry paste/powder 37

D

daiken *see* Chinese white radish
dark soy sauce 89
duck, pressed, Cantonese 142–3

E

egg dishes:
egg fried rice 193–4
eggs with stir-fried vegetables 165
omelettes 162–3

prawns stir-fried with eggs 166
Shanghai-style egg with crab meat 166–7
steamed egg custard with clams 163–4
steamed egg custard with meat sauce 164–5
stir-fried, with preserved vegetables 167
egg noodles 56
bean sauce noodles 189–90
braised, with bean sprouts and ham 188
hot and sour noodles 191
spring onion and ginger noodles 190–1
eggplant *see* aubergine

F

fats *see* oils
fermented bean curd 14, 150
fermented black beans *see* black beans
fish:
baked, Hong Kong style 110
braised, spicy 108–9
braised catfish casserole 115–16
crispy fish fillets 111
crispy sole 112
with meat sauce 112–13
red cooked 108
sauce 38
smoked 114–15
stir-fried, in tomato sauce 110–11
watercress fish soup 103–4
five spice powder 39, 181
flours 40–1

G

gaai choy *see* Chinese mustard cabbage
garlic 42–3
cold pork with garlic sauce 156–7
prawns in hot garlic sauce 119–20
stir-fried silk squash with 182–3
garlic shoots 43
ginger 44–5
spring onion and ginger noodles 190–1
ginger juice 45
gluten 94
glutinous rice 71–2
pearl meatballs 151
savory casserole 196
glutinous rice flour 40–1
groundnut oil 60–1

H

ham 46
and braised noodles with bean sprouts 188
hoisin sauce 48

J

Jicama 93
Jinhua ham *see* ham

L

leeks 49
lemongrass 50
light soy sauce 88
lily buds 51
    Cantonese-style braised chicken 141–2
    meat-filled omelette 162–3
    Mu Shu pork with Chinese pancakes 157–8
long-grain rice 71
lotus root 52, 179

M

maltose (malt) sugar 53
mangetouts 54
    vegetable egg flower soup 98–9
melon, bitter 17
monosodium glutamate 55
mooli *see* Chinese white radish
mung bean threads 58–9
mushroom soy sauce 89
mushrooms *see* Chinese dried black; cloud
    ears; tree ears; wood ears
mustard cabbage *see* Chinese mustard cabbage
mustard greens, preserved 68

N

nappa cabbage *see* Peking cabbage
noodles 56–9, 188–93
Northern Jiangxi style sauce 130–1
northern-style garlic-vinegar sauce 131

O

oils 60–2
omelettes 162–3
oxtail:
    oxtail-chicken soup 100
    red cooked oxtail stew 150
oyster sauce 64
    Chinese broccoli with 177
oysters, dried 63

P

pak choi *see* Chinese white cabbage
pancakes, Chinese 157–8
pea pod *see* mangetouts
peanut oil 60–1
peanuts 65
    bean sauce chicken 139–40
    with five spice 181
peas *see* mangetouts
Peking cabbage 66
    Chinese cabbage soup 99–100
    Chinese chicken noodle soup 192–3
    mixed green vegetables 185
    oxtail-chicken soup 100
    vegetarian dumplings 171

peppercorns *see* Sichuan peppercorns
peppers, fried stuffed 181–2
plum sauce 67
pork:
    beggar's chicken 138–9
    braised stuffed bean curd 173–4
    Chiu Chow style sweet and sour 158–9
    cold, with garlic sauce 156–7
    crispy fried chops 155–6
    fish with meat sauce 112–13
    home-style omelette 162
    meat-filled omelette 162–3
    Mu Shu, with Chinese pancakes 157–8
    pearl meatballs 151
    savory deep-fried wonton 151–2
    savory glutinous rice casserole 196
    shredded, in bean paste 153–4
    shredded strange-flavor 155
    steamed, with fragrant rice crumbs 154
    steamed egg custard with bean sauce 164–5
    stewed spareribs 152–3
potato starch 41
prawns:
    braised stuffed bean curd 173–4
    chicken wonton soup 101–2
    deep-fried prawn balls 117–18
    with honey-glazed walnuts 118–19
    in hot garlic sauce 119–20
    prawn dumpling soup 104–5
    savory deep-fried wonton 151–2
    and scallops:
        in honey sauce 120–1
        Sichuan-style 121–2
    stir-fried, with broad beans 116–17
    stir-fried with eggs 166
    with stir-fried rice noodles 188–9
    stuffed chicken slices 137–8
    stuffed Chinese mushrooms 179–80
preserved beans *see* black beans
preserved mustard cabbage (greens) 68
preserved vegetable 68
    see also Sichuan preserved vegetable
pressed seasoned bean curd 14
    vegetarian delight 170–1

R

rapeseed oil 62
red fermented bean curd 14
red rice vinegar 74
red in snow cabbage 69
regular fermented bean curd 14
rice 70–2
    aromatic chicken fried rice 195–6
    egg fried rice 193
    pork, with fragrant rice crumbs 154
    Shanghai vegetable rice 194–5
    steamed 194
rice flour 40–1
rice noodles 57–8
    stir-fried, with prawns 188–9

rice papers (wrappers) 73
rice vinegar 74
rice wine, Shaoxing 75
rock sugar 91, 143

 S

safflower oil 62
salt 76
    salt roasted chicken 135
salted beans *see* black beans
scallops:
    and prawns, in honey sauce 120–1
    and prawns, Sichuan-style 121–2
    stir-fried, with broccoli 122–3
seafood, dried 77–8
sesame oil 62
sesame paste 79
sesame sauce, with aubergines 172
sesame seeds 80
shallots 81
Shaoxing rice wine 75
shark's fin 82
short-grain rice 71
shrimp, dried 83
    bean curd casserole 174–5
    Chinese cabbage soup 99–100
shrimp roe, dried 83
shrimp sauce/paste 84
    stir-fried spinach with 184–5
shrimp-flavored soy sauce 89
Sichuan chilli sauce 20
Sichuan peppercorns 85
    crispy fried pork chops 155–6
    Sichuan peppercorn onion beef 149–50
Sichuan preserved vegetable 86
    chicken Sichuan vegetable soup 102
    vegetarian dumplings 171
silk squash 87
    stir-fried, with garlic 182–3
snow peas *see* mangetouts
soups 98–105
soy sauce 88–9
soybean condiment *see* bean sauce
soybean oil 62
spareribs 152–3
spice powder *see* five spice powder
spinach:
    prawn dumpling soup 104–5
    spicy salad 183–4
    stir-fried, with shrimp paste 184–5
spring onions, Lillian's spring onion and
    ginger noodles 190–1
squid, salt and pepper 124–5
star anise 90, 143
starches 40–1
sugar 91
sugar peas *see* mangetouts
sunflower oil 62
sweet rice flour (powder) 40–1
sweet rice vinegar 74
sweet and sour sauce 134, 152

 T

transparent noodles 58–9
tree ears 34
    beggar's chicken 138–9
    chicken wonton soup 101–2
    Mu Shu pork with Chinese pancakes 157–8

 V

vegetable, preserved *see* preserved vegetable
vegetable egg flower soup 98–9
vegetables, green, mixed 185
vegetarian delight 170–1
vegetarian dumplings 171
vinegars 74

 W

water chestnuts 92–3
    bean sauce chicken 139–40
    beggar's chicken 138–9
    chicken wonton soup 101–2
    Chiu Chow style sweet and sour pork 158–9
    deep-fried prawn balls 117–18
    fried stuffed peppers 181–2
    stuffed chicken slices 137–8
    stuffed Chinese mushrooms 179–80
watercress fish soup 103–4
wheat gluten 94
wheat noodles 56
    braised noodles with crab meat 191–2
    Chinese chicken noodle soup 192–3
    see also recipes under egg noodles
wheat starch 41
white rice vinegar 74
wonton wrappers (skins) 95
    chicken wonton soup 101–2
    savory deep-fried wonton 151–2
    vegetarian dumplings 171
wood ears 34
    Cantonese-style braised chicken 141–2

Y

yellow bean sauce *see* bean sauce
yellow lump sugar 91
Yunnan ham *see* ham